Michael Hauck

Automated Experiments for Deriving Performance-relevant Properties of Software Execution Environments

**The Karlsruhe Series on Software Design and Quality
Volume 13**

Chair Software Design and Quality
Faculty of Computer Science
Karlsruhe Institute of Technology

and

Software Engineering Division
Research Center for Information Technology (FZI), Karlsruhe

Editor: Prof. Dr. Ralf Reussner

Automated Experiments for Deriving Performance-relevant Properties of Software Execution Environments

by
Michael Hauck

Dissertation, Karlsruher Institut für Technologie (KIT)
Fakultät für Informatik
Tag der mündlichen Prüfung: 07. November 2013
Referenten: Prof. Dr. Ralf Reussner, Prof. Dr.-Ing. Stefan Tai

Impressum

 Scientific
Publishing

Karlsruher Institut für Technologie (KIT)
KIT Scientific Publishing
Straße am Forum 2
D-76131 Karlsruhe

KIT Scientific Publishing is a registered trademark of Karlsruhe
Institute of Technology. Reprint using the book cover is not allowed.

www.ksp.kit.edu

Print on Demand 2014

ISSN 1867-0067
ISBN 978-3-7315-0138-1

Karlsruher Institut für Technologie

Automated Experiments for Deriving Performance-relevant Properties of Software Execution Environments

Zur Erlangung des akademischen Grades eines

Doktors der Ingenieurwissenschaften

von der Fakultät für Informatik
des Karlsruher Instituts für Technologie (KIT)

genehmigte
Dissertation
von

Michael Alexander Hauck
aus Freiburg im Breisgau

Tag der mündlichen Prüfung: 07. November 2013
Erstgutachter: Prof. Dr. Ralf Reussner
Zweitgutachter: Prof. Dr.-Ing. Stefan Tai

KIT – Universität des Landes Baden-Württemberg
und nationales Forschungszentrum der Helmholtz-Gemeinschaft

www.kit.edu

Abstract

In software engineering, considering quality attributes such as software performance plays a crucial role. Approaches such as Software Performance Engineering (SPE) aim at systematically reflecting software performance during the whole software life-cycle. Using model-based performance analyses, predictions on the software performance, e.g. the expected software response times or the resource utilization, can already be conducted during design time.

The software execution environment heavily influences the performance of a software and thus has to be reflected in performance analysis. With the increased complexity of the execution environment (e.g. due to the introduction of virtualized environments or new operating system schedulers), performance analysis approaches have to be extended in order to continue to yield precise prediction results.

Existing performance prediction approaches usually abstract from most parts of the execution environment or do not deal with the problem of quantifying properties of the execution environment for performance prediction models. Hence, detecting execution environment properties and integrating such properties into performance analyses is a manual, error-prone task that requires expert knowledge on the execution environment.

The scientific contribution of this thesis is a novel approach for detecting performance-relevant properties of the software execution environment. These properties are automatically detected using predefined experiments and integrated into performance prediction tools. To detect the properties, performance experiments are conducted on the target platform. The experiments issue predefined load patterns on the system and observe certain performance metrics. Based on the measured results, performance-relevant execution environment properties are then derived. As the approach is solely measurement-based, it does not require access to low-level details of the execution environment.

For predefining experiments, this thesis introduces a metamodel for experiment specification. Using a model-based approach, experiment models can be directly transformed into executable experiments on the target platform. The metamodel facilitates the specification of experiment execution logic and the corresponding load patterns. In addition, the metamodel and the transformation encapsulate domain knowledge on experiment design, such as the execution of microbenchmarks or the automated termination of experiments once statistically sufficient measurements have been collected.

To validate the approach, different experiments have been developed in the scope of this thesis. The experiments aim at detecting performance-relevant properties of different parts of the execution environment, i.e. CPU, OS scheduling, and virtualization properties. The derived properties include for example the timeslice length of the OS scheduler or the used scheduling strategy for load-balancing, as well as different kinds of resource demand overhead introduced by a virtualization platform. The experiments are technology-independent and thus applicable to a multitude of target platforms.

The experiments presented in this thesis have been integrated into the Palladio Component Model (PCM), a model-based software performance analysis approach. By reflecting the derived execution environment properties in PCM, performance predictions can be improved. The experiments have been validated on different platforms and in different case studies: The first case study is based on a POV-Ray system that is used for ray tracing. The case study shows that reflecting the derived OS scheduling properties can lead to an increased prediction accuracy of software response times. In two other case studies, the experiments for detecting virtualization properties have been executed to enhance the performance prediction of two different systems: the TPC-W benchmark, an e-commerce platform, and the RUBiS benchmark, an online auction platform. In both cases, reflecting the experimentally derived properties yields an increased prediction accuracy compared to predictions where the derived details of the execution environment have been neglected.

By automatically deriving execution environment properties and integrating these properties into performance prediction approaches, performance predictions at design time are facilitated where details of the execution environment do not have to be derived and included manually. Software architects can conduct analyses without having to deal with identification of execution environment properties and the integration of such properties into performance analysis. In addition, since the experiments are automated, they can be repeated with little overhead, for example if parts of the execution environment have been changed and should be reflected in software performance analysis.

Kurzfassung

In der Software-Technik spielt die Berücksichtigung von Qualitätsattributen wie der Software-Performance eine wichtige Rolle. So wird im Software Performance Engineering (SPE) eine systematische Betrachtung der Performance über den gesamten Software-Lebenszyklus hinweg angestrebt. Modell-basierte Performance-Analysen ermöglichen bereits zur Entwurfszeit Aussagen über Antwortzeitverhalten und Ressourcenauslastung.

Da die Performance eines Software-Systems stark von der Ausführungsumgebung beeinflusst wird, muss diese in Performance-Analysen mit einbezogen werden. Mit zunehmender Komplexität der Ausführungsumgebung (z.B. durch den Einsatz von Virtualisierungsplattformen oder neuer Betriebssystem-Scheduler) müssen Performance-Analysen erweitert werden, um nach wie vor genaue Vorhersagen zu ermöglichen.

Existierende Ansätze zur Performance-Vorhersage abstrahieren meist von Teilen der Ausführungsumgebung oder befassen sich nicht mit der Quantifizierung von Plattformeigenschaften in Performance-Modelle. Das Erkennen von Plattformeigenschaften und die Integration dieser Eigenschaften in Performance-Analysen ist daher aufwändig, fehleranfällig, und erfordert Expertenwissen.

Der wissenschaftliche Beitrag dieser Arbeit ist ein neuer Ansatz, um performance-relevante Eigenschaften der Ausführungsumgebung automatisiert durch vordefinierte Experimente zu ermitteln und diese Eigenschaften in Werkzeuge zur Performance-Vorhersage zu integrieren. Zur Ableitung von Performance-Eigenschaften werden Experimente auf der Zielplattform ausgeführt. Diese Experimente erzeugen dann eine vordefinierte Last auf dem System und beobachten die dadurch entstehenden Performance-

Auswirkungen. Anschließend werden, basierend auf den Messresultaten, performance-relevante Eigenschaften für die Performance-Vorhersage abgeleitet. Interna der Ausführungsplattform müssen zur Anwendung des Ansatzes nicht bekannt sein, da dieser rein messbasiert vorgeht.

Um Experimente vorzudefinieren, wurde ein Metamodell für die Experimentspezifikation entwickelt. Experimentmodelle können so direkt in ausführbare Experimentinstanzen auf der Zielplattform transformiert werden. Das Metamodell ermöglicht die Spezifizierung von Experimentausführungslogik und Lastmustern. In dem Metamodell und der Transformation werden außerdem Details zur Experimentdurchführung gekapselt, wie z.B. die Ausführung von Mikrobenchmarks, oder automatische Abbruchkriterien nach Erreichen statistisch robuster Messwerte.

Zur Validierung des Ansatzes wurden im Rahmen der Arbeit verschiedene Experimente entwickelt, die eine automatische Ableitung verschiedener Eigenschaften der Ausführungsumgebung ermöglichen. Im Mittelpunkt standen hierbei CPU- und Betriebssystem-Eigenschaften, sowie Eigenschaften der Virtualisierungsplattform. Eigenschaften des Betriebssystems umfassen z.B. die Größe der Scheduler-Zeitscheiben oder die eingesetzte Strategie zur Lastverteilung auf mehrere Prozessorkerne. Die Experimente zur Ableitung von Eigenschaften der Virtualisierungsplattformen zielen unter vor allem darauf ab, den durch die Virtualisierungsschicht verursachten Overhead zu quantifizieren. Die Experimente sind plattformunabhängig und können dadurch auf einer Vielzahl von Zielplattformen eingesetzt werden.

Die in dieser Arbeit entwickelten Experimente wurden in das Palladio-Komponentenmodell, ein Ansatz zur modellbasierten Software-Performance-Vorhersage, integriert und ermöglichen so eine erweiterte Performance-Vorhersage unter Berücksichtigung der zusätzlichen Plattformeigenschaften. Die Experimente wurden auf mehreren Plattformen anhand verschiedener Fallstudien validiert: Die erste Fallstudie basiert auf einem POV-Ray-System zur Berechnung von 3D-Grafiken. Hier konnte gezeigt werden, dass die Berücksichtigung von Eigenschaften des Betriebssystem-Schedulers zu verbesserter Vorhersagegenauigkeit von Antwortzeiten führt. In zwei weiteren Fallstudien wurden die Experimente zur Ableitung von Virtualisierungseigenschaften durchgeführt und in die Performance-Vorhersage für den TPC-W-Benchmark, eine E-Commerce-Plattform, sowie den RUBiS-Benchmark, eine Online-Auktion-Plattform, integriert. Auch hier ergab eine Berücksichtigung der Experimente eine Verbesserung der Vorhersagegenauigkeit gegenüber einer Vorhersage unter Vernachlässigung der Ausführungsplattform.

Durch die automatisierte Ableitung von Parametern der Ausführungsplattform und Integration in Performance-Vorhersage-Werkzeuge werden so entwurfsnahe Vorhersagen möglich, ohne dass Details der Plattform manuell erhoben und berücksichtigt werden müssen. So können Software-Architekten die Analysen durchführen, ohne Fachkenntnisse zur Experimentdurchführung und der zugehörigen Performance-Modellierung besitzen zu müssen. Außerdem lassen sich die Experimente mit wenig Aufwand erneut durchführen, wenn sich z.B. Teile der Ausführungsplattform ändern und diese Änderungen in der Software-Performance-Vorhersage berücksichtigt werden sollen.

Acknowledgements

This thesis would not have been possible without the great support of many people.

First, I want to thank my two supervisors Ralf Reussner and Stefan Tai. Ralf has been a great advisor at all times and provided me with invaluable support. I always enjoyed working in his research group with its excellent working atmosphere. With Stefan I had great discussions concerning my PhD topic (and IT in general). His fruitful comments and insights really helped me to shape the topic and complete the thesis.

Furthermore, I am deeply thankful to Jens Happe and Dennis Westermann for the time we spent together doing research and for their feedback in the last years. Jens has supported me from the beginning in finding and shaping the topic and has always made time for discussing problems. I want to thank Dennis for the great discussions we had and the feedback he gave me when proof-reading the complete (sic!) thesis. I am looking forward to the next adventures we are going to take.

From the research group of SDQ and FZI, I want to thank my current and former colleagues I had the pleasure to work with. In alphabetical order: Christoph Becker, Steffen Becker, Martin Blersch, Franz Brosch, Fabian Brosig, Erik Burger, Oliver Denninger, Zoya Durdik, Michael Faber, Giovanni Falcone, Thomas Goldschmidt, Henning Groenda, Lucia Happe, Christoph Heger, Jörg Henß, Nikolas Herbst, Oliver Hummel, Matthias Huber, Nikolaus Huber, David Karlin, Benjamin Klatt (also thanks for the great food supply in our office!), Samuel Kounev, Anne Koziolek, Heiko Koziolek, Rouven Krebs, Klaus Krogmann, Max Kramer, Michael Kuperberg, Martin Küster, Michael Langhammer, Philipp Merkle, Aleksandar Milenkoski, Christof Momm, Qais Noorshams, Fouad ben Nasr Omri, Michal Papež, Pierre Parrend, Chris Rathfelder, Andreas Rentschler, Piotr Rygielski, Thomas Schuster, Simon Spinner, Johannes Stammel, Misha Strittmatter, Mircea Trifu, Robert Vaupel, and Alexander Wert.

I would also like to thank Susanne Agwaze, Elena Kienhöfer, Vanessa Martin Rodríguez, and Tatiana Rhode for their organizational support. Furthermore, I would like to thank Andrea Ciancone, Michael Kupsch, and Christian Stier, who supported me as students in various projects.

I am deeply grateful to my parents who have always been there for me. None of my achievements would have been possible without their support and encouragement.

Finally, I would like to thank Anne for her love, support and inspiration throughout the years. I dedicate this thesis to her.

Contents

1. Introduction

In 1966, IBM released the first version of the OS/360 operating system, a batch processing operating system with over 220,000 lines of code [Os]. Today, modern operating systems reach millions of lines of code: The Linux kernel 3.2 released in 2012 featured approx. 15 millions lines of code [Lee12], the complete codebase of Microsoft's operating system Windows XP released in 2001 features approx. 40 millions lines of code [Mar05].

This example illustrates how the complexity of the software execution environment increased over time. With the increased complexity, reflecting performance properties of the execution environment in software performance analysis gets more and more challenging. This thesis introduces a novel approach for automatically detecting such properties through experiments.

1.1. Motivation

Software Performance Engineering (SPE) is an approach to systematically reflect software performance during the whole software life-cycle [Smi90, SW02]. By considering performance early in software development, costly adaptations of the software at later stages in order to solve performance problems can be avoided. This can for instance be achieved by using model-based SPE approaches, which facilitate performance predictions of a software based on models (which can, in contrast to the implementation, already be specified at design time). Depending on the available information, models can be specified with different levels of granularity. Ideally, with more information available, fine-grained models can be created leading to more accurate performance predictions. However, this requires careful engineering of the performance model and often involves a lot of efforts.

The software performance can be influenced by multiple factors. Typically, many of them stem from the software execution environment. The execution environment encompasses the complete underlying infrastructure of the software such as hardware resources, controllers, the operating system, or further middleware.

Over the years, software execution environments became more and more complex. On the one hand, parts of the execution environment became more sophisticated and thus more extensive, such as operating systems (see example above). On the other hand, today's infrastructures typically consist of several layers through which resources are accessed by the software. For example, one major trend can be seen in the increased use of virtualized platforms. In a virtualized environment, software does not need to run on a dedicated server, but can also be deployed on a virtualized server which is running on top of a physical server. By using virtualization techniques, it is also possible to deploy multiple virtual servers on a single physical server. Software virtualization has a lot of benefits concerning costs, platform independence, security or reliability and is therefore used in more and more systems today. However, in virtualized systems the software accesses a hardware resource, such as the CPU or a hard disk, not directly through the operating system. Instead, resource calls may be passed from the operating system to the virtualization layer, which usually provides its own scheduling logic to handle the assignment of requests to resources.

In software performance analysis, execution environment properties have to be thoroughly reflected in order to yield acceptable analysis results. For example, Schroeder et al. showed that scheduling policies can have an impact on request response times by an order of magnitude or more [SWHB06]. Due to the increased complexity of the software execution environment, it becomes more difficult to accurately reflect the influence of the execution environment on the software performance during performance analysis. Of-

ten it is not possible to deploy the software on the target platform in order
to directly measure the performance impact of the execution environment
on the software.

For instance, at early stages of the software life-cycle, only initial performance models of the software might exist, but the software itself is not yet
fully implemented. In other scenarios, the deployment of a system on the
target environment might involve major efforts, so that it is not practical
to deploy the system during development time for performance measurements. In this case, the performance impact of the target system has to
be identified in a different way. Typically, small load tests or benchmarks
which are easy to deploy are typically executed in this case, but it remains
unclear how the results of such tests relate to the performance models of
the software.

Besides, performance analysis requires additional efforts at run-time,
when models have to be updated due to changes in the software and its environment. If the software execution environment changes, measurements
performed on older versions of the execution environment often cannot be
reused and might render software performance models unusable. In this
case, efforts are necessary to setup and repeat the measurements.

1.2. Problem

In order to accurately predict the performance of a software, the performance analyst has to reflect the performance-relevant properties of the execution environment in software performance analysis. This leads to various
issues:

- Typically, performance analysts are familiar with the concepts of performance engineering or with the software that is to be analyzed.
  Details on the domain of the software execution environment are often known to a much lesser extent. Hence, performance analysts are
  often only able to specify a limited set of performance-relevant exe-

cution environment properties for performance prediction, although the specification of additional properties might be beneficial.

- The execution environment is often simplified in performance analysis using basic queues and scheduling policies (e.g. in the performance analysis tools presented in [BKR09, FMW+12, KSM10]). In some performance analysis scenarios, for example for certain high-level predictions at early stages of design time, these properties are sufficient. However, sometimes fine-grained properties of the execution environment have to be supported as well in order to yield performance predictions with adequate prediction accuracy. This can for instance be the case if a software is running in a virtualized environment where the virtualization technology can have a significant impact on the response time of issued resource demands [Men05]. For such scenarios, support of deriving execution environment properties and including them in performance analysis is insufficient.

- Gathering information on the execution environment typically involves substantial efforts which often have to be carried out manually. This can be done by the performance analyst using specifications or by taking measurements. In the former case, gathering informations from specifications is a manual task. As performance-relevant information is typically not presented in a unified format, specifications have to be obtained and examined for the actual system manually. Some attributes, such as the performance overhead introduced by a virtualization platform, are typically not specified and thus can only be retrieved through measurements. When taking measurements, efforts are required in order to design experiments that are targeted towards the execution environment property in focus. For some properties, existing tools might be reused, but they are often platform-specific (and hence not always applicable).

- If certain execution environment properties can only be acquired with substantial efforts, some scenarios for performance prediction become infeasible: For example, the performance analyst might predict how the performance of a software changes when the software is deployed on different servers. If the execution environment differs for the different servers (for example, a different operating system, virtualization layer, or hardware resource setup is used), the time-consuming process of obtaining execution environment properties has to be repeated for every server in focus. If this has to be done manually, such efforts are rendered impractical.

- All manual efforts (either the efforts of gathering information on the execution environment properties or the integration of the properties in the performance analysis configuration) are notoriously prone to errors.

Based on these issues, three main challenges arise:

Shield the performance analyst from having to deal with details of the execution environment. In order to facilitate an efficient performance analysis, an SPE approach should encapsulate domain knowledge where possible so that the performance analyst can concentrate on specifying the information he is familiar with. For example, model-based performance engineering approaches such as the Palladio Component Model [BKR09] or the Core Scenario Model [PW04] introduced concepts for encapsulating details of performance analysis theory into tooling. In this case, the performance analyst can specify performance models using concepts from the domain of software system modeling. These models are then automatically transformed into low-level performance models. However, a comparable approach for encapsulating the process of retrieving and specifying information on the software execution environment is missing. In addition, automated integration into software performance analysis is also required in order to enable efficient performance analyses. Otherwise, the performance analyst has to manually insert the derived properties into the performance model. Not only implies such an approach more efforts, it also requires the performance analyst to deal with low-level details of the execution environment: Manual integration into performance analysis can only be done by the performance analyst if he is familiar with the execution environment properties and knows how to reflect such properties in performance analysis. Hence, it has to be investigated how the derivation and specification of performance-relevant execution environment properties as well as the integration into performance analysis can be encapsulated into an automated approach.

Find a proper abstraction level to deal with heterogeneous environments. As discussed above, retrieving information about the execution environment manually is cumbersome and requires in-depth knowledge about the platform. The performance analyst has to know on which properties he should focus on, and how property values can be detected. Automating this process requires to design an approach that can be applied to a wide range of execution environment properties. The approach should neither be limited to a certain part of the execution environment (e.g. operating system properties only), nor be restricted to an insufficient subset of platform technologies (e.g. Linux-based technologies only). The challenge is here to facilitate the design of automated experiments which are applicable to such heterogeneous environments.

Evaluate the impact of derived execution environment properties on software performance prediction accuracy. For some execution environment properties, it is difficult to specify how the property actually influences the performance of a software. For example, the performance overhead introduced by virtualization technology can strongly depend on the kinds of resource demands issued by the software. Detecting such overheads without measuring the software itself can for example be done by measuring the effect on synthetic load (i.e. microbenchmarks). In this case, the generated load has to be representative in order to derive a reasonable model of the execution environment. Hence, for experiments detecting such properties, it has to be validated whether the inclusion of the derived execution environment properties in a performance analysis can lead to significant improvements of the prediction results.

In order to address these issues, this thesis introduces an approach for the automated derivation of execution environment properties. Since not all properties can be easily detected through specifications, the approach regards the execution environment as a black box, i.e. it does not require access to internal information and derives all properties through measurements.

1.3. Shortcomings of Existing Solutions

Traditional approaches in software performance analysis (cf. [BKR09, BMdW⁺04, GMS07, PW04, SBHS06]) require the manual specification of execution environment properties in the performance models. They neglect the issue of how such information can be retrieved in the first place.

In order to enhance performance models with details that can be retrieved automatically, various approaches have been presented. Woodside et al. use measurements to derive a performance model that captures software resource demands as a function of the execution environment and user workload properties[WVCB01]. Zheng et al. use Kalman filters to derive a performance model through measurements [ZWL08]. While these approaches are based on measurements that can be potentially automated, they do not explicitly quantify the performance influences that stem from the execution environment—the derived properties are depending on the software model and cannot be reused for a different software model.

Other approaches that focus on the automated inclusion of performance properties of the execution environment are tailored towards a specific part of the execution environment. Krogmann et al. [KKR10] use measurements of Java bytecode instructions to extend a performance model automatically with information about the Java runtime environment. Liu et al. [LFG05] developed a benchmark-based approach for measuring the performance impact of the J2EE middleware platform. The measurements can be integrated into a performance model of the middleware for performance prediction of J2EE applications. While these approaches support the decoupling of the software performance model from a performance model of the execution environment, they are strongly targeted at specific parts of the execution environment and cannot be applied to other execution environment properties. For example, detecting properties of the operating system scheduler requires a different kind of measurements logic than predefined measurements that aim at detecting J2EE or JVM properties. Such approaches support the detection of specific execution environment properties which are important to be reflected in software performance prediction. However, since the approaches differ strongly in their structure and their implementation, applying multiple approaches in a software performance prediction can get complicated.

Finally, a large body of research exists on the performance evaluation of specific execution environment properties. These works typically address a certain performance-relevant property of the execution environment and provide a performance model of the property or an approach for quantifying the property. While the performance impact of the property under focus might be substantial, the problem of how to calibrate and translate the modeled property for inclusion into a software performance analysis approach is typically neglected. Furthermore, when it comes to detecting and modeling the properties, these works provide very specific approaches that cannot be transferred to different properties. In addition, many approaches do not focus on automated evaluation, but require manual investigation of measurement results. Thus, it requires in-depth knowledge in order to evaluate the properties and include them into performance analysts. For software performance prediction, such detailed properties are therefore usually neglected, although the prediction accuracy might strongly benefit from reflecting the properties. In Section 7.3 and 7.4, we provide a detailed discussion on related work w.r.t. the properties that are in the focus of this thesis.

Summing up, existing approaches are limited w.r.t. (i) the focus on the software level instead of the execution environment level, (ii) the automated execution of performance experiments, and (iii) the limited focus on a certain part of the execution environment. Chapter 7 discusses related work in detail.

1.4. Contributions

To ease the burden of detecting performance-relevant properties of the software execution environment and integrating such properties into performance analysis, this thesis introduces an approach called GINPEX (Goal-oriented INfrastructure Performance EXperiments). In the following, we present the contributions of the thesis in more detail.

An approach for the automated derivation of execution environment properties. The defined approach does not require that information on execution environment properties is available prior to performance analysis. Instead, it aims at retrieving such information automatically through predefined experiments. These experiments automatically conduct measurements on the target platform and analyze the measurement results to detect the value of the execution environment property under focus. The approach follows the idea of regarding the execution environment as a black box, i.e. it does not require access to internal details of the execution environment. This has the advantage of introducing technology-independent experiments that can be executed on all execution environments that meet the experiment requirements. In addition, the approach contributes

- a *workflow* for the design of automated experiments as well as the execution of automated experiments,

- concepts for *structuring execution environment properties* and *predefining automated experiments*,

- a concept for coupling experiments through *parametric experiment dependencies*.

A metamodel for the specification of execution environment experiments. The implementation of the approach is based on a metamodel which provides a domain-specific language for specifying experiments and the corresponding experiment logic. Experiments can be created as instances of the metamodel and stored in a repository for later application by performance analysts. For experiment execution, an experiment model is transformed into executable experiment code. This happens automatically through a model-to-text (M2T) transformation. Generating code based on metamodel instances facilitates the separation of experiment specification and experiment execution. In order to change details of how experiment logic has to be executed on a target platform (i.e. the structure of the experiment code), the metamodel and all specified metamodel instances do not have to be adapted; instead, only the transformation has to be changed. In summary, the contributions include

- a *metamodel* for specifying experiments, dependencies between experiments, as well as experiment logic,

- an *experiment template* for non-formal description of experiments,

- model-based concepts facilitating the *extension* of the approach with new experiments and new experiment logic.

Experiment designs for detecting CPU, OS scheduling, and virtualization properties. In this thesis, we validate the applicability of the approach by applying it to different parts of the execution environment. We define experiments to detect CPU, operating system scheduling and virtualization properties. Here, the thesis contributes

- *CPU and OS scheduling experiments* covering CPU simultaneous multithreading (SMT), the number of CPU cores, the operating system timeslice length and operating system load-balancing policies,

- *Virtualization experiments* detecting different kinds of virtualization overhead introduced by the virtualization platform, as well as the concept of an experiment for detecting additional load present in a virtualized environment.

An integration of experiment results into an approach for software performance prediction. This thesis provides an exemplary integration of the experiment results into the Palladio Component Model, an approach for model-based software performance prediction. Using the Palladio Component Model, we evaluate the impact of the experiment results on performance prediction.

1.5. Validation

The validation of the contributions of this thesis comprises the validation of the general approach and the validation of the presented experiment designs.

As mentioned above, we validate the applicability of the general approach by defining experiments that illustrate how correct execution environment properties can be detected automatically. The defined experiments demonstrate how the model-based approach can be used to define the corresponding experiment logic using the presented metamodel. In order to evaluate that the approach can be applied to different parts of the execution environment, we define experiments for different parts (CPU, OS scheduling, and virtualization properties).

The experiments for detecting CPU and OS scheduling properties are validated by executing the experiments on different platforms and evaluating the detected experiment result. The result is compared to the actual platform specification to show that the experiment detects the correct property value on all used platforms. To illustrate how the detected properties influence performance analysis, we conduct a case study where we show that the prediction error can be decreased by including the experimentally detected properties into performance analysis.

In contrast to the CPU and OS scheduling properties, the virtualization experiments do not detect properties that are available in specifications (i.e. different kinds of virtualization overhead). Hence, we cannot directly assess whether the experiments detect the property values correctly. However, we can analyze whether the performance prediction accuracy can be increased by including the detected properties in performance prediction (compared to a traditional prediction neglecting the detected properties). This is done using different case studies. The case studies show that the prediction error can be decreased significantly using the detected properties in performance analysis. In addition, they demonstrate that the experiment results are not directly connected to a single software application, but can be used for different applications: The same model of detected properties is used in different performance analyses conducted for two independent applications. In both cases, increased prediction accuracy can be observed.

1.6. Outline

The remainder of this thesis is structured as follows.

Chapter 2 deals with the foundations of this thesis. They are concerned with software performance analysis, model-driven software development, as well as operating system scheduling and virtualization as parts of the software execution environment that are in the focus of the presented experiments. Section 2.1 presents concepts from the domain of software performance analysis. It discusses software performance as an important quality attribute in software engineering, gives an introduction to software performance engineering (SPE), and discusses concepts of experiments and performance benchmarking. Finally, the section gives an overview on the Palladio Component Model (PCM), which is used in this thesis for integrating experiment results into performance analysis and for conducting software performance predictions. Section 2.2 discusses concepts from the area of model-driven software development on which this thesis builds on. It introduces the concepts of models and metamodels and presents some technological approaches from the Eclipse Modeling Project which are used for the implementation of the thesis approach. Finally, Section 2.3 gives an overview on some concepts from the domain of operating system scheduling and virtualization. It first discusses operating system scheduling and highlights various existing approaches for detecting CPU and OS scheduling properties. Afterwards, the concept of system

13

virtualization is introduced which is the basis of the execution environment properties detected by the virtualization experiments.

Chapter 3 introduces GINPEX (Goal-oriented INfrastructure Performance EXperiments), the overall approach presented by this thesis. In Section 3.1, the research context is set by defining the execution environment, presenting performance influences of the execution environment, and discussing how and why the execution environment model should be separated from the software architecture model. Section 3.2 continues with a discussion of the scientific challenges for the approach. In Section 3.3, the approach is presented in detail. Section 3.4 deals with the different scenarios in software performance engineering which can benefit from the presented approach, and Section 3.5 discusses limitations and assumptions of the approach.

Chapter 4 deals with the GINPEX approach in detail and shows how the approach can be implemented using concepts from model-based software engineering. Section 4.1 is focused on the concepts of experiment automation, presents requirements for such experiments, and deals with the structure of experiment execution. Section 4.2 introduces the concepts of experiment libraries and experiment domains, and Section 4.3 presents a concept for parametric experiments. The metamodel of the approach is presented in detail in Section 4.4. Section 4.5 is focused on the experiment execution and results analysis, and Section 4.6 presents a template that provides a common format for describing experiments. Section 4.7 continues with a discussion of the extensibility of the approach and Section 4.8 deals with the performance overhead of executing experiments.

Chapter 5 shows how the approach can be applied in order to define experiments for detecting CPU and OS scheduling properties. Section 5.1 gives an overview on the experiments presented in the chapter and Section 5.2 lists the scientific challenges that are related to these experiments. Section 5.3 to Section 5.6 cover the experiments in detail. In these sections, the results of executing the experiments on different platforms are also presented. Section 5.7 discusses how the experiment results can be integrated into a performance prediction approach. In Section 5.8, the detected properties are used in a case study to evaluate how the prediction accuracy can be increased when reflecting the properties in performance analysis. Section 5.9 continues with a discussion on the limitations and assumptions of the presented experiments.

Chapter 6 has a different focus on the execution environment: It features experiments to detect properties of virtualized environments. Again, the chapter starts with an overview on the presented experiments in Section 6.1. Section 6.2 discusses the scientific challenges for those experiments. In Section 6.3, an experiment is presented to derive a simple model of virtualization overhead. This overhead model is extended by another experiment in Section 6.4. Both sections feature case studies where the resulting prediction accuracy of the detected model is analyzed. Section 6.5 sketches another experiment for detecting additional load in virtualized environments and discusses limitations and assumptions of the presented experiments.

Chapter 7 discusses related work. Related work can be grouped into approaches dealing with the modeling of the execution environment in performance prediction (Section 7.1), approaches for deriving performance models through automated measurements (Section 7.2), and work that covers the performance analysis of CPU and OS scheduling properties (Section 7.3) and the performance analysis of virtualized environments (Section 7.4).

Chapter 8 concludes the thesis. It summarizes the contributions in Section 8.1 and briefly outlines the limitations and assumptions in

Section 8.2. In addition, it presents additional application areas of the GINPEX approach in Section 8.3, and discusses future work in Section 8.4.

2. Foundations

In this chapter, we introduce some concepts and terms from the different domains this thesis is based on. First, we give an overview on the field of software performance analysis. We continue with presenting some concepts from the area of model-driven software development. Finally, we explain some concepts of the software execution environment that are relevant for the experiments presented in this thesis; these concepts deal with operating system scheduling and virtualization.

2.1. Software Performance Analysis

In the following, we first give an introduction to some basic software performance concepts. We then explain the Software Performance Engineering approach (SPE), and give an overview on concepts for conducting performance experiments and benchmarks. We conclude this section with a presentation of the Palladio Component Model, an approach for architecture-based software performance prediction.

2.1.1. Software Performance

Performance is a software quality attribute that plays a role for nearly every software system that has been or has to be developed. In this work, we use the following definition of the term performance (from Smith and Williams [SW02]):

Definition 2.1. *Performance* is the degree to which a software system or component meets its objectives for timeliness.

Performance deals with the responsiveness of a software, i.e. how a software system meets its given objectives for response times or throughput, and with the scalability of a system, i.e. with its ability to meet performance objectives with an increased demand [SW02]. Typical metrics used in performance analysis are

- the response time of executed functionality,

- the throughput of a system, i.e. the number of requests processed during a specified time,

- and the utilization of the system's resources, i.e. the proportion of the time a resource was busy processing software requests.

Based on [BHK06], Becker [Bec08] identifies four factors influencing the performance of component-based software systems (see Figure 2.1):

Implementation. The implementation of a component has an influence on its performance, because the issued resource demands depend on the chosen algorithms and data structures.

Deployment. The execution environment the software is running on, has an performance impact, as processing or transfer rates of hardware resources influence the software response times.

External services. The performance of a component also depends on the performance of external services accessed. If an external service forms a performance bottleneck and yields slow response times, the performance of the accessing component can suffer as well.

Usage profile. The workload issued to a component also influences its performance. A component might yield different response times depending on the number of users accessing the component in parallel. Also the type and amount of data users issue to or request from a component can have a performance impact.

Analyzing the performance of a software means that all four factors have to be taken into consideration. In this thesis, the main focus lies on the performance impact of the software execution environment which is covered by the "Deployment" influencing factor.

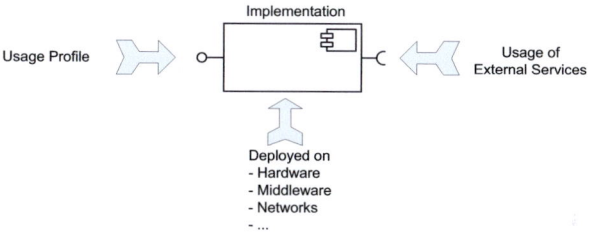

Figure 2.1.: Influence factors on the performance of component-based software systems (from [Bec08])

2.1.2. Software Performance Engineering

Software Performance Engineering (SPE) is a systematic approach to reflect the performance of a software during its development. The approach and a corresponding process was extensively presented back in 1990 by Smith [Smi90]. From this book, we quote the following explanation of SPE:

> Software performance engineering (SPE) is a method for constructing software systems to meet performance objectives. The process begins early in the software lifecycle and uses quantitative methods to identify satisfactory designs and to eliminate those that are likely to have unacceptable performance, before developers invest significant time in implementation. SPE continues through the detailed design, coding, and testing stages to predict and manage the performance of the evolving software and to monitor and report actual performance against specifications and predictions. [Smi90, p. 1].

19

While the complexity of software systems has changed radically during the last decades, this quote is still up-to-date.

In [SW02], the approach was extended to distributed and embedded systems. In addition, the SPE process was adapted to include the following 9 steps:

1. *Assess performance risk:* Identify the amount of SPE effort that is needed in a software development project.

2. *Identify critical use cases:* Select the most important use cases w.r.t. the system operation or the perceived responsiveness.

3. *Select key performance scenarios:* For each critical use case, select the most important performance scenarios.

4. *Establish performance objectives:* Provide performance requirements for each identified scenario using performance metrics such as response time, throughput, or resource utilization.

5. *Construct performance models:* Transform the identified performance scenarios into a model for performance analysis. The authors of the SPE process use execution graphs as a performance model.

6. *Determine software resource requirements:* Specify the amount of work that is performed during the steps of an performance model

7. *Add computer resource requirements:* Map the software resource requirements to hardware resource demands, such as CPU instructions or disk I/O.

8. *Evaluate the models:* Calculate performance values by solving the model and evaluate whether the specified requirements are met. If the evaluation reveals performance problems, steps 5 through 8 are repeated.

9. *Verify and validate the models:* In parallel to the complete process, determine whether the model is an accurate reflection of the software system and its performance.

2.1.3. Performance Experiments and Benchmarking

In [CS01], an experiment is defined as a method to check an assumption or a theory, to analyze an effect or to demonstrate possible fields of application. In computer science, experiments also comprise series of measurements [CS01, p. 234]. In the are of performance evaluation, Ferrari [Fer78] defines an experiment as a "set of empirical (or simulation) tests performed to obtain answers to questions which arise in an evaluation study". Based on these definitions, for this thesis we define a performance experiment as follows:

Definition 2.2. A *performance experiment* is a methodical procedure to assess the value of a performance characteristic or the validity of a hypothesis on the performance behavior of a system.

Experimental design deals with the statistical design of experiments. It aims at reducing the number of experiment runs while still obtaining results with adequate accuracy. The outcome of an experiment is called *response variable*. It is influenced by various variables which are called *factors*. The *levels* of a factor constitute the values for which a factor can be varied. Experimental designs aim at reducing the number of needed runs by reducing the number of factors, levels, or a combination of them. We will revisit experimental design in Chapter 6. For more details on the concepts of experimental design in performance analysis, see [Jai91].

Benchmarking denotes the process of performance comparison for two or more systems by measurements [Jai91]. The programs used for this are called *benchmarks*. A benchmark is a program which resembles a real-world workload. Sometimes, a synthetic workload (or *microbenchmark*) is used instead of a real-world benchmark for a more fine-grained, specific workload generation. Gray [Gra93] defines four properties a useful domain-specific benchmark has to provide:

1. *Relevance:* The benchmark must measure the performance (or price per performance) when the system performs typical operations in the problem domain.

2. *Portability:* It should require little effort to implement and deploy the benchmark on many different systems.

3. *Scalability:* The benchmark should work on small and on large systems.

4. *Simplicity:* The benchmark must be understandable.

The same properties also hold for microbenchmarks. Microbenchmarks are typically used to meet the second and fourth criteria: Due to its limited amount of code and benchmark logic, it is generally easier to understand and to implement. In this thesis, microbenchmarks are used for generating a certain type of workload on a target system, and to observe certain performance effects while this workload is executed.

2.1.4. The Palladio Component Model

The Palladio Component Model (PCM) comprises a domain-specific language for modeling component-based software architectures and related QoS properties [BKR09], as well as integrated tooling for model-based QoS predictions. It supports software performance analysis by following the SPE approach and aims at encapsulating knowledge on performance analysis as much as possible in attached tools. Therefore, the software architect or performance analyst does not have to understand how performance models can be analyzed or simulated using constructs from performance theory, such as queues, tokens, Instead, he can focus on modeling the software architecture using concepts from the software architecture domain, such as components, connectors, or servers. The software architecture model is then automatically transformed into a performance analysis model. Depending on the chosen prediction approach, this can be an analytical layered queueing network solver, or a simulation based on queueing networks. The PCM approach has been presented in [BKR09] and is shown in Figure 2.2.

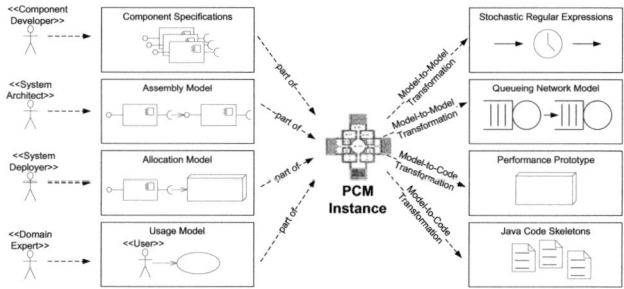

Figure 2.2.: PCM performance prediction process (from [BKR09])

Compared to other approaches for model-based performance prediction, the PCM is aligned with different developer rules, allowing for using performance prediction in a development process of component-based software engineering (CBSE). In addition, it supports the specification of parametric dependencies in the model, which facilitates the reuse of parts of a model in different contexts. In the following, we give more details on the structure of PCM models and explain how performance prediction can be carried out with the PCM-based simulation.

Modeling software for performance prediction with the PCM

The PCM is based on the CBSE development process presented [KH06]. The process distinguishes four different developer roles: The *component developer* is responsible for specifying and implementing software components. In a PCM model, he provides component models that include QoS-relevant component specifications, such as an abstract behavior specification called service effect specification (SEFF) or resource demands for performance analysis. The *software architect* assembles components to build the overall software architecture, which is called system in the PCM. The assembled components are then deployed by the *system deployer*. In the PCM model, he specifies the resource environment, i.e. the setup of the execution environment, servers, and hardware resources, and the allocation of components to servers. Finally, the *domain expert* is responsible for specifying the user workload, i.e. the frequency of user requests to the system, or the parameters which are passed by the users to the services.

The PCM separates the information from the different developer roles in different models. For example, the component specifications are stored in a component repository that is located in a different model than the system containing the software architecture. This way the different parts of the models can be developed independently of one another. It also means that information related to the software execution environment only has to be specified in the resource environment model. This is one of the reasons why the PCM was chosen as the software performance analysis tool for this thesis.

Conducting a performance prediction with the PCM-based simulation

In order to conduct a performance prediction for a PCM model, analytical solvers or a simulation based on queueing networks can be used. While analytical solvers provide fast analyses that can usually be executed within seconds, the simulation yields more detailed results. Compared to analytical solvers, it does not only report average performance response times but facilitates the calculation of fine-grained distribution functions for these metrics. In addition, the simulation supports more modeling constructs, such as multiple user scenarios [BKR09] In this thesis, we use the PCM-based simulation for performance predictions.

The PCM performance simulation is available as a simulation framework SimuCom. It is a Java-based simulation engine that is based on a generic event-based simulation engine such as Desmo-J [DES]. To execute a simulation for performance prediction, the performance analyst has to provide a complete PCM model including the component repository, the system, the resource environment, the allocation and the usage model. When a simulation run is launched, the PCM model is then transformed into Java code that represents the modeled system in a structure which can be used for simulation. The code directly plugs into the simulation framework; the combination of generated code and simulation frameworks forms a runnable simulation instance.

After code generation, a simulation run is immediately initiated. During a simulation run, the simulation engine iteratively executes simulated requests based on the modeled user workload. The requests lead to the execution of component specifications, which in turn access the simulation framework, for example when an issued resource demand is to be simulated. The resource demand that occurs in a component is mapped to a simulated resource management by the simulation framework. This resource simulates the performance behavior of the hardware resource which is responsible for executing the demand. During simulation, the framework calculates the response times of such a demand and collects performance metrics (such as response times or resource utilization) in corresponding sensors. For details on how the elements are mapped to SimuCom constructs and how the performance of the model is simulated in SimuCom, see [Bec08].

2.2. Model-driven Software Development

Model-driven software development (MDSD) is an approach in software engineering that puts a strong focus on the creation of software through models. Models are considered equal to code, as their implementation is automated [SV06]: Based on models, executable code is automatically generated through model transformations or code generators. Using model-driven engineering approaches in software development can have several benefits. For example, it can increase productivity if it takes less time to provide a model instead of the corresponding software implementation. Typically, code generation is used to encapsulate recurring code constructs. This code can then be generated automatically, leading to an improved development speed and fewer bugs created by manually writing code. As an example, take a web-based software application where part of the data structure is represented through models. In this case, a lot of "glue code" dealing with data management and database access, can be created automatically and does not have to be written manually. Another advantage of using models is that, due to the abstract level of models, the understandability of the software can be increased if the models hide software complexity in a reasonable way.

2.2.1. Models and Metamodels

The term *model* has been defined by Stachowiak as a formal representation of entities and relationships in the real world (abtraction) with a certain correspondence (isomorphism) for a certain purpose (pragmatics) [Sta73]. Abstraction means that only those details of the real-world, that serve the purpose of being modeled are included in the model; other details are removed. Isomorphism means that properties of the model elements also hold for the real world properties. In other words, the projection of real-world elements onto model elements has to be isomorphic. Finally, a pragmatic model means that it serves a certain goal, and has not been created only for the sake of its own.

Models are created using a formal specification called metamodel. In [Ern], a metamodel is defined as a precise definition of the constructs and rules needed for creating semantic models.

As an example, consider the Unified Modeling Language (UML) specified by the OMG for modeling object-oriented software systems [Obj11b, Obj11c]. The UML serves as the metamodel that specifies the elements and relationships that can be used to create UML models. For example, the metamodel provides constructs to model classes, attributes, and references between classes. Based on the UML metamodel, a UML model can be created for a certain software application. This model can for example contain the object-oriented classes of the software – these classes are instances of the class metamodel element. Finally, the implemented software can again instantiate the modeled classes.

To illustrate these dependencies, the OMG has specified a four-level metamodel hierarchy [Obj11b]. The lowest level (M0) consists of the actual instances of the model, such as object-oriented runtime instances of the classes. The next level (M1) features the object-oriented software model, i.e. the modeled classes, attributes, references and so on. Again, the model at the M1 level is an instance of the metamodel, which is located at the metamodel level (M2). For every level holds that the elements in this level are instances of the model specified in the next upper level. In addition, the OMG defines a fourth level (M3) which consists of a so-called meta-metamodel which can be used to model metamodels such as the UML. For this case, the OMG has defined the Meta Object Facility (MOF) [Obj11a]. This level is self-referencing, i.e. the metamodel of the meta-metamodel MOF is also the MOF. In other words, the MOF is modeled using MOF elements.

Figure 2.3 illustrates the four metamodel levels with the example of modeling persons in an object-oriented software. The "Person" class is modeled

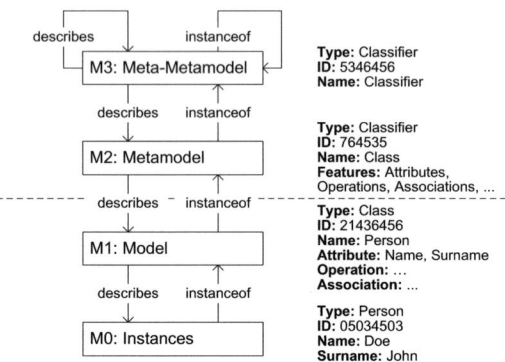

Figure 2.3.: The four-level metamodel hierarchy of the OMG (based on [SV06])

using UML constructs, i.e. the UML "Class" element. An actual instance of the "Person" class, i.e. a runtime instance of a person during execution of the software, is denoted at the lowest level M0. For the sake of completeness, it should be noted that the UML also provides modeling constructs to model class instances at the same level as classes using UML object diagrams (not shown in the figure).

2.2.2. The Eclipse Modeling Project

The Eclipse development environment features a variety of technologies and tools to support model-driven software development. These items are bundled in the Eclipse Modeling Project [Thef]. In this thesis, we make use of two Eclipse MDSD frameworks: the Eclipse Modeling Framework for metamodeling, and the Eclipse Model to Text (M2T) project for code generation.

The Eclipse Modeling Framework features a meta-metamodel called Ecore [Thec]. Ecore is based on a subset of OMG's meta-metamodel MOF and can be used to create metamodels for the Eclipse platform. A subset of the Ecore metamodel elements is shown in Figure 2.4.

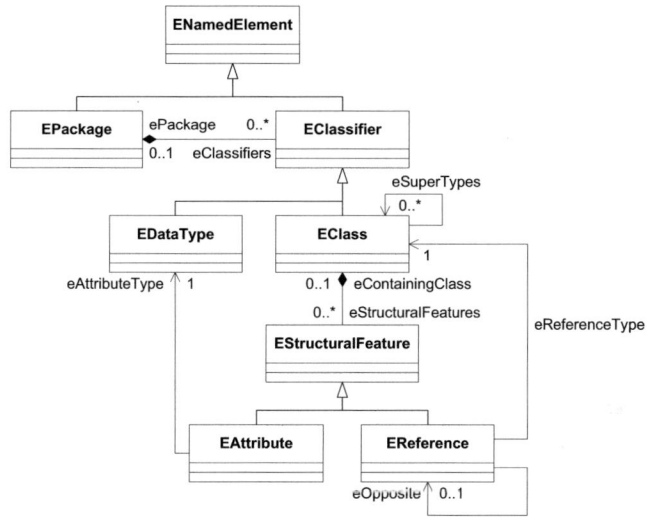

Figure 2.4.: Excerpt from the Ecore metamodel (based on [Gro09])

Based on an Ecore metamodel, the EMF framework can be used to automatically generate model editors which facilitate the creation and editing of metamodel instances. Furthermore, various framework for the automated generation of additional graphical editors.

In model-based software engineering, models are not created for documentation purposes only, but are integrated into an executable software toolchain. One possibility of using models in a software system could be the modeling of a data structure. The structure can then for example be transformed into a database schema. Another option is to model some kind of software behavior which is then transformed into executable software. In this thesis, we define a metamodel for specifying experiment logic. The concrete metamodel instances are then transformed into executable Java code, facilitating the specification of experiments without the need to write any Java code.

To generate code based on metamodel instances, so called model to text (M2T) approaches are used. For this purpose, the Eclipse Model to Text

(M2T) project [Thee] provides various libraries for code generation. The approach presented in this thesis has been implemented using the XPand language of the M2T framework. In XPand, code generation templates are specified that define which kind of source code has to be generated for every element of the metamodel.

2.3. Operating System Scheduling and Virtualization

In this thesis, we discuss how to derive performance-relevant properties of software execution environments. In particular, we present experiments to derive CPU and OS scheduling properties as well as properties of virtualized environments. To facilitate the comprehension of these experiments, we discuss some concepts regarding OS scheduling and virtualization.

2.3.1. Operating System Scheduling

The operating system is a software that serves as a layer between the hardware resources and the software applications. It encapsulates hardware access and provides additional functionality for program execution, such as simultaneous execution of applications.

The basic concept of an operating system for executing a software is a *process* [Tan01]. A process is a program in execution managed by the operating system. The operating system schedules the program on hardware resources. It assigns the program to a CPU to perform CPU calculations, or to a network or disk device to perform I/O operations. The operating system can manage multiple processes at the same time. If multiple resources of the same kind are available, such as CPU cores, true hardware parallelism can be exploited for parallel execution of processes. If the hardware resource does not permit to be used by multiple processes at the same time, such as a single-core CPU or a simple hard disk device, the operating system switches between the processes, giving each process access to the resource for a short time period (tens to hundreds of milliseconds) and thus creating the illusion of parallelism to the user (also called pseudoparallelism) [Tan01].

Besides processes, operating systems provide the constructs of *threads*. A thread is a light-weight process that involves less overhead in creating and executing. Multiple threads can be executed in the context of a process; they share the resources of the process, such as the address space or open files.

In performance analysis, the differentiation between processes and threads is often not necessary [Hap08]. This is also the case for the experiments presented in this thesis. Hence, in this thesis we use the term *task* as a generic term that covers both processes and threads.

When multiple tasks are to be executed in parallel, the operating system is responsible for assigning the tasks to the available CPU cores. If more tasks are available for execution than CPU cores, the operating system has to decide when and which task to schedule on which CPU core. This operation is called *scheduling*. For this purpose, different scheduling strategies exist. While real-world operating systems typically use more complex strategies, we briefly discuss two basic scheduling policies, which are also commonly used in performance analysis approaches:

- The *first come, first served* scheduling policy assigns a CPU core to the tasks in the order the tasks request it. If a task does not voluntarily stop running on the CPU, other tasks have to wait until the tasks completes. This policy is typically used in batch systems where interactive behavior (which is typically achieved through pausing running tasks and moving other tasks to the CPU) is not needed.

- The *round robin* scheduling policy is a widely used scheduling policy which supports a fair scheduling of parallel tasks. Each task is executed on the CPU for a specified duration, which is called *timeslice* or quantum. After a timeslice is completed, the scheduler pauses the currently running task and switches to the next one. The timeslice

31

length differs between different scheduler implementations. Short timeslices lead to a higher overhead for context switching, longer timeslices can cause poor response times for interactive requests. In performance analysis approaches, for example in performance simulations, a modification of the round-robin policy called *processor sharing* often is used. Processor sharing assumes a theoretical infinitely short timeslice length, abstracts from context switches, and simulates real parallel execution of all running processes.

Most scheduling policies used in general-purpose operating systems (GPOS) are based on some kind of round robin scheduling. Typical enhancements include priorities to favor certain tasks (especially in interactive systems, where responsive UI tasks are desired), or the introduction of additional scheduling queues. Real-time schedulers for embedded systems often use different scheduling policies, because in real-time systems the meeting of deadlines is an important requirement. As embedded systems are not in the focus of this thesis, we refer the reader to [Kop11] for further information on real-time scheduling policies. Details on GPOS scheduling and general concepts of operating systems can be found in [Tan01].

2.3.2. Detecting CPU and OS Scheduling Properties

In this thesis, we present an approach to detect CPU and OS properties in a automated, platform-independent way. Without such an approach, platform-specific tasks have to be performed. Some of them are discussed in the following.

For detecting CPU properties, OS-specific operations can be executed. Linux and other Unix-based systems provides the virtual file \proc\cpuinfo that contains information about the available CPU processors. On Windows systems, the user can consult the Windows Device Manager. Obtaining CPU information this way requires manual efforts and performing procedures that cannot be applied across different operating system families. In addition, OS-specific operations can sometimes return incorrect CPU information. For example, some AMD or Intel processors might use certain flags to indicate simultaneous multithreading (SMT) availability although SMT is not available [Wik].

Instead of issuing calls to the operating system API for querying CPU information, various tools exist that report information about the available CPU hardware. The Intel Processor Identification Utility [Intc] is a tool that identifies different properties of the CPU processor. In addition to other CPU properties, it also identifies the number of CPU cores as well as whether simultaneous multithreading (SMT) is supported by the processor. However, the tool reports SMT availability even if it has been disabled in the system setup. In addition, the tool is only applicable to newer Intel processors. For older processors, a legacy product has to be used [Intb]. The tools only work on Windows machines, or can be installed as a bootable version which does not require an operating system, but the access to rebooting the machine. It is not executable from within different operating systems, such as Unix-based systems.

A third-party tool that works with CPUs of different vendors is for example CPU-Z [CPU]. It detects, among others, the number of available virtual and physical cores. From this information, SMT availability can be derived manually. However, this tool can also only be used on Windows machines.

A platform-independent approach for querying CPU information can be taken by querying CPU information from within the programming environment, for example the Java Virtual Machine. The Java library provides the API call `Runtime.getRuntime().availableProcessors()` which returns the number of virtual CPU cores. However, if SMT is available, the number of available physical CPU cores cannot be retrieved this way.

In all cases, the user has to query this information manually (or automate the queries on his own), and provide an integration of the detected information in performance analysis. The experiments presented in this thesis for detecting CPU properties run automatically on all platforms supporting

Java and yield results that can be directly used in the Palladio Component Model for performance analysis.

Regarding OS scheduling properties, no uniform approach exists for detecting such properties on the different general-purpose operating systems that are usually installed on servers. In this thesis, we focus on different Windows and Linux operating systems. Here, no uniform approach exists for detecting certain OS scheduling properties. In general, obtaining information on the scheduler requires manually researching OS specifications and in-depth OS documentation which is usually spread among various websites on the Internet. Neither does a uniform approach or classification for documenting scheduler properties exist, nor can such properties queried automatically inside the different operating systems.

For the OS scheduling properties that are in the focus of this thesis, we used various primary sources for obtaining information on the different schedulers ([Aas05, Mol07, RS05]). Additional details on the OS schedulers can be found in [Jon] and [SQ]. In [Hap08], different operating system schedulers are presented and their performance-relevant properties are compared.

2.3.3. Virtualization

Gartner defines virtualization as an abstraction that masks the physical nature and boundaries of those resources from resource users [Gar]. An IT resource can for example be a server or a hardware device, but also an application. For instance, the Java Virtual Machine (JVM) provides a virtual runtime environment in which Java programs can be executed. The JVM software can be installed on various operating systems, facilitating the OS-independent development of software applications. Another form of virtualization called system virtualization provides a complete system environment [SN05]. System virtualization makes it possible to run multiple operating systems in parallel on the same machine. This requires that a virtualization software called hypervisor (or virtual machine monitor) is installed on the server instead of a conventional operating system. The hypervisor serves as the virtualization layer. On top of this layer, multiple virtualized operating systems (called Guest operating systems or Guest virtual machines) can be installed. Just like the operating system manages the execution of parallel processes, giving each process the illusion of running on the machine alone, the hypervisor supports execution parallel operating systems (in which the running applications do not have to know that they run in a virtualized environment). In this thesis, we mean system virtualization when we use the term virtualization.

Figure 2.5 illustrates the concept of system virtualization. It shows how the hypervisor serves as a layer between the hardware and the virtualized operating systems.

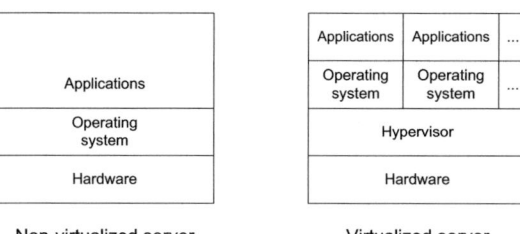

Figure 2.5.: System virtualization

The system virtualization structure shown in the right part of Figure 2.5 is called a native VM system [SN05] or type-1 virtualization resp. type-1 hypervisor [BKNT11]. In this case, the hypervisor is directly installed on the hardware and not running on top of a host operating system. Type-2 virtualization denotes a system virtualization technique where the hypervisor is installed on top of an operating system. Typically, the hypervisor runs as a process in the operating system like other applications, but still serves the purpose of running multiple guest operating systems.

Figure 2.6 illustrates these two concepts of system virtualization. Both concepts may have different implications on the guest applications running in such virtualized environments, such as the performance overhead induced by the virtualization layer. However, for this thesis it is not necessary to further distinguish these virtualization types.

Virtualizing operating systems can have several benefits. First of all, multiple servers can be consolidated on one server if the server's operating systems are transferred to Guest operating systems on the virtualized server. This is often done in the area of server consolidation, where servers with little resource utilizations are replaced by a single virtualized server, yielding a better resource utilization and a reduced number of server machines.

In addition, virtualization can be used to run different types of operating systems in parallel. For example, a virtual machine can run an older operating system to support the execution of legacy software that does not run on newer operating systems anymore. Or virtual machines can be used to separate the development and testing environment from the production environment.

Another benefit of virtualization is the improved maintainability of the execution environment. Virtual machines can be migrated from one server to another. Virtualization solutions also provide the functionality of taking virtual machine snapshot, i.e. storing the state, disk data and configuration

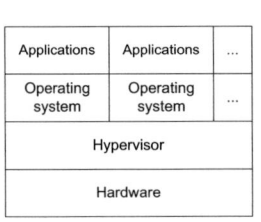

Type-1 virtualization

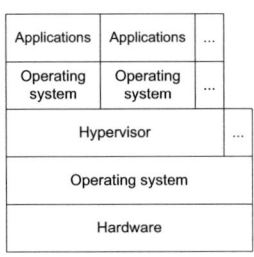

Type-2 virtualization

Figure 2.6.: Type-1 and type-2 virtualization

of a virtual machine as a file. Such techniques enable a simple setup and rollback of operating system installations as well as a easy way of transferring operating systems from one server to another.

Virtualization also provides the technical foundation for cloud computing, where virtual machines are used to provide infrastructure, middleware, or software services on a pay-per-use basis.

Virtualization is not a new technology. Initial virtualization techniques have been developed in the late 1960's and a lot of research has been carried out at that time [Gol74]. Back then, mainframe servers were expensive and therefore multiple Guest operating systems had to be supported. With the advent of low-cost computing power in the 1980's, the importance of virtualization declined. In the 1990's the computing power of the x86-based machine was high enough to support virtualization on mainstream machines. This led to an increased number of virtualization installations and paved the way for the cloud computing trend that could be observed in recent years. For more details on virtualization techniques, see [SN05].

3. An Approach For Deriving Execution Environment Properties

This chapter introduces the approach to derive performance-relevant properties of execution environments that is contributed by this thesis. In Section 3.1, we first give a definition of the term execution environment and discuss the relevance of including execution environment properties in software performance analysis. We then present the scientific challenges for an automated approach to derive such properties in Section 3.2. The method of the approach itself is introduced in Section 3.3. Afterwards, we present scenarios in which the approach can be applied (Section 3.4) and discuss limitations and assumptions of the approach (Section 3.5). Section 3.6 recapitulates the chapter and summarizes the core benefits of the approach. Parts of the approach have been initially published in [HHR11], [HKHR11], and [HKHR13].

3.1. Research Context

The work of this thesis aims at enhancing architecture-based software performance analysis. In the following, we illustrate the research context on which the work of this thesis is based on.

We first give a definition on the term "execution environment" in Section 3.1.1. In the following Section 3.1.2, we present and group different performance-relevant properties of the execution environment. Finally, Section 3.1.3 illustrates how the execution environment has to be reflected in software performance analysis in by separating the execution environment model from the software architecture model.

3.1.1. A Definition of the Execution Environment

In related work, there is no clear definition of the term "software execution environment". Instead, the term is used in different meanings. Often, a clear definition is omitted. In addition, other terms, such as "infrastructure" or "platform" are used as well, sometimes referring to slightly different parts, sometimes denoting the same thing.

The specification of the Unified Modeling Language (UML) defines the execution environment as "a node that offers an execution environment for specific types of components that are deployed on it in the form of executable artifacts" [Obj11c]. A node is defined as a "computational resource upon which artifacts may be deployed for execution" [Obj11c]. An execution environment in the UML denotes software components but no hardware resources; those are represented by the "device" element.

A different definition can be found in the area of real-time systems: Burns and Wellings [BW01] describe the execution environment as the "components that are used together with the application's code to make the complete system: the processors, networks, operating systems and so on." Here, both hardware resources, such as processors and the network, and software middleware, such as operating systems, are included in the term "execution environment".

Another definition is used in [Mal12], a work rooted in the area of component-based software development. Here, the term 'execution environment' is used for denoting a component platform on which components can be deployed and executed. The underlying operating system and hardware resources are not part of the execution environment (the term "system execution infrastructure" is used for subsuming resources, operating system and the component platform).

As no uniform definition of the term "software execution environment" exists, we use the following definition in the scope of this thesis:

Definition 3.1. The *software execution environment* denotes the infrastructure on which the software is running on. It comprises hardware resources and software, such as operating systems and middleware technologies.

For the sake of readability, the terms "software execution environment" and "execution environment" are used interchangeably in this thesis.

3.1.2. Performance-relevant Properties of the Execution Environment

Based on Definition 3.1, we group the various parts into the following categories:

Hardware resources. Hardware resources include all physical resources that are accessed when executing the software. For business information systems, such resources include CPU processors, the available main memory, as well as hard disk and network devices. Certain systems might involve additional special resources, such as tape data storage systems or barcode readers.

Performance-relevant properties of a CPU resource include the processing rate, the number of cores, and simultaneous multithreading capability (for more details, see Chapter 5). Hard Disk properties include disk throughput and the scheduling policy of the hard disk controller. The performance impact of the network depends on various factors, such as network bandwidth, network load, but also on the type of network communication used (packet size, network overhead, etc.).

Hardware virtualization. In order to run multiple guest operating systems on a single physical server, virtualization mechanisms can be used. A typical scenario for virtualization of operating systems involves a hypervisor running on the hardware which manages the execution of virtual machines (VMs) and the scheduling of demands occurring in VMs to the available physical resources. In addition to the guest operating systems, the software performance is influenced by the employed virtualization. Performance-relevant properties include hypervisor and virtual machine properties (such as resource priorities) as well as virtualization overheads. Chapter 6 deals with the integration of such properties in performance prediction.

The provisioning of computing resources over a network, which is denoted by the cloud computing paradigm, also falls into this category, as cloud computing approaches heavily utilize hardware virtualization mechanisms. Here, additional properties might have to be regarded, such properties of elastic systems, or additional system load stemming from the fact that resources are shared with other users.

Operating systems.   Depending on the number of servers, different kinds of operating systems can be involved in a software setup. Business information systems usually run on so-called general-purpose operating systems (GPOS), which are targeted at software applications that are not time-critical (compared to real-time systems). A major impact on software performance that stems from the operating system is the scheduling policy: operating systems differ in how tasks are scheduled on the available CPU processors. The scheduling policy can influence the response time of a software by several orders of magnitude [SWHB06]. Details on deriving GPOS scheduling policy properties for performance prediction can be found in Chapter 5.

Middleware.   On top of the operating system, additional software can be deployed which is usually not considered part of the business application, but, like operating systems, reused off-the-shelf. Such software involves middleware approaches and application servers providing functionality for distributed systems, runtime environments facilitating the execution of programs such as the Java Virtual

Machine, and database management systems. Middleware provides logic that can be reused for different software applications. Hence, it can be distinguished from business components that make use of or are deployed on middleware, and thus be considered as another part of the execution environment.

Apparently, various performance-relevant properties can be found in those systems. For example, consider the thread pool functionality of an application server that is used to handle incoming requests. Properties related to thread pool logic include the invocation costs of process or thread creation, or the invocation costs of accessing the thread pool. In addition, contention effects when accessing the thread pool can occur as well as performance delays, when the request is blocked because the maximum number of running threads has been reached.

Influence factors of the execution environment, such as the ones mentioned above, occur in various kinds even for small systems. As an example, consider the simple three-tiered software architecture shown in Figure 3.1. The software consists of four components: a database component,

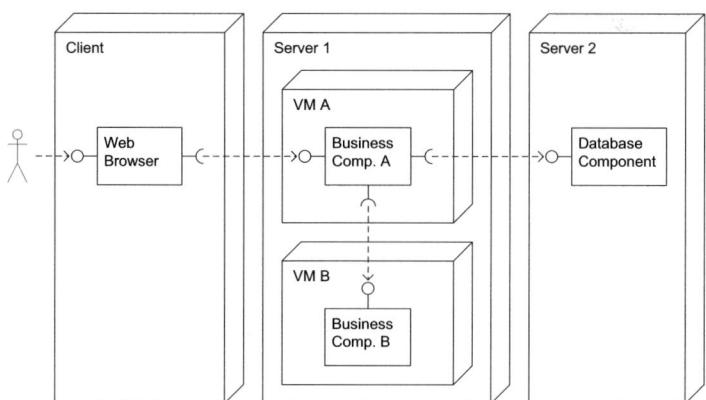

Figure 3.1.: Exemplary three-tier architecture

two components forming the business layer, and a user interface component executed in the web browser on the client machine. The user calls are propagated to the business component *Business Comp. A*, which delegates the calls to another business component *Business Comp. B* and to the database layer component *"Database Component"*. While the database component is deployed on a different physical server (for example, a server equipped with sufficient disk storage), the business components share the same physical server, but are deployed in separate virtual machines.

Even though the considered architecture is kept simple, various potential performance impacts of the execution environment on the system's performance can be observed in the architecture:

- *Client* machine: On the client machine, the *Web Browser* component requires system resources, typically memory and CPU, to provide the presentation logic (e.g. UI rendering). While these effects are irrelevant for server performance management (such as capacity planning or server performance bottleneck analysis), they can influence the overall software response time observed by the end user.

- Call *Client* to *Server 1*: Calls from a browser to the server tier occur over a network, which can be a limited area network, such as a local area network (for example, if server and all client machines are located in the same office building), or a broad network, such as a wide area network or the internet. While performance analysis is much easier for the former type of network, systems typically involve the latter type of networks for communication.

- Delegating call to *Business Comp. A*: Once a call to *Server 1* has been transmitted over the network, additional steps may occur which induce performance overhead due to the execution environment. First, the call has to be dispatched from the network device of *Server 1* to the local network device of the virtual machine *VM A*. This can include contention effects (for example on a limited resource such as a network device) or CPU resource overhead (for example due to virtualization hypervisor activity for mapping sever network device requests to virtual machine network devices).

In many software systems, business components are deployed inside an application server, which provides additional functionality. In this case, additional performance impact can occur, such as accessing a thread pool, as described above.

- Execute service of *Business Comp. A*: When a service of *Business Comp. A* is executed, resource demands occur. Depending on the amount of issued demands, they have to be regarded in performance analysis to gain accurate analysis results. Typical resource demands include CPU and disk resource demands. Performance-relevant properties include properties of the accessed hardware resources, OS scheduling properties, and virtualization properties.

  While *Business Comp. B* shares the same properties, differences to *Business Comp. A* can stem from different reasons: For example, a certain resource type access might by negligible in *Business Comp. B*. If the component does not perform any disk accesses, disk properties can be neglected here. In addition, some execution environment properties might have different values compared to *Business Comp. A*, for example if the component is deployed on a different guest operating system, or if a part of the infrastructure is configured in a different way.

- Call *Business Comp. A* to *Business Comp. B*: These calls occur on the same physical machine, and thus do not go over a network connection. However, as *Business Comp. B* is deployed on *VM B*, calls have to pass the virtualization hypervisor, which might incur performance overhead. In addition, performance influences can be caused by additional communication overhead, such as marshalling and demarshalling operations.

45

- Call *Business Comp. A* to *Database Component*: These calls occur between two physical machines. Thus the performance of the call is influenced by the network adapters involved (including mapping a virtual machine network device to a physical machine network device) and the network connection. In addition, marshalling and de-marshalling overhead can influence the performance.

- Execute service of *Database Component*: The component deployed on *Server 2* provides data access. Similar to the application server, the underlying database is a part of the execution environment that introduces further performance-relevant properties. For performance analysis, disk access typically needs to be reflected, but database functionality often involves a mixture of CPU and disk accesses (for example, when evaluating database queries), as well as transaction properties. Accurate analyses thus need to reflect the corresponding properties.

Additional properties can be observed if the software (or a part of the software) is running in a cloud computing environment.

To sum up, even for the small example shown in Figure 3.1 various performance infrastructure properties can be observed that may need to be reflected in software performance analysis. The list of properties and impact factors presented above is by no means exhaustive; further properties can for example be found in different infrastructure libraries or frameworks, such as middleware communication systems or MapReduce [DG08] implementations for highly parallelized applications. In addition, the system presented above is an example of a Client-server system with synchronous calls; other properties can for example arise in systems with P2P communication or other asynchronous calls.

In this thesis, we focus on server-based systems as the one described in the example above, but the general approach can be applied to different systems as well. We also do not cover database and network properties in this thesis, although they can play an important role in performance analysis, as discussed in the example. An extension of the approach to these properties is out of the scope of this thesis and regarded as future work (see Section 8.4).

3.1.3. Separating the Execution Environment Model from the Software Architecture Model

Software Performance Engineering helps in detecting performance problems of a software system at early stages of the life-cycle. Architecture-based performance prediction can be used to analyze the software performance by using architecture models. To reflect the impact of the execution environment in such predictions, a model of the execution environment has to be available.

In the following, we discuss how the execution environment model has to be separated from the software architecture model. We argue that this is necessary in order to (i) get accurate performance prediction results and (ii) conduct performance predictions in a feasible way.

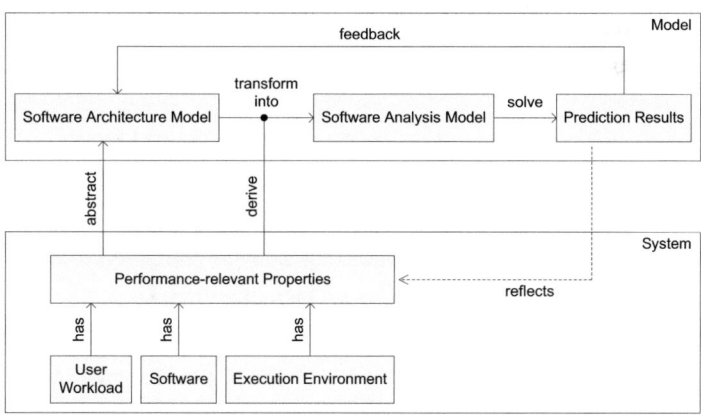

Figure 3.2.: Reflecting performance-relevant properties in model-based software performance prediction

47

The integration of performance-relevant properties of the execution environment is illustrated in Figure 3.2. The upper part of the figure depicts the traditional model-based software performance engineering approach, where the software performance model is transformed into a software analysis model for performance analysis. Based on the analysis results, performance questions can be answered, which then reflect in changes to the software system and the corresponding software performance model. Performance-relevant properties that have to be reflected can stem from the software itself (both the architecture and the implementation), the user workload, and the execution environment [LFG05]. To include performance-relevant properties in software performance analysis, they can either be included in the software architecture model, or in the analysis model. In the former case, the degree of abstraction used in the performance model determines which information can already be included in this model. As the performance model is constructed from architectural and design-level information, the architecture model often provides an abstract view. It is typically not designed to include fine-grained properties. In the latter case, derived performance properties are directly included in the analysis model during or after the transformation of the software architecture model. In this case, it depends on the features of the analysis model which kind of performance-relevant properties can be included. As the analysis model typically consists of a more fine-grained model on a different abstraction level (for example, a simulation of a queueing network, implemented in a high-level programming language), in general more properties can be included and reflected during analysis compared to including properties on the level of the software architecture model.

Many existing performance analysis approaches neglect most influences of the execution environment and use only abstract representations of the environment. Hence, depending on the scenario, arbitrarily high prediction errors can be introduced in the analyses. Other approaches are tailored towards a certain part of the execution environment, but neglect other parts of the execution environment. In addition, existing models have to be instantiated manually, which requires domain knowledge about the execution environment and is a cumbersome and error-prone approach.

Other approaches fail to include certain execution environment properties, as platform-dependent information is directly encoded in the software model. For example, ROBOCOP [BMdW+04] and CUTS [SBHS06] provide component models with support of performance prediction, but component resource demands have to be specified in milliseconds in both models. Thus, when using these models for performance prediction, resource demands are only valid for a certain platform. If one is interested in predicting the performance of a component deployed in a different execution environment, he or she has to adapt the resource demands in the model, which is typically only possible by deploying the component and taking resource demand measurements on the new platform. For performance prediction, this has several disadvantages:

- For analyzing the software's performance on multiple different execution environments, resource demands have to be obtained for every execution environment, for example by conducting measurements. If different software is to be analyzed, measurements have to be repeated.

- The software has to be deployed on the target execution environment environment to predict its performance. This is not possible in all cases, for example when the software performance is to be predicted in a migration project. Here, typically effort has to be put first into adapting the software before it can be deployed on the target platform. Performance predictions at early stages of a migration project are not possible in this case, if properties of the execution environment have to be reflected in prediction. Another problem arises when the deployment itself requires much effort, for example because of the size and complexity of the software system. In this case, if performance models already exist, but resource demands have to be adapted, deployment efforts are required in order to take new resource demand measurements.

To overcome the issue of having to deploy the software on the target platform in order to make accurate predictions, infrastructure-specific information has to be separated from the software-specific information in the performance model. For example, performance prediction approaches such as PCM [BKR09], *SPE·ED*/PMIF [SL04], or KLAPER [GMS07] support the specification of platform-independent demands that occur during execution of a component's service, such as number of operations or number of resource instructions. Such specifications are then transformed into a performance analysis model, where concrete, platform-specific execution times are calculated by incorporating information of the execution environment, such as resource processing rates.

The separation of platform-independent and platform-dependent information in software performance models is for example utilized by Krogmann et al. [KKR10]. The authors specify resource demands of Java components by quantifying platform-independent bytecode instructions and map the duration of bytecode instructions to specific platforms by employing bytecode benchmarking. However, the approach only aims at quantifying a specific property of the execution environment and cannot be reused for deriving different execution environment properties. The same holds for other existing approaches (see also the survey on related work in Chapter 7).

3.2. Scientific Challenges

In the previous sections, we discussed the influences of the execution environment on performance prediction and how the execution environment has to be integrated in performance prediction approaches. To reflect performance-relevant execution environment properties in software performance prediction, this thesis presents an automated approach to derive such properties by predefined experiments. In the following, we present the scientific challenges for the approach.

1. **Structuring performance-relevant properties out of the huge amount of execution environment properties.** As described in Section 3.1.2, the execution environment typically consists of various middleware and hardware systems, all featuring different properties. Without a useful structure, the software architect may be overwhelmed with a vast amount of execution environment properties and corresponding experiments. Thus, to ease the integration of such properties into performance analysis, it has to be investigated how properties of different parts of the execution environment can be structured in a meaningful way in order to be derived using an automated, uniform approach.

2. **Automating the derivation of performance-relevant execution environment properties for software performance prediction.** Software performance prediction is usually conducted by software architects or performance analysts. Manual derivation of execution environment properties is error-prone and cumbersome. In addition, it involves domain knowledge on how to retrieve the properties. To overcome these issues by using an automated approach, it has to be investigated which concepts are necessary that support the specification of automated experiments.

3. **Deriving execution environment properties through experiments that are reproducible and have a good performance.** An automated approach to derive performance properties only becomes feasible if the experiments yield reproducible results and run with acceptable performance. Thus, it has to be investigated how the approach can support the experiment designer in specifying experiments that meet these requirements.

4. **Integrating performance-relevant execution environment properties into software performance analyses.** In order to reflect execution environment properties, software performance prediction approaches have to be enhanced. For example, current model-based performance prediction approaches only provide limited means for configuring execution environment properties. A generic approach to integrate derived properties into software performance analysis, for example by using a configuration model, should be developed. As the approach should run in an automated way where possible, analysis tool configuration should also happen in an automated way.

More detailed scientific challenges are presented in Section 5.2 and Section 6.2.

3.3. A Method for Automated Derivation of Execution Environment Properties

In order to face the identified research challenges, we introduce an approach called GINPEX (Goal-oriented INfrastructure Performance EXperiments). This approach features

(i) the automated derivation of performance-relevant properties based on goal-oriented measurements and

(ii) the integration of the derived properties into a performance analysis approach. By embedding the approach into SPE approaches, model-based performance predictions can be enhanced.

The idea of the approach is to provide a set of predefined experiments that can be executed by the performance analyst on the target platform with little effort. The experiments encapsulate the logic of performing actions on the platform, such as issuing load and taking appropriate measurements. They also contain predefined analysis logic, which is executed to derive certain properties of the execution environment based on the measurement results. The derived properties of the execution environment are then fed into a performance prediction tool, leading to an automated procedure of deriving performance-relevant execution environment properties and augmenting performance prediction approaches with those properties.

The approach features two different levels: the level of experiment design, and the level of experiment execution.

3.3.1. Experiment Design

In order to detect performance-relevant properties through automated experiments, those experiments have to be designed and predefined at first. This can be done using the workflow shown in Figure 3.3.

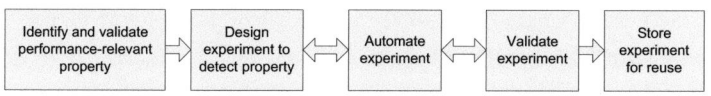

Figure 3.3.: Experiment design workflow of the approach

The workflow consists of the following five steps: In the first step ("Identify and validate performance-relevant property"), a property of the execution environment has to be identified as performance-relevant. It should then be validated that reflecting the property in performance prediction is appropriate (e.g. that reflecting the property leads to significantly improved prediction accuracy). It also has to be checked how the property can be supported in a performance prediction approach (e.g. a simulation of performance models). Existing approaches can be applied to execute this step, for example the method for experiment-based performance model derivation introduced in [Hap08]. This method aims at employing experiments to identify and validate properties of a system and design a performance model based on the experiment results.

Afterwards (step "Design experiment to detect property"), a manual experiment should be designed in which the experiment designer evaluates how the value of the property can be detected by issuing certain load patterns and taking measurements on the platform. As a result of this step, the designer has learned how to specify experiment logic and analysis in order to derive the property value. In the following step ("Automate experiment"), the designer implements an automated experiment to derive the property value. Compared to the previous step, the designer might have to provide an parametric experiment that depends on certain input parameters, or he might have to fine-tune the experiment logic so that it runs robust and on a variety of platforms. Automating the experiment also involves embedding the experiment into the framework that is used later by performance analysts. For issuing load and taking measurements on the target platform, a small and lightweight tool called "Load Driver" is deployed on each machine on which measurements are to be taken.

These two steps might have to be executed multiple times, as implementing automated experiments might lead to new insights for which the experiment design has to be adapted. To derive performance-relevant properties, the load patterns in the experiments have to be designed in a way that the measured results allow to infer the properties through statistical analyses. This requires domain knowledge and careful experiment design. Which load exactly is issued depends on the type of experiment (i.e. the execution environment property under focus). In this thesis, mainly microbenchmarks are used for generating load, but different kinds of load can be issued as well.

Afterwards, the experiment should be validated (step "Validate experiment"), i.e. the experiment designer should check that the experiment is able to detect the value of the corresponding property correctly on a variety of platforms, runs in reasonable time, and is robust enough so that it can be executed by performance analysts who are not familiar with experiment design. Again, if the validation shows that the experiment does not work properly, the experiment designer should go back to the previous step in order to improve the experiment.

Once the experiment has been validated successfully, the experiment designer can complete the process of developing the experiment. In the last step ("Store experiment for reuse"), the designer moves the implementation of the automated experiment in a repository where it can be reused later by performance analysts. Besides, the designer should provide a documentation of the experiment. In Chapter 4, we present a template that can be used for experiment documentation.

3.3.2. Experiment Execution

After experiments have been predefined for automated execution, the performance analyst can use such experiments in order to derive properties of the execution environment for performance prediction. An overview of this workflow is given in Figure 3.4 and explained in the following.

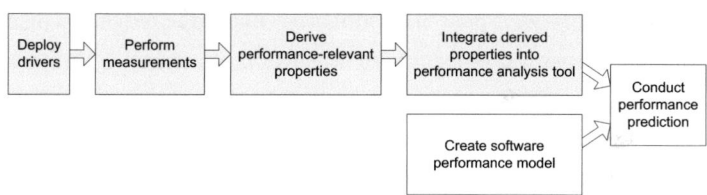

Figure 3.4.: Experiment execution workflow of the approach. The gray boxes indicate the steps that are explicitly covered by the approach

In the first step ("Deploy drivers"), the Load Driver tool has to be deployed on each machine on which measurements are to be taken. Once the Load Drivers are deployed, experiments can be selected for execution.

In the second step ("Perform measurements"), different patterns of load are issued by the Load Driver(s) and certain measurements (e.g. response times or CPU utilization) are taken for specific parts of the issued load. The predefined experiment logic specifies in detail which load patterns are to be issued and during which parts of the experiment measurements are to be taken.

In the third step ("Derive performance-relevant properties"), the measurement results serve as input for an analysis to derive the performance-relevant properties. Like the experiment execution logic, the analysis logic is predefined and is executed without user interaction. During analysis, the properties are derived using statistical methods. If necessary, further experiment runs can be triggered during analysis in order to obtain additional analysis input.

Finally, in the fourth step ("Integrate derived properties into performance prediction tool"), the detected properties are integrated into the performance prediction processes and tools. The performance prediction tool has to support configuration of the relevant execution environment parameters, which can for example be done by using a configuration model. In this case, the detected properties would be passed to the prediction tool as a configuration instance.

Once the performance prediction tool is configured based on the detected performance properties, the software architect can conduct a performance analysis using a software performance model. This is done following the traditional SPE approach (steps "Create software performance model" and "Conduct performance prediction"). During prediction, the experimentally derived execution environment performance properties are taken into account to increase prediction accuracy. The GINPEX approach explicitly covers the steps denoted by the gray boxes in Figure 3.4. In the following chapters, we show how the approach can be realized by tooling that provides automated execution of the four steps.

We also show how the approach works with a software performance prediction tool, namely the Palladio Component Model (PCM) [BKR09]. To include execution environment properties into performance prediction tooling, we use a configuration model to export the detected properties. The configuration model is then used to automatically configure the PCM performance analysis tooling. To use a different performance prediction tool, only the output format of the detected properties would have to be adapted. The integration of the execution environment properties via a configuration model into performance analysis then follows the scenario presented in Figure 3.2 from Section 3.1.3.

By storing predefined and validated experiments in an experiment library, the approach facilitates the execution of experiments on different platforms and by different performance analysts who do not have to take care of experiment design anymore. Each experiment makes certain assumptions on the condition of the system: Some experiments may require idle systems to yield meaningful measurement results. Other experiments may be designed more robust against measurement noise or can explicitly take additional load on the system into account. The description of the experiment in the experiment library supports the analyst in selecting suitable experiments.

3.4. Scenarios

In the following, we discuss different scenarios in software performance engineering where applying the GINPEX approach can enhance performance analysis.

First of all, the approach can be used to yield more accurate performance analyses due to a more sophisticated model of the execution environment used in analysis. Here, all well-known SPE scenarios are affected where software performance is analyzed (i) based on software models and (ii) at early stages of the software life-cycle. These scenarios include the following:

Assessing performance implications of decisions regarding software design and architecture. Model-based performance analysis can be used for modeling high-level decisions, such as architectural patterns or design decisions. Examples include the performance impact of architectures such as Client-server vs. Peer-to-peer communication, and component design decisions such as thin client vs. rich client solutions. A multitude of papers have been published using design-time performance predictions to answer questions on architecture design, for example Gomaa and Menascé [GM00], Cortellessa et al. [CDI01], or Becker et al. [BKR09].

Predicting the performance impact of changes in deployment or workload. Another group of scenarios includes the variation of certain parameters, such as the workload profile of the software or deployment settings. This helps in analyzing whether a software architecture can handle a certain amount of parallel user requests, or predict the impact on resource utilization due to component deployment changes. Such scenarios can be found in the work on SPE conducted by Sharma et al. [SJT05] (varying user workload) or Wu and Woodside [WW04] (varying deployment environment).

Identifying potential performance problems in the architecture. Performance models can be used to identify architectural flaws which should be corrected in order to improve performance, or components whose implementation can lead to a low performance of the overall system. For instance, if the performance model reflects how the different components are invoked during the processing of user requests, performance analysis can be carried out in order to identify the component or connection that forms a performance bottleneck in the software architecture. Examples can be found in Sharma et al. [SJT05] and [MM07].

Capacity planning or resource utilization analysis. Finally, design-time performance prediction can be carried out in order to reason about the overall system utilization or the amount of resources needed. Case studies on performance predictions con-

ducted for capacity planning can be found in Kounev and Buchmann [KB03] or Menascé et al. [MAD04].

If performance analysis takes place at early stages of the software life-
cycle, typically only coarse-grained models can be provided. However,
performance analysis still can yield useful results (for example, to compare alternatives based on relative quantification of performance metrics).
Nevertheless, performance impacts of the execution environments can still
be significant in order to be considered at early analyses, for example in
the scenarios outlined above. If the execution environment is available, the
GINPEX approach can be used to derive performance-relevant execution
environment properties and include them into performance analysis.

In addition to the SPE scenarios described above, the approach can be
used in scenarios where the performance impact of the execution environment is of particular importance. In the following, we present such scenarios in detail.

**Predicting the performance impact of changes in software deploy-
ment.** This scenario has already been described above as part of
the typical SPE scenarios. However, we also list this scenario here,
as the execution environment is directly involved when software is
deployed and thus has to be considered in performance analysis.
Typical architectural questions regarding software deployment are:
*On which servers or virtual machines should the components be
deployed in order to yield acceptable performance? What is the
best configuration of the execution environment for the target software application? What is the performance impact when a certain
part of the execution environment (e.g. a middleware solution) is
replaced by a different but feature-equivalent solution?* To answer
such questions, the performance impact of the execution environment has to be reflected in performance analysis. Depending on
the granularity of the software (analysis) model, fine-grained per-

formance properties of the execution environment may have to be supported in analysis.

Predicting the effect on performance when components are migrated to a different system. When a software application is migrated to different resources, execution environment properties often change. For example, a migration to a different server can involve new hardware resources like faster disks or new CPU processors. On the other hand, migration projects often involve migrating a software to run on a newer version of a middleware technology (e.g. a virtualization technology or an application server). In both cases, the performance of the software can be affected due to the changed execution environment. Sometimes, the changes in the execution environment can easily be integrated in performance analysis, such as an improved throughput due to a new hard disk resource. However, other causes for may be harder to detect, such as for example changes in the scheduling policy of operating systems, virtualization hypervisors, or middleware containers. Such properties are usually not reflected in coarse-grained performance models of the execution environment, but have to be integrated in order to allow for the performance impact.

Predicting the effect on performance when a new infrastructure technology is introduced. A typical scenario for this case can be found in systems that are running on non-virtualized servers and for which performance analyses are available. If a virtualization technology is now being introduced, for example in order to consolidate servers, existing performance analyses cannot be reused, because the new technology (in this case, the virtualization solution) has not been considered yet. As already mentioned above, the performance impact of this technology should be reflected in performance analysis.

Reasoning on architectural patterns related to execution environment access. Certain architectural decisions are heavily tailored towards certain properties of the execution environment. For example, consider the decision whether to keep certain data in-memory or store the data on a hard disk during normal system operation. In this case, the decision can depend on the properties of the used disk. The architect might for example consider SSD drives compared to traditional HDD drives in order to avoid storing data in volatile memory while still yielding adequate performance. However, as the performance speedup of an SSD compared to an HDD also depends on the access pattern (see [PSG08]), the architect has to model the target workload properly and conduct a performance analysis where the performance influences due to the used disk resources are taken into account.

In the following section, we discuss limitations and assumptions of the approach. In contrast to the scenarios presented above, we also discuss some scenarios for which the approach is less suitable.

3.5. Limitations and Assumptions

The GINPEX approach presented in the previous section is integrated in the area of model-based software performance engineering. Thus, in order to apply the approach, a model of the software and its performance-relevant factors has to be available. This includes components and their performance specifications, architectural information on how the components are connected and deployed, and a usage model describing the workloads of the system.

Furthermore, we assume that the target environment is available, as the properties of the execution environment are derived by taking measurements. In some cases, this assumption does not hold, for example in early stages of the software life-cycle, when the target environment is not yet set up, or if the target environment cannot be used for taking measurements due to other restrictions. If the target environment is not available, an equivalent platform can be used, given that this platform shares the same properties as the target environment. In this case, the derived properties can be adopted for performance prediction of a software running on the target environment.

In Section 3.1, we provided a definition of the software execution environment and a categorization of the different parts that make up the execution environment. While the GINPEX approach is not restricted to a certain part of the execution environment, some parts can include properties that are more suitable for automated detection and inclusion in performance analysis than others. In Chapter 5 and Chapter 6, we apply the approach to detect performance-relevant CPU, OS scheduling and virtualization properties. These properties can be easily included in a performance analysis model while maintaining the separation of execution environment properties from software architectural properties. Hence, the properties can be easily reflected in a performance analysis of a different software, where the execution environment properties stay the same. Execution environment properties that are not suited for automated experiment-based derivation are properties that are strongly connected to software application behavior. As an example, take a relational database which is accessed by a software through SQL queries. SQL queries can get very complex and the performance of a query (i.e. its response time as well as its impact on resource utilization) strongly depends on both how the software specifies the query and how the database handles it. In this case, our approach might not be useful as the major challenge here is to find a model of the software and how the software accesses the database for answering performance-related questions. The approach could however be used to detect different database properties which are not tightly coupled to the software, such as database connection pool or cache sizes.

Similarly to execution environment properties that are strongly connected to the software behavior, the approach is also not suited for detecting performance-relevant properties of a software instead of the execution environment. In this case, an experiment detecting such a property would probably not be applicable to a different software. Hence, the benefits of including such an experiment with the GINPEX approach would be limited. This motivation can also be used for specifying the border between the software and the software execution environment w.r.t. the GINPEX approach: Every part of the infrastructure, whose performance-relevant properties might be relevant for multiple software applications, can be regarded as part of the software execution environment for which GINPEX experiments can be specified. Every property that is directly related to a single software is not in the scope of GINPEX execution environment experiments.

In Section 3.4, we discussed various approaches where the GINPEX approach can help to ease software performance engineering. In contrast, the following scenarios do not benefit from the approach:

Analyzing the performance impact of changes not related to the execution environment. If the execution environment is already modeled with sufficient granularity, additional execution environment properties do not have to be included in performance prediction. This can for example be the case when analyzing the impact of changes in the component implementation or component assembly, as well as changes in the user workload.

Analyzing performance on a level where infrastructure can be neglected. In certain scenarios, for example for very coursegrained predictions in early stages of the life-cycle, the influence of the infrastructure can be neglected. In such cases, the rough estimates made with the predictions do no require including execution environment properties that need to be derived automatically. Instead, abstract performance models of the execution environment, e.g. simple queues, suffice.

Analyzing the performance of a deployed software. If the software is already deployed on the target platform, run-time analysis and monitoring approaches are usually utilized. Our approach is not applicable here, as we aim at deriving a performance model for conducting performance predictions (without having to deploy the software on the target platform).

In the remainder of this thesis, we focus on business information systems, as performance prediction based on software architecture models is highly applicable for such systems. However, the approach could also be adopted for real-time systems. In this case, concepts of automating the execution of experiments and the derivation of performance-relevant properties can be transferred to the domain of real-time systems. Usually, different performance questions and performance-relevant properties are considered for such systems. Hence, different experiments would have to be defined, which is outside the scope of this thesis.

3.6. Summary

In this chapter, we motivated and introduced a novel approach called GIN-PEX for deriving performance-relevant execution environment properties for software performance prediction. The approach employs measurements on the target platform by conducting automated experiments. The measurement results are then analyzed in order to derive the properties under focus. In summary, this approach has the following benefits:

Enhancing performance prediction accuracy. Performance predictions using a simple model of the execution environment fail to include certain kinds of performance impact of the execution environment and thus have to be enhanced. By including performance-relevant properties of the execution environment into performance prediction, the presented approach aims at increasing the prediction accuracy.

Automation.   The GINPEX approach facilitates automated experiment execution and result analysis. Little effort is required for the performance analyst to run the experiments. In addition, due to the high level of automation, the experiments can easily be repeated if platform properties have changed, or if the experiments are to be conducted on a different execution environment.

Encapsulating domain knowledge.   As the approach aims at providing predefined experiments to the performance analyst, a lot of domain knowledge can be encapsulated in the experiments. This spares the performance analyst from having to set up experiments correctly, reasoning on what and how to measure, analyzing and interpreting the experiment results, and configuring the performance prediction tooling.

Structuring performance-relevant properties.   As discussed in Section 3.1.2, today's software systems run in a complex execution environment that features a variety of performance-relevant properties on different granularities and infrastructure levels. With the presented approach, we introduce an experiment library that can be used to classify experiments targeting different parts of the execution environment. In Section 4.2, we deal with this concept in detail.

Supporting execution environment design / operation.   Although the focus of this thesis is on supporting the software performance analyst, the approach can also be used during the development or operation of middleware or execution environment software. For example, predefined experiments can be used as test cases that check whether certain implementations or configurations of a certain part of the execution environment have a certain impact or do not induce any unwanted side effects.

We apply the approach in Chapter 5 and Chapter 6 to derive various properties of different parts of the software execution environment. In the following chapter, we present the approach in detail.

4. Model-based Definition and Execution of Execution Environment Experiments

In the previous chapter, we introduced the GINPEX approach and highlighted several research challenges that have to be addressed when deriving execution environment properties automatically. This chapter tackles the research challenges by providing a structure for defining automated experiments. This structure involves (a) a metamodel for modeling experiments and grouping them, (b) a domain-specific language (DSL) for experiment execution, and (c) a template for a structured, non-formal experiment description.

In Section 4.1, we elaborate on the concept of automated GINPEX experiments and state some requirements such experiments have to fulfill. We then introduce experiment libraries and experiment domains for structuring experiments in Section 4.2 and the concept of parametric experiments in Section 4.3. Section 4.4 presents a metamodel for the specification of automated experiments. Afterwards, we refine experiment automation and result analysis in Section 4.5. We continue with a discussion on how to describe experiments in Section 4.6. We describe in Section 4.7 how the presented approach can be extended and discuss the performance overhead of experiments in Section 4.8. Finally, Section 4.9 summarizes the chapter and discusses how the approach addresses the identified research challenges. Some contributions of this chapter have been initially published in [HKHR11] and [HKHR13].

4.1. Automated Execution Environment Experiments

Before discussing automated execution environment experiments in detail, we first give a definition on the term "automated execution environment experiment":

Definition 4.1. An *automated execution environment experiment* is a procedure that aims at detecting the value of an execution environment property without user interaction. The procedure involves measuring observable execution environment parameters based on generated goal-oriented load, and analyzing the measurement results to obtain the resulting value.

In this thesis, we use the term "experiment" interchangeably with "automated execution environment experiment" for the sake of readability.

As an example for an automated experiment, consider a simple experiment that detects the number of available CPU cores. The experiment procedure contains logic to generate CPU load and measure load response times and CPU utilization for the issued load. Based on the measurements, the experiment analysis can calculate the number of available CPU cores. This value is then returned by the experiment. Details for this experiment are given later in Chapter 5.

To enable experiment reusability and automated experiment execution, experiments have to be predefined. In the following, we first highlight requirements for automated experiments. We then present the structure of such experiments and conclude the section with an illustration of the system setup for experiment execution.

4.1.1. Requirements

Predefining an experiment means that both the execution of experiment logic and the subsequent analysis of the taken measurements are encapsulated within the experiment and can be executed automatically without user interaction. Those parts of the experiment have to be specified in advance so that the experiment can be reused later. Predefined, automated experiments have to fulfill the following requirements:

1. **Adequacy.** The experiment has to aim at deriving a meaningful property of the execution environment. This is either a performance-relevant property, i.e. a property that should be reflected in performance analysis, or a preliminary property whose value has to be identified first before deriving an actual property in a later step.

2. **Automation.** The experiment has to be executed automatically, i.e. ideally without any user interaction. This requirement is needed in order to facilitate the work of the software architect or performance analyst, who may have little experience in performing or analyzing measurements to identify execution environment properties.

3. **Broad range.** The experiment has to be designed to derive all eligible values for the execution environment property under focus. For example, if an experiment aims at detecting a load-balancing strategy of operating systems, it should not be designed for only detecting strategy A (which might by very popular on operating system X), but should also be applicable on a different operating system Y, where the strategy can be B. Likewise, the range of possible property values that can be derived by the experiment should be wide enough so that frequent experiment adaptations to future systems are avoided.

4. **Independence.** In order to reflect properties of different execution environments, automated derivation must not be tailored towards a specific execution environment. Instead, the experiment should be designed with as little platform and technology dependencies as possible. Such a design enables the experiment to run on a wide range of platforms. For example, when comparing different execution environments in a performance analysis, it is desirable to execute an experiment on different execution environments (e.g. different oper-

ating systems, or different virtualization hypervisors). Thus, generating load and taking measurements should not restrict the experiment to run on a small set of systems. Experiment logic can be specified in a platform-independent way by using platform-independent programming languages such as Java. However, parts like special sensors for taking measurements are often only available in platform-specific libraries. While means to measure time spans are available on many systems, some metrics such as resource utilization can only be obtained in a platform-dependent way. Experiments should avoid using platform-specific libraries where possible.

5. **Robustness.** The experiment has to be robust against measurement noise, so that meaningful properties can be derived.

In this chapter, we will discuss how experiments can be implemented within the GINPEX approach that fulfill these requirements.

4.1.2. Experiment Structure

In order to implement the GINPEX approach featuring predefined, automated experiments, we identified three parts of the experiment that can be predefined:

Experiment execution logic.   The main part of the experiment is the execution logic that defines the tasks of the experiment, i.e. which kind of load is issued and where measurements are taken. To fulfill requirements 1 and 2, the experiment logic has to be designed in such a way that, after experiment execution, meaningful conclusions can be drawn from the measurement results, i.e. the value of the performance-relevant property under focus can be derived from the experiment, and it can be derived in an automated way.

Experiment analysis logic.   After measurements are taken, the results are analyzed in order to derive the property value. Automating this step means that measurement results are directly fed into analysis methods. Predefined analyses might also determine whether additional kind of experiment logic should be executed based on retrieved measurement results.

Experiment metadata. Experiment metadata describes certain experiment properties that can be used for querying and selecting experiments. In addition, experiment metadata can be used to describe experiment dependencies (see Section 4.4.1).

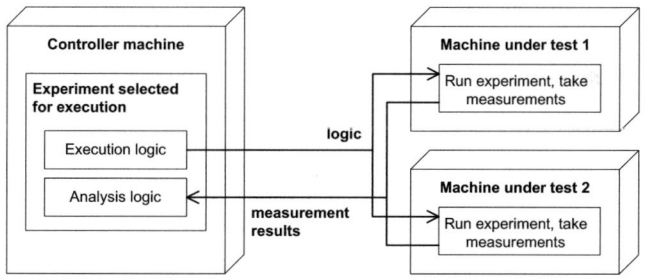

Figure 4.1.: Exemplary experiment setup

Figure 4.1 shows how a system looks like during experiment execution. Running experiments are managed on a controller machine. As experiment management should not disturb the issued load and taken measurements during an experiment, this machine should not be part of the system under test. After selecting one or multiple experiments for execution, the predefined experiment logic is executed on the system. The system can consist of one or multiple machines that are accessed during the experiment depending on the defined logic. After the logic is executed, measurements that have been taken on the machines are transferred to the controller machine. Note that measurements might also be taken on the controller machine, but in order to yield fine-grained measurement results, certain experiments might require taking measurements directly on the machines under test, as shown in Figure 4.1. Once the measurement results are transferred, they are analyzed based on the predefined experiment analysis logic. This step aims at deriving the value of the execution environment property under focus.

A complete experiment might require multiple steps of running experiment logic and analyzing measurement results. We call such a step an "experiment run":

Definition 4.2. An *experiment run* denotes the execution of experiment logic and subsequent analysis of measurement results. An experiment can consist of multiple experiment runs in order to detect the value of an execution environment property.

Hence, an experiment run of a predefined experiment features predefined experiment logic and predefined analysis logic. Including multiple experiment runs into an experiment facilitates the execution of experiment logic based on prior analysis results. The value of the execution environment property is then derived after the last experiment run has been executed.

If all three predefinable parts of an experiment are available, the experiment can be executed by the software architect or performance analyst. What remains to be specified manually is the actual system structure, i.e. the IP addresses of the machines under test so that experiment logic can be distributed.

4.2. Experiment Library and Experiment Domains

Section 3.1.2 listed various performance-relevant properties of the software execution environment and pointed out that the execution environment can be very complex since a lot of properties exist that may have to be reflected in performance analyses. In addition, performance analysts or software architects often do not have a detailed knowledge of the execution environment. To conduct a performance analysis, they have to specify certain information of the execution environment, such as the server structure and how components are deployed on servers. To include detailed performance-relevant information in a performance analysis, a performance analyst has to

- know that these properties exist and are performance-relevant,

- know how to obtain the property values on the target platform, and

- include the values in performance analysis.

As this requires detailed knowledge and efforts, the GINPEX approach aims at automating the part of deriving detailed properties and including them in performance analysis.

Since the execution environment features a lot of potential properties that may have to be detected automatically, the list of predefined GINPEX experiments can become very large as well. In order to help the performance analyst in selecting suitable experiments, we define two concepts for structuring and grouping predefined experiments: the *experiment library* and the *experiment domain*.

The experiment library facilitates the storage of predefined experiments. By accessing the experiment library, experiments can be selected for execution. When accessing experiments, two scenarios can be possible (see Figure 4.2): In the first case, the performance analyst creates a software architecture model for performance analysis and manually selects a set of experiments for execution from the experiment library (a). In the second case, the performance analyst has to create the software architecture model only. Based on an automated analysis, a set of suitable experiments is then selected from the library for execution (b). Such an analysis could for example scan the architecture model for certain kinds of resource demands that require specific experiments. For instance, if no disk requests are modeled to occur on a certain machine, no disk properties have to be reflected during performance analysis for that machine, and hence no disk experiments are needed on this machine. Automated architecture model analysis could also be used to detect the model granularity and the granularity of modeled resource demands. Depending on the granularity, certain experiments might be selected for execution, where the detected properties can improve prediction accuracy.

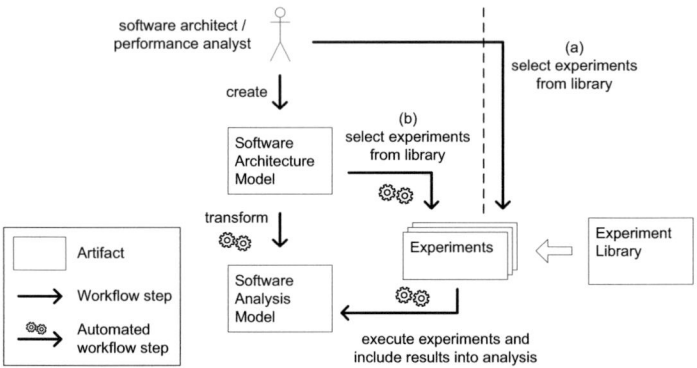

Figure 4.2.: Manual and automated experiment selection from the experiment library

In the former case, the performance analyst can of course select all experiments from the experiment library for execution; however, this might take a very long time. Another option would be to support the performance analyst by grouping experiments and presenting experiments in a way so the analyst can figure out whether an experiment is appropriate for execution or not. In the latter case, it has to be investigated how the software architecture model can be analyzed in order to derive a set of necessary experiments. This is outside the scope of this thesis, but might be a useful extension of the approach (see discussion on future work in Section 8.4).

To support the performance analyst in selecting experiments for execution, we specify a structure for grouping experiments called experiment domain.

The use of an experiment domain is twofold: First, it groups experiments that aim at detecting properties of the same part of the execution environment. For example, experiments detecting virtualization properties should reside in a different experiment domain than experiments detecting hard disk properties. All experiments in one experiment domain should also aim at detecting properties that are on the same level of granularity. For example, detailed properties of the operating system scheduler are more important for fine-grained analysis of demands. On the other hand, some performance models feature more coarse-grained demands and thus may not benefit from reflecting fine-grained execution environment properties during analysis. In this case, abstract models can be augmented with experiments aiming at coarse-grained properties. Even if the fine-grained and coarse-grained properties belong to the same part of the execution environment, they should reside in different experiment domains.

Second, as all experiments in one experiment domain belong to the same part of the execution environment, the experiment domain can be used to specify the common machine setup that is required by all included experiments. Here, the machine setup denotes information on the different machines involved in the experiment. When executing experiments, the user has to specify the machine locations (e.g. by providing IP addresses) and prepare the machines for experiment execution (in our case, by deploying Load Drivers on the machines). For example, consider a set of experiments aiming at OS scheduling properties, grouped in an experiment domain "OS Scheduling". Typically, such experiments run on a single machine only, as they neglect execution environment properties involving multiple machines, and they do not require other machines for experiment execution. In this case, the machine setup stated by the experiment domain is very simple, the user selecting this experiment domain has to provide information for one machine only. On the other hand, consider experiments that aim at detecting virtualization overhead of a virtual machine compared to a physical machine. Such experiments might require to run on both a physical machine and a virtual machine, in order to calculate the resource demand slowdown due to virtualization overhead. In this case, the corresponding experiment domain would state that different types of machines are involved in the experiment; a physical machine and one or multiple virtual machines.

A predefined experiment is kept independent from concrete execution environments, only machine types are known to predefined experiments. The specifics of the execution environment (e.g. machine IP addresses) are mapped to predefined machine types once the performance analyst has selected an experiment domain and specified the machine information.

Thus, to support the specification of experiments within experiment domains, the experiment structure has to separate infrastructure-specific information from infrastructure-independent information. This is supported by the metamodel we created for specifying automated experiments. Section 4.4 deals with the metamodel in more detail.

The number of experiments per experiment domain depends on the number of performance-relevant properties for this domain that should be derived through experiments. In this thesis, we introduce experiments for three different experiment domains: CPU, OS Scheduling and Virtualization. In the following chapters, we show that for these domains, only a handful of properties can suffice to increase the performance prediction accuracy. If the number of experiments and experiment domains increases, automated selection of experiments might be useful to support the performance analyst. This extension of the GINPEX approach is regarded as future work (see Section 8.4).

4.3. Parametric Experiments

In this section, we introduce the concept of *parametric experiments*, which we use for specifying experiment configuration parameters and experiment dependencies.

When running experiments, there might be some information the user has to specify in advance. Such information can then be used by the experiments when setting up the experiment execution and analysis logic; in other words, the user should be able to specify *configuration parameters* for experiments. Such a configuration parameter might be the maximum duration of a certain experiment. It could be used to abort long-running experiments where the time of abortion influences the precision of measurement results, but yields a valid experiment result anyhow. Such a parameter could be used to give the user the possibility to specify the trade-off between accuracy and experiment runtime.

Another kind of configuration parameter for an experiment might be a certain property of the execution environment which the experiment needs to know in order to generate suitable execution logic. For example, certain experiments aiming at deriving OS scheduling properties need to take into account the number of available CPU cores on the system. In this case, this parameter can also be detected by a different experiment executed beforehand. The experiment is then parametrized with the detected execution environment property value of another experiment.

By specifying the detected parameter (i.e. the execution environment property) and an optional set of required configuration parameters for an experiment, multiple experiments can be executed successively. A later experiment can take parameters into account that are detected in earlier experiments and adapt the execution logic if necessary.

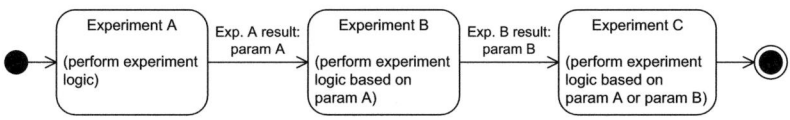

Figure 4.3.: Joined execution of parametric experiments

Figure 4.3 illustrates how multiple experiments can be executed successively based on parametric dependencies: Experiment *A* detects a parameter "param *A*" which is required by experiment *B*. Experiment *B* performs experiment logic that depends on configuration parameter "param *A*" in order to detect "param *B*". Finally, experiment *C* depends on "param *B*" and can access both "param A" and "param B" in order to adjust its experiment logic.

For parametric dependencies, we assume that among the dependent experiments no cyclic dependencies exist. More formally, consider a set of experiments E and a binary relation R on $E \times E$, with $(e_1, e_2) \in R$ if experiment e_1 depends on the detected parameter of experiment e_2, then we require (E, R) to be a partially ordered set.

If (E, R) is a partially ordered set, the order of executed experiments can be easily obtained through topological sorting.

By using parametric dependencies, the user does not have to select all experiments required for execution. If he selects only a subset of experiments for execution, additional experiments can be detected by calculating the execution order based on the parametric dependencies. In this case, the user could be presented with the adapted selection of executed experiments, and he could then either specify the missing parameters by hand or execute all required experiments.

To give an example, consider the simple experiment from the example given in Section 4.1. The experiment detects the number of available CPU cores. This parameter now can serve as a configuration parameter for a different experiment. Such an experiment can be defined for detecting certain property values of operating system schedulers, such as the scheduling timeslice length. This experiment and its logic are presented in detail in Chapter 5. Here, we only need to know that the experiment logic consists of putting CPU load on all available CPU cores. Hence, the experiment has to start a certain number of parallel threads, where each thread issues load, and the total number of threads depends on the number of available CPU cores. As this parameter cannot be fixed during experiment design time, it is specified as an configuration parameter for the experiment. When executing the experiment, the user can either specify the number of cores, if he knows this information, or select an experiment for prior execution that detects the number of CPU cores. In the latter case, that experiment is executed and its output value, the number of available CPU cores, is used for specifying the configuration parameter of the experiment detecting the OS scheduling timeslice length.

As illustrated above, the detected parameter of an experiment is always the value of an execution environment property. Experiment configuration parameters might refer to such properties as well, but can also be used to specify additional input parameters for an experiment. In this case, the parameter value has to be specified in a different way, for instance manually by the user executing the experiments.

4.4. A Metamodel for Specifying Experiments

In order to systematically set up new experiments, we developed a metamodel which is used for specifying the experiments in detail. Both predefined GINPEX experiments and additional experiments defined by the performance analyst are based on this metamodel.

Before we explain the metamodel in detail, we first discuss why a model-based approach is appropriate for specifying GINPEX experiments:

- A model-based approach provides an easy and elegant foundation to specify experiment configurations. Additional experiments and their specifications can easily be added by creating additional instances of the metamodel. Furthermore, existing modeling frameworks come with extensive tool support regarding the creation, display, and processing of metamodel instances.

- Based on the modeling framework, modeling editors can be derived which can be used to display experiments in a convenient way, and allow for easily creating new experiments. When changing or enhancing the metamodel, these derived editors can be easily updated. The GINPEX framework also provides programmatic access to the model, which can be used for automated generation of experiment descriptions, rather than manual GUI-based DSL editing. Automated generation of experiment descriptions is used for predefined experiment logic and can be used for specifying large amounts of experiments, which would be a cumbersome task if done with a GUI editor. On the other hand, the GUI editor enables manual specification of experiments, which can be appropriate for conducting initial measurements.

- By using a metamodel for the experiments, we separated the specification of an experiment from its execution: the (often platform-specific) way of how an experiment is executed and interpreted is not encoded in the model. For example, measurement of timing values and resource utilization are highly platform-specific. The mapping of metamodel constructs to executable experiment code is encapsulated in the transformation and not in the metamodel. In this thesis, a transformation to Java code has been implemented which facilitates the direct execution of experiments based on instances of the experiment metamodel. In addition, the implementation and the metamodel of GINPEX itself can be extended in a systematic way, since we used established model-driven technologies and transformation languages.

The GINPEX metamodel consists of four parts: The *Experiments* part contributes to the experiment metadata and specifies the overall structure of an experiment as well as dependencies between experiments. The *Experiment Logic Definition* denotes the central element of the experiment logic specification. The other two parts constitute the experiment logic in detail, namely *Experiment Tasks* and *Experiment Sensors*. The metamodel parts are explained in detail in the following subsections.

4.4.1. Experiments

The first part of the GINPEX metamodel provides a structure for modeling experiment domains and experiments. An overview of the metamodel part is given in Figure 4.4.

To structure experiments, we introduced the concept of experiment domains in Section 4.2. An experiment domain is modeled with the ExperimentDomain object. It contains a set of Experiments and a set of MachineTypes. The Experiment element is used to describe a predefined experiment which will be covered in the following sections. The MachineType element is an abstract representation of the machines on which the experiments of the domain are to be executed. A machine type can either be *single machine* type or an *unbounded machine* type.

A SingleMachineType denotes one machine, whereas an UnboundedMachineType denotes a set of multiple machines. To give an example, consider an experiment domain "OS Scheduling" that features experiments detecting OS scheduling properties. These experiments only need a single machine for execution. In contrast, an experiment domain "Virtualization" might require different machine types for executing experiments. For example, virtualization experiments could run on an arbitrary number of virtual machines to detect certain virtual machine properties in a virtualized server. In this case, the unbounded machine type can be used to indicate that these experiment run on an arbitrary number of (virtual) machine instances. If the optional attribute of a MachineType is set to *true*, experiment logic may make use of the corresponding machine if it is specified, but should not depend on it. In other words, a machine type should only be marked as optional for an experiment domain if the parameters that are to be detected in this experiment domain can be detected by experiments that can run without this machine type.

Note that the MachineType element and its child elements denote a type of a machine. Hence, on the instance level, machine types are modeled,

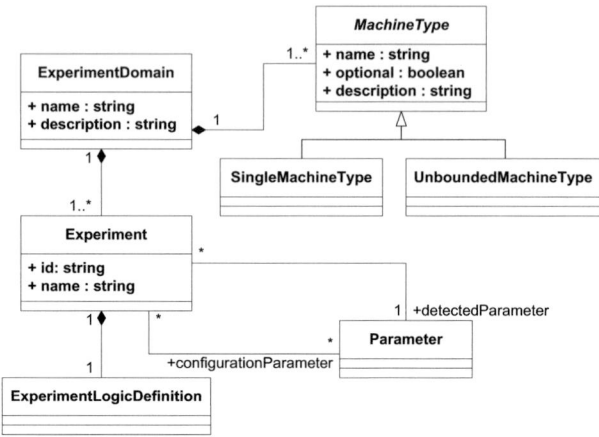

Figure 4.4.: GINPEX experiments metamodel

not machine instances. This is due to the fact that the metamodel focuses on modeling predefined experiments. When modeling predefined experiment, the information regarding machine instances is not available. This information becomes available later when predefined experiments are executed. During experiment design, experiment logic can only differ between different machine types.

Parametric dependencies that have been introduced in Section 4.3 can be modeled with the `Parameter` element. Every `experiment` references exactly one detected parameter and optionally one or multiple configuration parameters. The detected parameter represents the execution environment property whose value is derived by the experiment. Finally, an `experiment` contains an `ExperimentLogicDefinition` which specifies the experiment logic in detail. This part of the metamodel is presented in the following section.

4.4.2. Experiment Logic Definition

An `ExperimentLogicDefinition` denotes the container for experiment logic modeled with the GINPEX metamodel. It is either generated on-the-fly when predefined experiments are selected for execution, or generated by a user who manually models an experiment using the modeling editor. As shown in Figure 4.5, it consists of three parts:

First, an `ExperimentLogicDefinition` contains a set of `MachineReferences` that are used to denote the target machines on which the experiment is to be executed. Second, the referenced `AbstractTask` denotes the root task of experiment logic, i.e. the entry point for executing experiment tasks. The root task typically contains other tasks, spawning a fine-grained task structure of experiment logic. Section 4.4.3 deals with tasks in detail. Third, the `SensorRepository` contains sensors that indicate which measurements have to be taken for which tasks. Sensors are presented in detail in Section 4.4.4.

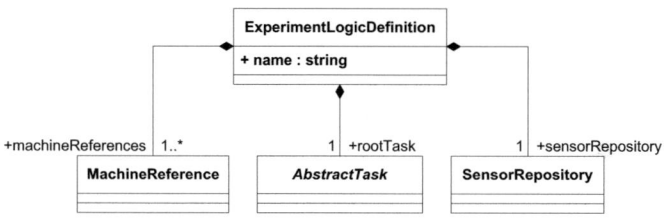

Figure 4.5.: GINPEX experiment logic definition metamodel

In contrast to the experiment structure presented in the previous section, this part of the metamodel is used to model experiment runtime instances. This means that a `MachineReference` denotes a machine instance, whereas a `MachineType` denotes a machine on the type level. For example, consider an experiment domain containing an unbounded machine type. When specifying predefined experiment logic, it is unknown how many machine instances will be specified during experiment execution. Instead, the predefined experiment logic has to generate the experiment logic definition and its machine references depending on the specified number of machine instances. If the user specified three machines when executing the experiment, this would lead to three machine references in the generated experiment description instance.

4.4.3. Experiment Tasks

Executable GINPEX tasks fall into two groups. The first groups denotes all tasks that specify the control flow of the experiment. These tasks inherit from the abstract `ControlFlowTask` element. The second group denotes all task that perform a certain logic on one of the target machines. Those tasks inherits from the abstract `MachineTask` element.

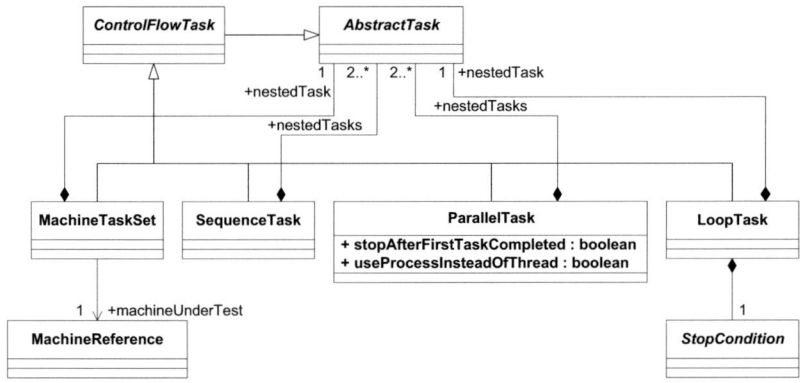

Figure 4.6.: GINPEX control flow tasks metamodel

The different control flow tasks are shown in Figure 4.6. Control flow tasks contain nested tasks that are to be executed in a certain way. A SequenceTask executed all nested tasks one after another, while a ParallelTask executes nested tasks concurrently. For the latter task, the useProcessInsteadOfThread attribute can be used to specify how nested tasks are parallelized. If it is set to *true*, a new process is forked for each nested tasks. Otherwise, a thread is used for executing parallel tasks. Using processes instead of threads can be useful when separating the address space of load issued in parallel in order to avoid mutual interference. The stopAfterFirstTaskCompleted attribute of a ParallelTask indicates whether its nested tasks should be aborted once the first nested task has completed.

The LoopTask executes a nested task multiple times. By putting a task into a loop task, repetitions can be modeled, which are for example necessary to obtain multiple measurement values of the same task. The stop condition of a LoopTask is modeled with the abstract StopCondition element. The concrete elements inheriting from StopCondition (not shown in the figure) include the following:

FixedNumberOfIterationsReached   Denotes a loop that repeats the nested task for a fixed number of iterations. The number of iterations is specified by the numberOfIterations attribute.

InternalTimesStable   Denotes a loop that repeats until the measured response times of a nested task are stable, i.e. until a specified level of confidence is reached. This facilitates taking stable measurements while keeping the number of needed iterations low. This stop condition is specified using the two attributes confidence (the confidence level) and halfWidth (half the width of the confidence interval).

InternalTimesChanged   Denotes a loop that repeats until a change in the measured response times of a nested task is observed. This stop condition contains the attribute numberOfLastTimesRegarded that indicates the number of previous iterations that should be taken into account when determining a difference in response times. A higher number means that the condition is more robust to outliers.

EndlessLoop   Denotes a loop that runs without a specific stop condition. Instead, the loop has to be aborted from outside. Endless loops can for example be used in a `ParallelTask` that aborts the loop after another nested task has been completed.

`UserAbort`   Denotes a loop that executes until the user manually aborts the loop. This stop condition can be used in experiment design for manually specified experiments, but should be avoided in predefined experiments that strive for high automation.

Finally, a `MachineTaskSet` denotes a control flow task that executes the nested task on a certain target machine. The target machine is specified using the `machineUnderTest` reference pointing to a `MachineReference`. By modeling experiment logic definitions containing multiple `MachineTaskSets` which reference different `MachineReferences`, the executed experiment logic can be distributed to different target machines.

Only tasks that are nested inside a `MachineTaskSet` are executed on the corresponding target machine. All other tasks are executed on the controller machine.

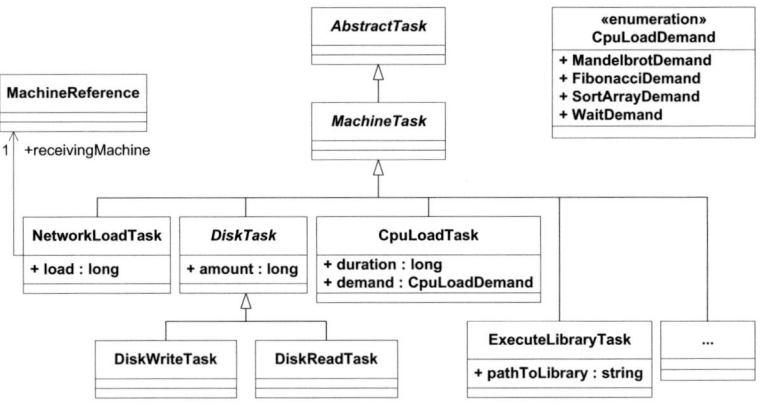

Figure 4.7.: GINPEX machine tasks metamodel

In addition to control flow tasks, `MachineTasks` can be specified (see Figure 4.7). While control flow tasks can be nested inside a `Machine-TaskSet` (but do not have to), `MachineTasks` have to be nested inside a

MachineTaskSet. This can be ensured by a metamodel constraint. For specifying constraints, we use the OCL language [Obj12], which results in the constraint

```
self->closure(parentTask)->select(task |
task.oclIsTypeOf(MachineTaskSet))->size() = 1
```

for the MachineTask metamodel element. We have specified different tasks for load generation that are detailed in the following.

CpuLoadTask   This task aims at issuing CPU load on a machine in a single thread. It features an attribute duration that indicates the amount of load to be issued, and a demand attribute denoting the type of demand to be issued. The type of demand is specified with the enumeration element CpuLoadDemand and can be chosen out of MandelbrotDemand, FibonacciDemand, mmSortArrayDemand, and WaitDemand. The issued MandelbrotDemand performs Mandelbrot Set calculations which have a strong focus on floating point operations, whereas FibonacciDemand calculates Fibonacci numbers basically consists of integer operations. Compared to these demands, the SortArrayDemand performs memory-bound array sort operations. A WaitDemand does not directly issue CPU load, but waits for the specified duration and can thus be regarded as an "empty demand" type.

The specified duration of a CpuLoadTask denotes the duration the task takes on the target machine on a single CPU core without contention. This is achieved by a calibration step that is done prior to experiment execution. This calibration determines the input parameters for the load generation algorithms to match the specified duration times. Details on this approach are explained in [BDH08].

DiskTask, DiskReadTask, DiskWriteTask   The abstract DiskTask denotes tasks that issue certain hard disk load. The amount of issued disk load (in bytes) is specified with the amount at-

87

tribute. The concrete tasks specify the kind of load that is issued: a `DiskReadTask` reads the amount from the hard disk, a `DiskWriteTask` writes the amount to disk. In order to avoid caching effects that affect the runtime of disk tasks, random bytes are read and written.

`NetworkLoadTask` This task sends network load from one machine to another machine. The source machine issuing the network load is the machine referenced by the `MachineTaskSet` the `NetworkLoadTask` is nested in. The target machine receiving the load is denoted by the machine referenced by the task through the `receivingMachine` reference. The amount of network load (in bytes) is specified with the `load` attribute. During task execution, random bytes are transferred over the network.

`ExecuteLibraryTask` This task aims at executing additional logic that is not encoded in the metamodel, but available in an external library (e.g. a Java JAR library). This task facilitates execution of task logic without extending the metamodel. Section 4.7 deals with GINPEX extensibility in detail.

4.4.4. Experiment Sensors

Specifying the load that is issued during a predefined experiment is not sufficient for automated analysis. It is also necessary to specify at where and when measurements are to be taken during experiment execution. This means that the experiment designer has to specify (i) where in the experiment logic measurements are to be taken, i.e. on which machine at which point of time, and (ii) which kind of counter or performance metric is read to take a measurement. For this purpose, the GINPEX metamodel supports the specification of sensors. During code generation, corresponding code for taking measurements is then generated at the appropriate places in the experiment code.

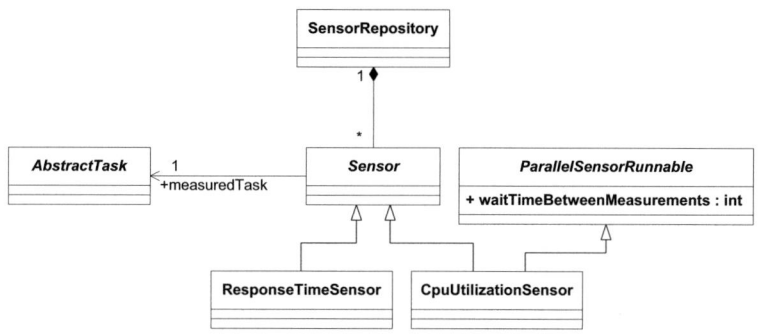

Figure 4.8.: GINPEX sensors metamodel

The GINPEX sensor metamodel is shown in Figure 4.8. All specified sensors are located in the SensorRepository. Concrete sensor types inherit from the abstract Sensor element. Every sensor references a task it belongs to. In the metamodel, the measuredTask reference of the Sensor element is used for this. Sensor logic is only executed while the referenced task is executed. The GINPEX metamodel distinguishes between two kinds of sensors: sensors that run in the same thread as the referenced task, and sensors that run in parallel to the referenced task. Sensors running in the same thread simple inherit from the Sensor element; such a sensor can take measurements right before or right after the task logic. An example of this sensor can be found in the ResponseTimeSensor which measures the response time of the referenced task's duration. A sensor that runs in parallel to the referenced task has to inherit from ParallelSensorRunnable as well. The sensor logic is executed repeatedly in a different thread as long as the referenced task is executed. The waitTimeBetweenMeasurements attribute can be used to denote the time between sensor logic execution, i.e. the wait time between measurements. An example of such a sensor is the CpuUtilizationSensor that measured the overall CPU utilization on the machine on which the task is executed. Typically, CPU utilization is calculated by repeatedly measuring CPU busy and idle time counters. By using the `waitTimeBetweenMeasurements` attribute, the granularity of the CPU utilization results can be set. Additional sensors exist; we cover all implemented sensors in the metamodel overview given in Appendix A.

Similar to GINPEX tasks, additional sensors can be added to the GINPEX metamodel. Extending GINPEX sensors is covered in Section 4.7. The following section deals with executing experiments based on GINPEX metamodel instances and analyzing experiment results. An overview on all GINPEX metamodel elements can be found in Appendix A.

4.4.5. Example

To give an example for a metamodel instance, we go back to the simple experiments presented in Section 4.1 and 4.3. We introduced two experiments, one for detecting the number of CPU cores, and one for detecting the timeslice length of the operating system scheduler.

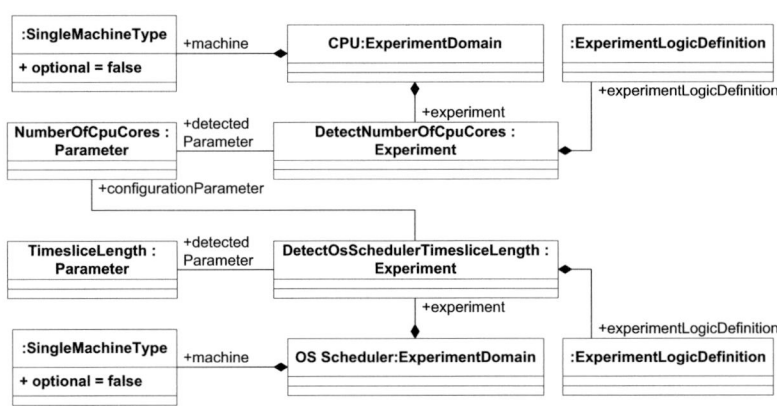

Figure 4.9.: Object diagram for an excerpt of a GINPEX metamodel instance

Figure 4.9 shows an excerpt of the corresponding GINPEX metamodel instance in a UML object diagram. The two experiments reside in different experiment domains, each featuring a `SingleMachineType` which denotes the machine on which the experiment is executed. The first experiment for detecting the number of CPU cores is modeled with the `Experiment` element named "DetectNumberOfCores". It references a parameter called "NumberOfCpuCores" which is the detected parameter of the experiment. In addition, the experiment contains an `ExperimentLogicDefinition` which holds the experiment logic with its tasks and sensors. This part of the metamodel instance is omitted here. A metamodel instance example covering tasks and sensors is given in Section 4.6.2. Besides, a detailed description of the experiment logic for the experiments in this example is given in the corresponding sections in Chapter 5.

The second experiment for detecting the OS scheduling timeslice length is modeled in a similar way in the lower part of the figure. As explained in Section 4.3, this experiment depends on the detected parameter of the first experiment. Hence, it references the parameter "NumberOfCpuCores" as a configuration parameter.

4.5. Experiment Execution and Results Analysis

In the following, we explain how experiments specified with the GINPEX metamodel can be executed and analyzed.

4.5.1. Experiment Execution

For implementing experiment execution, different design alternatives exist. One option would be to interpret a GINPEX experiment instance using a visitor pattern on the instance. The interpreter would traverse the experiment instance on the controller machine and issue certain commands in order to execute experiment logic on the appropriate machines of the system under test (SUT). However, interpreting the model can introduce performance overheads, for example due to additional communication between the controller machine and SUT machines. In order to keep such overheads low, we decided to chose a second option for experiment execution. Instead of interpreting the model, executable code is directly generated based on a model instance which is then directly executed on the SUT machines. In detail, for each `MachineTaskSet`, Java code is being generated that conforms to the specified tasks inside the `MachineTaskSet`. The generated code includes both the task logic to be executed, as well as sensor logic (such as response tome or CPU utilization measurements), if sensors have been specified for the tasks.

The generated source code is then transferred to the SUT machines. On each machine, a program called Load Driver is running which is responsible for receiving the generated code, compiling it, and executing the initial preparation part of the experiment.

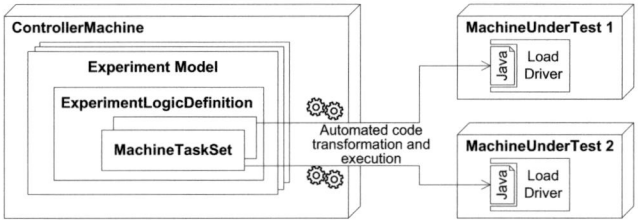

Figure 4.10.: Executing experiments through code generation

Figure 4.10 gives an overview on how an experiment is executed through code generation based on the experiment setup shown in Figure 4.1.

The preparation part of an experiment, which is executed prior to the experiment logic, is used for object initialization, different checks (for example, to ensure that needed network connections are working etc.), or calibration, such as the calibration step for `CpuLoadTasks` explained in Section 4.4.3. As calibration might take some time, the calibration results are stored in calibration files which are then reused in later runs.

After the code for all `MachineTaskSets` has been generated and compiled and the preparation phase has been completed, the experiment logic is executed. Depending on the specified experiment control flow, the controller machine asks the Load Drivers to execute the corresponding `MachineTaskSets`. Once the overall experiment control flow is completed, each Load Driver reports all measurement results for the executed Ma-chineTaskSets to the controller machine.

4.5.2. Results Analysis

Experiment results are available for every specified sensor. For example, if a response time sensor has been specified for a task nested inside a Loop-Task, the measurement results for this task consist of multiple response times. The amount of response time results depends on the number of task iterations.

If the experiment has been specified and executed manually, the results can be visualized to the user. If the experiment had been predefined, au-tomated analysis is executed once the results are available. In this case, the analysis step is executed in order to derive performance properties for later performance predictions. For automated analysis, different kinds of analysis methods can be executed:

- Statistical functions, such as mean, median, or variance calculations for the result set of one sensor;

- Clustering methods such as k-means clustering or QT clustering for the result set of one sensor;

- Prediction models such as MARS, Kriging, or CART, that can be de-rived for sensor results of multiple experiment runs, yielding a per-formance prediction function from measurement data.

GINPEX provides access to statistical libraries, for example the R statis-tical computing engine [R F]. By using an engine for statistical computing such as R, GINPEX can be easily enhanced with additional analysis logic. We cover the extensibility of GINPEX in Section 4.7.

The output format of the detected parameters depends on the scenario in which GINPEX is used. In this work, we apply GINPEX in the scope of model-based performance prediction with the Palladio Component Model (PCM) [BKR09]. To integrate properties of the software execution environment into performance prediction, GINPEX stores the detected properties in a configuration model that can be used by the PCM for performance prediction. However, the GINPEX approach is not linked to a specific performance prediction approach, but can also be enhanced to export detected parameters in a different format.

4.6. A Template for Experiment Description

In Section 4.4, we introduced the GINPEX metamodel that can be used for specifying the experiments that aim at deriving parameters of the software execution environment. A GINPEX metamodel instance provides a formal representation of an experiment. Code generation templates specify how executable code has to be produced for a specified experiment.

However, a metamodel instance alone might not be sufficient for the software architect in order to understand what the experiment does and whether he should execute it. Also, an experiment designer might need additional information about existing experiments when specifying new experiments. Hence, we developed a template that provides a common format for describing the experiments. By using the templates, the experiments can be presented in a structured way to performance analysts and software architects. The templates can also support people that do not have substantial experience with measuring and/or performance analyses. By capturing domain knowledge of the experiment domain, the templates can ease the understanding of existing experiments as well as the process of defining new experiments.

Note that the template is currently used to structure the experiments in a non-formal way. The major focus of the template concept lies on presenting a taxonomy for structuring the experiments. However, the template could also be used by tools to parse the experiment description and present it in an appropriate way to the user. Another option might be to extend the template to an ontology for a formal specification of various experiment properties.

In the following, we present the template in detail. To describe the experiment logic, we use UML activity diagrams, which is explained in Section 4.6.2.

4.6.1. Sections of the Experiment Template

The experiment template defines several sections which are presented below. In Chapter 5 and Chapter 6, we use the template to present various experiments in detail.

Experiment identifier The identifier of the experiment.

Experiment name The name of the experiment.

Experiment domain Used to group multiple experiments that aim at detecting properties of the same type of infrastructure.

Detected experiment parameter The parameter whose value is to be detected by the experiment. The experiment comes with predefined execution logic as well as predefined analysis logic to analyze the experiment results in order to detect the parameter value. A parameter has a type (e.g. int, double, boolean) and can provide a default value in case the experiment execution fails.

Importance for performance analysis Explains why the detected experiment parameter is performance-relevant and should be regarded in performance prediction.

Configuration parameters Parameters that are used as input for the experiment logic. Such parameters can be identified by other experiments which would then be executed prior to this experiment. If a parameter is already known, the user can specify the parameter value. A parameter has a type (e.g. int, double, boolean).

Experiment execution logic   Describes the idea behind the experiment and how the parameter is being detected based on the experiment results.

Assumptions   Assumptions that are made in the course of the experiment design and requirements that have to be met in order to get meaningful experiment results. Based on the assumptions and requirements, the experiments have been designed to derive the experiment parameter.

Assumptions and requirements can be distinguished in the following groups:

- **General infrastructure assumptions:** Lists assumptions on the infrastructure that have to be met, i.e. fundamental properties or platform behavior that have to be fulfilled.

- **Assumptions for performance analysis:** Lists assumptions that have to be met by the performance analysis approach in order to make use of the derived experiment parameter. For example, a certain parameter can only be considered for performance analysis if the performance analysis approach supports an analysis scenario where the parameter has an influence on the analysis.

- **Required sensors:** Sensors that are to be used during the execution of the experiment. Often needed sensors like response time sensors and CPU utilization sensors are available on most platforms and should not be a problem. However, in some cases an experiment might depend on a different sensor which might not be available on all target platforms.
  Common sensors for which implementations on most platforms (Windows, Linux, Solaris, Mac) are available include:

– Response time sensor: Uses Java `System.nanotime()` to get time stamps with nanosecond accuracy.

– CPU utilization sensor: Queries the system's counters of the CPU being in idle state, system processing state, or user processing state. Based on the counters, the CPU utilization can be calculated.

The amount of specified sensors has also an impact on data persistence when storing experiment results on the controller machine. In this case, assumptions on data persistence can also be listed here. For example, certain experiments may feature multiple experiment runs collecting a lot of sensor data. Such an experiment might require sensor data to be stored in a file instead of memory.

Experiment robustness   Describes actions that have been taken to ensure the experiment results are robust and not prone to measurement noise or other errors. Experiments might provide logic to detect whether the results can be considered stable or not. In the latter case, the user might want to re-run the experiment or manually check the experiment results.

Experiment performance   Information about the experiment performance can be given by using the following categories:

- **Critical properties:** Lists critical properties that may influence the performance (i.e. the runtime) of the experiment execution or analysis.

- **Ideal execution times:** Gives an estimation on the experiment duration including dependencies to critical parameters (if present).

- **Exemplary execution times:** Lists duration times of the executed experiment in a specific environment.

4.6.2. Describing the Experiment Logic

The template presented above contains a section "Experiment execution logic" which aims at describing the logic that is executed in an experiment run and how the measurement results are used to derive the value of the execution environment property under focus. However, plain text is not always suitable for illustrating experiment logic. For a visual representation of experiment logic, we decided to adopt UML activity diagrams [Obj11c], as they are easy to understand, widely used by software architects, and suitable for visualizing GINPEX control flow tasks.

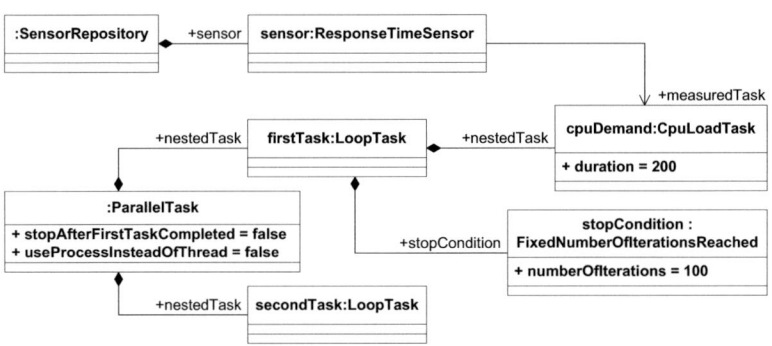

Figure 4.11.: Object diagram for an excerpt of a GINPEX experiment instance (tasks and sensors)

As an example, consider the excerpt of a GINPEX experiment execution logic shown in Figure 4.11. It consists of a `ParallelTask` that contains two nested `LoopTasks`. The first `LoopTask` contains a `CpuLoadTask` that is executed 100 times. The contents of the second `LoopTask` are not specified in detail for this example. In addition, a `ResponseTimeSensor` has been specified in the `SensorRepository` referencing the `CpuLoadTask` nested in the first `LoopTask`.

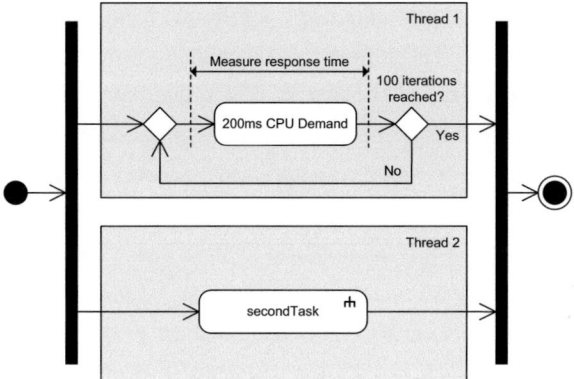

Figure 4.12.: UML activity diagram for the task logic shown in Figure 4.11

The corresponding UML activity diagram for the task logic is shown in Figure 4.12. The `ParallelTask` is denoted by the UML fork node bars. The two nested `LoopTask`s are displayed using a gray box as container. The first `LoopTask` contains a `CpuLoadTask`, which is denoted with a UML action element. By using the UML control flow and a UML merge node, the `LoopTask` logic is displayed. The second `LoopTask` is not specified in detail, hence we use a collapsed task notion to omit the details of this task. Finally, the specified sensor for the `CpuLoadTask` is indicated using two dashed bars around the task's UML action element. The shown execution logic is not targeted at detecting the value of a certain property, but only serves for illustrating the usage of experiment tasks and sensors. In the following chapters, experiments for detecting different execution environment properties will be presented.

A detailed presentation of various GINPEX metamodel elements using UML activity diagrams can be found in Appendix A.

4.7. Extensibility of the Approach

The GINPEX approach aims at deriving parameters of various parts of the software execution environment using a common format for specifying automated experiments. The approach is designed to be extendable in several ways. First, a main goal of the approach is to facilitate the specification of new experiments and experiment domains. In addition, in some cases one might want to extend GINPEX with additional experiment tasks, sensors, or analysis logic.

In the remainder of this section, we explain how GINPEX supports the specification of such extensions. To illustrate extensibility, we use as a running example experiments that derive database properties.

4.7.1. Experiments

GINPEX is integrated into the Eclipse Equinox platform that is based on the Eclipse OSGi architecture [Thed]. Eclipse Equinox supports the specification of modular extensions within the Eclipse IDE using an extension registry. We used this framework to implement GINPEX extensibility w.r.t. experiments and experiment domains. For both experiments and experiment domains, Eclipse extension points have been defined, i.e. new experiment domains and experiments can be added by specifying the corresponding Eclipse extensions.

As an example for extending experiments and experiment domains, consider the area of databases where a lot of database properties might be worth including in software performance prediction.

GINPEX provides an API that indicates the methods that have to be implemented by new experiments. Such methods include the specification of the configuration parameters and the detected parameter, the generation of the experiment model, and the analysis of the experiment results. Adding a new experiment specification and the corresponding analysis logic certainly requires detailed domain knowledge as well as some knowledge in experiment design. Domain knowledge is necessary in order to assess which execution environment properties are adequate, i.e. they are relevant in order to be reflected in performance prediction, and they can be derived by automated measurements. In addition, an experiment has to be defined in a way to detect infrastructure properties without being tailored towards a certain platform, as the experiment should be applicable to a variety of platforms. For example, specifying an experiment that detects the throughput of write requests to a storage device should be applicable to platforms equipped with hard disks as well as solid state disks. Predefined experiments for detecting database properties should work with multiple existing database implementations. Second, the experiment designer has to be familiar with experiment design in order to design robust experiments. The GINPEX approach aims at supporting the experiment designer as much as possible when it comes to these requirements. For example, robust measurements can be specified by a `LoopTask` with an appropriate stop condition.

Considering the example of database experiments, the experiment designer would specify a new experiment for each relevant database property. Typical performance-relevant properties could be how multiple executed queries slow down query response time, whether inserting large amounts of data scales linearly, overhead of transaction management, and so on.

In addition to the specification of automated experiments, GINPEX can be used to execute experiments manually. Manual experiments support the developer in performing explorative measurements which precede the definition of new experiments and automated analyses.

4.7.2. Experiment domains

To group predefined experiments, a new experiment domain can be specified. Similarly to extending GINPEX with new experiments, new experiment domains can be specified by implementing the predefined Eclipse extension point for experiment domains.

To group experiments for detecting performance-relevant properties of relational databases, a new experiment domain "Relational Databases" could be specified to group database experiments.

4.7.3. Experiment tasks and sensors

Enhancing experiment tasks and sensors is possible through established model-driven technologies provided by the Eclipse platform. The GIN-PEX experiment metamodel is specified in Ecore [Thec]. Using the Eclipse Modeling Framework, developers can add new tasks or sensors to the metamodel. Extending the GINPEX metamodel by adding new tasks or sensors can be done without changing the core metamodel. As new elements inherit from existing ones, the existing implementation of the experiment controller, for example editor support for tasks and sensors, does not have to be adapted in order to support new task and sensor elements.

For tasks, we restrict the extensibility of tasks to tasks that run on a certain target machine (and not on the controller machine). This is due to the fact that the logic of such tasks is solely defined in code generation templates (not to be confused with the experiment template presented in Section 4.6). The templates are specified using the Xpand language of the Eclipse Model-To-Text (M2T) framework [Thee]. Here, extensibility can be achieved by adding new templates only. If a new task should be executed on the controller machine as well (as it is the case for all control flow tasks), adding the tasks would require access to the controller machine implementation. Hence, adding a new task can be done by specifying a new task metamodel element that inherits from `MachineTask`. In order to support the task execution on a Load Driver, the code generation templates have to be enhanced in order to generate source code for the added task. For adding a new task, four templates are available specifying the source code to be generated:

- The `TaskVariablesDeclaration` template contains all variable definitions that the task accesses.

- The `TaskPreparation` template contains preparation logic. This logic is called prior to the task execution in the preparation phase.

- The `TaskExecution` template contains the actual execution logic. This logic is called in the execution phase.

- The `TaskCleanup` template contains cleanup logic which is called after the experiment has been executed.

New task logic can also be added without adapting the metamodel. Instead, the `ExecuteLibraryTask` can be used to execute task logic that is available in a library. In the case of generated Java code, we use JAR libraries for this purpose. The library has to provide an implementation of a simple API that is aligned to the templates above and defines preparation, execution, and cleanup methods. These methods are then called at the corresponding phases of the running experiment.

Specifying tasks that execute libraries facilitates the encapsulation of new task logic while avoiding metamodel extensions. On the other side, metamodel extensions can be packaged and shipped separately from the GINPEX core, but can directly plug into existing GINPEX editors, and thus can be easily used when specifying experiments.

Adding a new sensor to the metamodel can be done in a similar way to adding new tasks. New sensor elements simply inherit from the `Sensor` element. If the new sensor is to be executed in a parallel thread to the annotated task, it has to inherit from `ParallelSensorRunnable` as well. To specify the sensor logic, the following Xpand templates have to be specified:

- The `SensorVariablesDeclaration` template contains all variable definitions that the sensor accesses.

- The `SensorPreparation` template contains preparation logic. This logic is called prior to the execution in the preparation phase.

- The `SensorLogicBeforeTask` template contains sensor logic that is executed before the annotated task is executed. This template is not needed if the sensor inherits from `ParallelSensorRunnable`.

- The `SensorLogicAfterTask` template contains sensor logic that is executed after the annotated task is executed. The template is also not needed if the sensor inherits from `ParallelSensorRunnable`.

- The `ParallelSensorLogic` template is only needed if the sensor inherits from `ParallelSensorRunnable`. It contains the sensor logic that is called during the execution of the sensor. How often this logic is called depends on the specified value of the sensor's `wait-TimeBetweenMeasurements` attribute.

- The `SensorCleanup` template contains cleanup logic which is called after the experiment has been executed.

Going back to the example of database experiments, adding new experiment logic for database access might become necessary. For instance, the performance analyst could start with encapsulating database access logic in a library. Afterwards, he would use this library in an `ExecuteLibrary-Task` in initial database experiments. In order to facilitate the specification of database experiments, he could then provide new task metamodel elements which can be used to issue certain database load. For example, typical database load could be generated by invoking database microbenchmarks such as the DBmbench microbenchmarks [SAF05]. To plug together tasks in order to generate database access patterns, new tasks encapsulating microbenchmark logic could be used in combination with existing control flow tasks.

4.7.4. Analysis logic

In addition to extending predefined experiment domains, predefined experiments, tasks and sensors, experiment analysis logic can also be enhanced by adding arbitrary analysis logic. This is not done in a model-driven way. Instead, evaluating experiment results in order to derive an execution environment property value is done programmatically. During experiment evaluation, any analysis code (e.g. Java code or R scripts) can be invoked.

4.8. Experiment Performance Overhead

When executing performance experiments, the performance overhead of such experiments typically has to be considered in order to assess the performance impact of experiments on the system under test and on the controller machine. The performance overhead of experiments includes two different aspects; (i) performance overhead that incurs due to experiment preparation and analysis, and (ii) overhead that incurs during experiment execution.

Experiment preparation occurs partly on the controller machine and partly on the system under test. On the controller machine, experiment specifications are loaded or generated programmatically. Based on the specification, source code is generated for the different `MachineTaskSets`. The source code is then transferred to the Load Driver(s) on the system under test, where the code is compiled and its preparation logic is executed.

Code compilation incurs some overhead on the target machine, but might be performed on the controller machine as well. In the latter case, already compiled experiments would be transferred to the Load Drivers. The experiment preparation might incur some overhead on the target machines as well. For instance, a `CpuLoadTask` requires a calibration that is performed on each target machine the first time a `CpuLoadTask` is executed on the machine. This calibration is based on the library presented in [BDH08]. In our experiments, we experienced the calibration to take 20 to 30 minutes per CPU demand.

The experiment analysis is completely performed on the controller machine, hence no performance overhead occurs on the system under test at this point. The runtime of the analysis depends on the type of analysis and the amount of data that has to be processed.

Communication between the controller machine and the Load Drivers only occurs before and after experiment execution. This is due to the fact that the complete experiment logic is transferred to the Load Drivers before experiment execution. Thus, we avoided additional communication overhead that would otherwise occur during experiment execution and might influence experiment results.

The performance impact of the experiment during its execution, i.e. the resource consumption of an experiment on the target machines, strongly depends on the modeled experiment logic. Some experiments might put a strong load on the target platform, and might require the platform to be idle in order to obtain useful experiment results. Other experiments might have a stronger focus on performing monitoring logic instead of issuing resource load. Such experiments can be used to detect certain properties on a system where additional software is running. In such cases, a performance degradation of running software due to performance experiments might not be desired.

The actual performance overhead due to experiment execution also depends on the experiment design, for example on the number of iterations of a certain part of the experiment, or the number of experiment runs needed when varying a parameter. Here, careful experiment design is needed in order to keep the overall experiment runtime and the involved performance overhead low while aiming at robust experiment results (for more details on experiment design, see [Jai91]). The GINPEX metamodel already includes certain logic to help the performance analyst in specifying experiments. For example, the number of loop iterations can be kept low by specifying a stop condition based on the confidence level of measurements.

As the performance overhead of an experiment during execution depends on the experiment logic and the experiment design, no general statements on the overhead can be made. Besides performing careful experiment design, the template presented in Section 4.6 should be used for documenting the performance impact. For example, the section "Experiment performance" can be used to document the experiment runtime, and the section "Assumptions" can be used to indicate whether an experiment requires a system under test where no additional load is present, or if an experiment can be executed on a production system.

4.9. Summary

In this chapter, we presented a model-based implementation of the GIN-PEX approach. We defined a metamodel for the specification of automated execution environment experiments. The metamodel can be used to specify experiments and parametric dependencies between experiments, as well as experiment execution logic. In order to provide a structured presentations of experiments to software architects and performance analysts, we developed a template format that captures the relevant information. In the following chapters, we will use this template for presenting various experiments. Finally, we explained how experiments are executed and analyzed based on GINPEX metamodel instances, how the approach can be extended, and discussed the performance overhead that incurs due to experiment execution.

In the following chapters, we demonstrate how the approach can be applied to different experiment domains. We will first present experiments that aim at deriving CPU and OS scheduling properties in Chapter 5. In Chapter 6, we focus on experiments that aim at deriving properties in virtualized systems.

5. Deriving CPU and OS Scheduling Properties

In this chapter, we demonstrate how the approach presented in the previous chapters can be applied to CPU and OS-related properties of the execution environment. We chose this domain, as it features properties for which the performance impact is well-known [Hap08]. We provide an automated experiment for each property and show for every experiment that it is able to derive the correct property value on multiple platforms featuring a different characteristic of the property. Afterwards, we discuss how the derived properties can be reflected in performance prediction. We then validate the experiments by conducting a case study where we predict the performance of a software system, using the derived properties in performance analysis, and compare the prediction results with measurement results. Finally, we discuss limitations and assumptions of the presented experiments and summarize the chapter. Some experiments presented in this chapter have been initially published in [HHR10], [HKHR11], and [HKHR13].

5.1. Experiments Overview

In Chapter 3, we introduced a workflow for executing GINPEX experiments (see Section 3.3.2). By using the experiments in this chapter, this approach can be instantiated for detecting certain CPU and operating system properties. Let us assume that a performance analyst wants to conduct a performance prediction for a software while reflecting such execution environment properties. For this prediction, he has created a performance model of the software architecture, and has set up the execution environment, e.g. a server of the production environment with the dedicated operating system installed. He would then deploy the Load Driver on the target machine which is used by GINPEX for automatically generating load and taking measurements. The experiments in this chapter are grouped into experiment domains which are selected by the analyst for execution. The GINPEX tool would then execute the experiments and analyze the experiment results which are available through measurements taken on the target machine. The analysis of the results would yield the values of the analyzed execution environment properties for the target machine. These values are then passed to the performance analysis tooling, where they are reflected during performance prediction for the software architecture model.

The experiments presented in this chapter can be grouped into two experiment domains. The first experiment domain "CPU" encompasses experiments that aim at detecting CPU properties. Here, we present two experiments aiming at detecting CPU simultaneous multithreading (SMT) availability (CPU.01) and the number of CPU cores (CPU.02). The detected SMT property of CPU.01 serves as configuration parameter for the CPU.02 experiment. The second experiment domain "OS Scheduler" is used to group three experiments aiming at detecting properties of general-purpose operating system schedulers. The properties under focus are the timeslice length of the scheduler (OSSCHEDULER.01) as well as strategies for load-balancing, i.e. initial load-balancing (OSSCHEDULER.02) and dynamic load-balancing (OSSCHEDULER.03). The number of cores property detected by experiment CPU.02 is used as configuration parameter for all three OS scheduling experiments.

Figure 5.1 gives an overview on the experiments of this chapter. The arrows between the experiments denote a detected parameter that is used as configuration parameter. Hence, they are indicating a possible order for experiment execution (execute CPU.01 before CPU.02; execute CPU.02 before OSSCHEDULER.01, OSSCHEDULER.02, OSSCHEDULER.03).

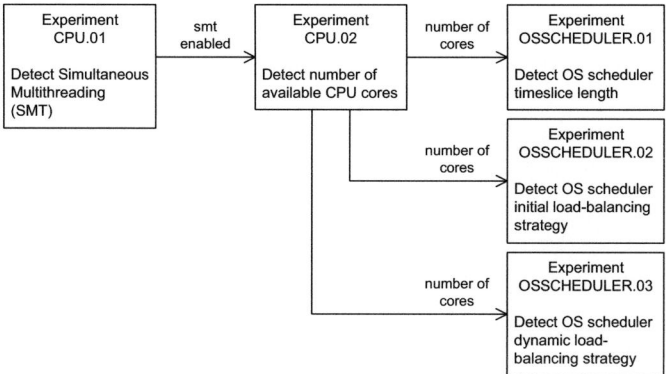

Figure 5.1.: Overview on the experiments presented in this chapter

5.2. Scientific Challenges

In this chapter, we present experiments for deriving CPU and OS scheduling properties automatically. While the scientific challenges outlined for the overall approach in Section 3.2 apply to these properties as well, the scientific challenges w.r.t. deriving CPU and OS scheduling properties in particular are:

- How can CPU and OS scheduling properties be derived through automated experiments?

- How can the detected properties be integrated into software performance prediction?

- What is the impact of the different properties on performance prediction accuracy?

In the following sections, we present the different experiments in detail.

5.3. CPU Simultaneous Multithreading

In this section, we present an experiment that detects whether the a machine is equipped with a CPU that has simultaneous multithreading (SMT) enabled. Detecting this CPU feature can be useful if performance prediction approaches support SMT in the prediction tooling. Besides, the fact whether SMT is available or not has an impact on other experiments presented in this chapter. For those experiments, the results of this experiment serves as an input parameter.

5.3.1. Motivation

Simultaneous multithreading (SMT) is a technique to provide hardware-based multithreading. A processor supporting SMT is able to concurrently execute multiple threads on the available cores. That is done by executing multiple instructions of different threads in different functional units in the same cycle [TEL95].

SMT can have several effects on performance. First, a speedup can be observed for software applications which feature workloads that benefit from SMT, e.g. applications with multiple CPU-bound threads in parallel. However, the observed speedup strongly depends on the workload. The performance of CPU-bound workloads can be increased by 10% to 40% [MMM+05], but as the parallel threads share the same resources such as cache, branch prediction, or execution units, for certain workloads no performance gain or even a performance degradation can be observed [EHK+02].

Second, a SMT CPU usually appears to the system as multiple CPUs (depending on the number of parallel threads that can be executed concurrently. Thus, if a system is equipped with a dual-core CPU that supports simultaneous multithreading of two parallel threads per core (two-way SMT), four CPU cores are visible to the system. As the operating system takes all available cores into account when calculating and displaying the overall

CPU utilization, the information whether SMT is available on the system matters when interpreting the CPU utilization.

For example, consider the dual-core system with two-way SMT described above. If one thread is running a CPU-bound workload on the system (the other threads being idle), the operating system would record a CPU utilization of approximately 25%. However, one must not conclude that four identical threads can be executed in parallel with similar response times for each thread, as only two physical cores are available and SMT might not lead to a full parallel execution of the available threads.

To show how CPU demand response times vary depending on the availability of SMT, we executed a manual experiment with GINPEX on a machine with four physical cores running the Linux 2.6.31 kernel[1]. The first run was executed on the machine while SMT was disabled (run A), in the second run, SMT was enabled (run B). The experiment consisted of a sequence of `ParallelTasks`, each `ParallelTask` containing a set of `CpuLoadTasks`. Every `CpuLoadTask` is executed multiple times and issued a fixed amount of CPU demand (200 ms `FibonacciDemand`). As explained in 4.4, the specified duration of a `CpuLoadTask` demand is based on the task calibration and denotes the time the task would run if executed on a machine's core without contention. In every step of the experiment run's sequence, the number of parallel tasks is being increased from 1 to 10. For every step, the response time for one nested `CpuLoadTask` as well as the CPU utilization was measured.

Figure 5.2 shows the measured results for the two runs. In Figure 5.2 (a), the results for run A where SMT was disabled are plotted. One can see that the measured task response times match the specified task duration, if the number of parallel executed CPU-bound task is not larger than the number of available (physical) cores (in this case, if no more than 4 tasks are executed in parallel). For 1 to 4 parallel executed tasks, the CPU utilization increases from around 25% to 100% which shows that the operating

---

[1] Intel Core i7-860, 2.80 GHz, 8 GB RAM

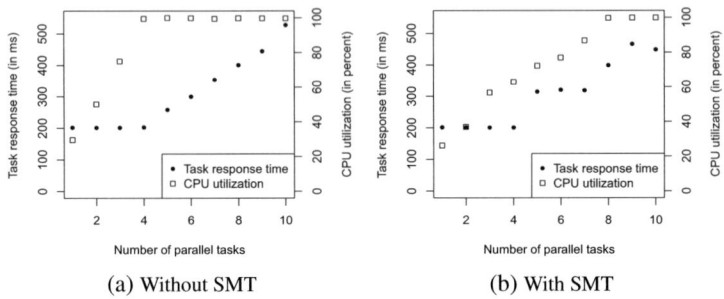

(a) Without SMT   (b) With SMT

Figure 5.2.: SMT effects on CPU-bound tasks

system utilizes the available CPU cores. For a larger number of parallel executed tasks, the CPU stays fully utilized, but as more tasks are executed than CPU cores are available, the measured response times increase due to CPU contention. For 8 parallel tasks, the measured response times are approximately twice as high as for 1 to 4 parallel tasks, as two parallel tasks share one CPU core.

For the experiment run B on the machine with SMT enabled, the results differ, as shown in Figure 5.2 (b). Similarly to the run with SMT disabled, the measured task response times increase once the number of parallel executed tasks is larger than the number of available CPU cores. However, the increase of response times is not as smooth as observed in run A, which indicates that the availability of SMT already has an effect on the observed response time. A significant difference in the measured results for the two runs can be seen in the reported CPU utilization. In run B, the system reports a lower CPU utilization for 1 to 7 parallel tasks compared to run A, as the system calculates CPU utilization depending on the visible CPU cores, which is the number of virtual cores and thus higher than the number of physical cores. For 5 to 7 parallel tasks, run B reports a CPU utilization that is lower than 100%, whereas the observed response time for the tasks are increased indicating that CPU contention was present during the runs.

5.3.2. Experiment Design

The experiment to detect whether SMT is available on the machine under test is structured as follows. For a graphical description of the experiment logic, see Figure 5.3.

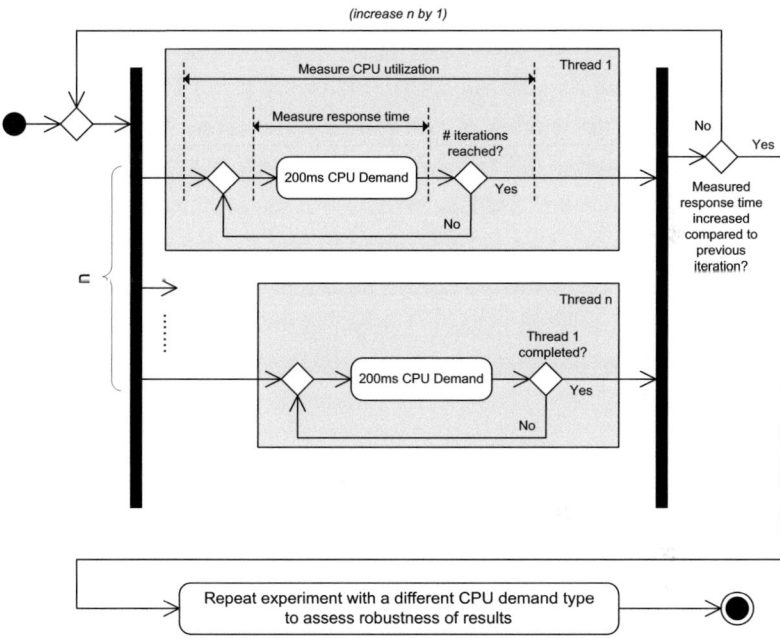

Figure 5.3.: Simultaneous multithreading experiment logic

The experiment consists of multiple runs. In each run, a `ParallelTask` is executed consisting of `LoopTasks` that are to be executed in parallel. Each `LoopTask` contains a `CpuLoadTasks` specifying the CPU load to issue (500 ms, `FibonacciDemand`). For the first nested `CpuLoadTask` (called *TaskMeas* in the following), the response time is measured. This task is iterated 100 times to gain stable response time measurements. During the execution of the `CpuLoadTasks`, the CPU utilization is measured as well. The remaining parallel `LoopTasks` are iterated until the first `Loop-Task` completes (stop condition `EndlessLoop`). In every experiment run, the number of parallel executed tasks is increased by one. After every run, the results are analyzed. Once the measured mean response time of an experiment run's *TaskMeas* is significantly higher than the measured mean response time of the previous experiment run, the first part of the experiment is completed. An increased response time indicates that CPU contention occurred during the run, i.e. the number of parallel `CpuLoadTasks` was higher than the number of available physical cores. If the measured CPU utilization during this run was significantly lower than 100%, the experiment concludes that SMT is available on the machine under test, as the operating system reported a system that was not fully utilized due to present virtual cores. Otherwise, if the measured CPU utilization was near or at 100% for increased measured response times, the system seems to fully utilize all physical cores and thus, no SMT is assumed.

5.3.3. Experiment Template

In the following, we use the experiment template from Section 4.6 to give a brief overview on the experiment.

Experiment ID: CPU.01

Experiment name: Detect simultaneous multithreading (SMT)

Experiment domain: CPU

Detected experiment parameter: SMT available (true/false); default: false

Importance for performance analysis: A performance speedup for parallel CPU-bound workloads possible due to virtual CPU cores. However, the performance gain of x virtual cores is typically lower than x physical cores. If SMT is available, the observed

CPU utilization of a software application is based on the available virtual cores.

Configuration parameters: None.

Experiment execution logic: Iteratively increase the number of parallel executed CPU-bound tasks and measure its response times and the CPU utilization. If response time increases, stop. If the measured CPU utilization has not reached 100% once increased response times have been measured, we assume that SMT is available. For details, see Section 5.3.2 or the graphical description shown in Figure 5.3.

Assumptions:

- The machine is idle.

- The operating system reports CPU utilization based on the number of available virtual cores.

- Required sensors: Response time sensor, CPU utilization sensor.

Experiment robustness: The experiment is being executed twice with different types of CPU demands, one focusing on integer operations, one focusing on floating-point operations. If at least one of the demands yields measurements that indicate SMT availability, the experiment result is set to true (SMT available).

Experiment performance: $O(n)$ where n is the number of available CPU cores. If the number of cores is larger than 8, the number of parallel tasks is doubled instead of linearly increased, which leads to a duration that lies in $O(\log(n))$.

5.3.4. Experiment Robustness and Performance

In order to assess the robustness of the experiment results, the experiment runs described in Section 5.3.2 are repeated with a different CpuLoadTask demand. For these runs, the demand is set to `MandelbrotDemand`. Compared to the `FibonacciDemand` which generates CPU load containing integer operations for the most parts, the `MandelbrotDemand` generates load with a focus on floating-point operations. By using different CPU operations, we assume that the availability of SMT has an effect on at least one of the executed demands. Thus, if SMT is being detected by the experiment analysis of either part 1 or part 2, SMT availability is assumed by the experiment and the experiment result is set to true.

The runtime of the presented experiment mainly depends on the number of needed iterations when the number of parallel tasks is increased. As the experiment completes once full utilization of the system is reached, the runtime depends on the number of available CPU cores. The runtime of one iteration is approximately $100 \cdot 500$ ms (100 iterations of a `CpuLoadTask` taking 500 ms), i.e. 50 seconds. From this follows that the duration of the experiment is $O(n)$ where n is the number of available CPU cores.

As the experiment runtime increases linearly with the number of parallel tasks, the experiment is suited for systems where the number of available CPU cores is not too high. This is the case for many server systems, where the number of available CPU cores can be considered to lie between 1 and 8. However, for systems with a higher number of available cores, the runtime of the experiment can become very long due to the linear increase of parallel tasks. To improve experiment runtime, we adapted the experiment logic that increases the number of parallel tasks as explained in the following.

The adapted experiment logic starts with 1 task in the first run and increases the number of parallel tasks from 1 to 8 as described above. If the experiment does not complete after the run in which 8 parallel tasks have been executed, a higher number of physical cores has to be assumed. Now, the experiment starts to double the number of parallel tasks until increased response times are measured. Once an experiment run has been executed for which increased response times are measured, the experiment completes if the measured CPU utilization was significantly lower than 100% for this run. Otherwise, the experiment continues for the range $[x_a, x_b]$ where x_a is the number of parallel tasks in the last experiment run that did not measure increased response times and x_b is the number of parallel tasks in the experiment run for which increased response times were measured. By performing a binary search within the range, the experiment continues executing experiment runs until it detects $x_{new} \in [x_a, x_b - 1]$ for which holds that the experiment run with x_{new} parallel tasks did not yield increased response time measurements, but the experiment run with $x_{new} + 1$ parallel tasks did. As described above, the experiment assumes SMT availability if the CPU utilization for the run with $x_{new} + 1$ parallel tasks was below 100%, and no SMT availability otherwise.

By using a combination of doubling the parallel tasks and binary search, the duration of the experiment is $O(\log(n))$ if executed on a system where the number of available cores is higher than 8. By avoiding a linear increase of parallel tasks for the experiment runs with a higher number of parallel tasks, the experiment still completes with a tolerable amount of needed experiment runs. For example, an experiment running on a 48-core machine yielded 17 runs in part 1 (compared to 49 runs for a simple setup with linear increase of parallel tasks) with a summarized part 1 execution runtime of 18 min 11 seconds.

5.3.5. Example

In the following, we illustrate how the experiment detects SMT availability for different platforms.

We executed the experiment on five different machines:

- Machine A: A dual-core machine with no SMT support (Intel Core 2 Duo, 2.66 GHz, 3 GB RAM) running Windows 7 (run A)

- Machine B: A dual-core machine with no SMT support (AMD Athlon64 X2 Dual Core 4600, 2.4 GHz, 4 GB RAM) running the Linux 2.6.32 kernel (run B)

- Machine C: A quad-core machine (Intel Core i7-860, 2.80 GHz, 8 GB RAM) running Windows 7, with SMT disabled (run C1) and SMT enabled (run C2)

- Machine D: A quad-core machine (Intel Core i7-860, 2.80 GHz, 8 GB RAM) running the Linux 2.6.31 kernel, with SMT disabled (run D1) and SMT enabled (run D2)

- Machine E: A 48-core machine with no SMT support (4x AMD Opteron 12 Core 6100, 2.1 GHz, 64 GB RAM) running the Linux 2.6.32 kernel (run E)

Run A and run B execute the experiment on CPUs of different vendors which do not provide SMT support. Run C1, C2, D1 and D2 execute the experiment on quad-core CPU machine with SMT support, but with different operating systems. The last run E was executed on a server machine equipped with four 12-core CPUs, which results in 48 available cores. We executed the experiment on this machine to show how the runtime of the experiment can be kept low by adapting the increase of parallel executed tasks.

For machine A and machine B, the results for the experiment are shown in Figure 5.4 (a) and Figure 5.4 (b), respectively. These machines feature a CPU from different vendors (Intel CPU for machine A, AMD CPU for machine B), both CPUs are not supporting SMT. As each experiment consisted of two parts (to assess robustness of results), the results for the two parts are separated by the vertical line in each plot. From the results one can see that the experiment detects missing SMT support after three runs in each part. In the third run, both increased response times and a fully utilized CPU were detected. Based on the experiment logic presented in Section 5.3.2,

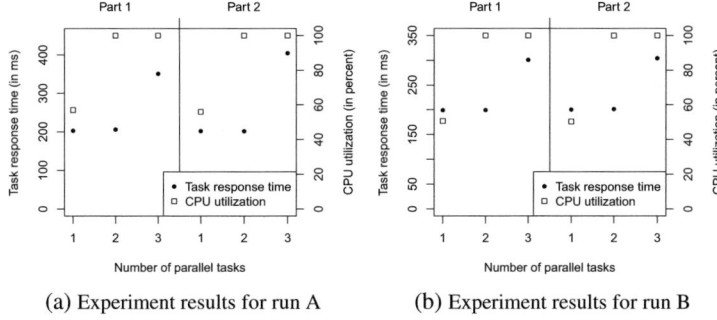

(a) Experiment results for run A   (b) Experiment results for run B

Figure 5.4.: Exemplary experiment results for experiment CPU.01 (SMT):
          run A, run B

this leads to an experiment result indicating no available SMT support. For both experiments, the second part yielded the similar measurements as the first part and thus lead to the same experiment result which indicates robust results. These results show that for a CPU without SMT support, the experiment works.

Machine C and machine D feature a CPU that supports SMT, but run a different operating system. We executed the experiment on these machines to show that SMT is detected once it is available and enabled.

Figure 5.5 shows the results for run C1 and run C2 on the Windows 7 quad-core CPU machine. If SMT is disabled, the machine reaches a CPU utilization of approx. 100% for four and more parallel tasks. An increased response time is observed for more than four parallel tasks, and thus SMT is derived in both experiment parts. Interestingly, as the threshold for detecting increased response times has been set to 30 ms for the experiment, the experiment detects increased response times not before the 6th run in the first part. However, the detected results are correct for both parts. If SMT is enabled, the experiment detects increased response times before a full CPU utilization is reported (after 7 runs in the first part and after 5 runs

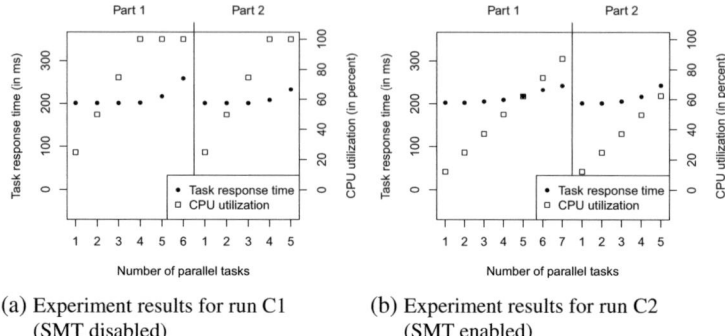

(a) Experiment results for run C1
(SMT disabled)

(b) Experiment results for run C2
(SMT enabled)

Figure 5.5.: Exemplary experiment results for experiment CPU.01 (SMT): run C1, run C2

in the second part). These observed results lead to an experiment result indicating available SMT support.

Figure 5.6 shows the results for run D1 and run D2 on the Linux 2.6.31 quad-core CPU machine. The results are similar to the results of run C1 and C2. Missing SMT support is detect in D1 and available SMT support

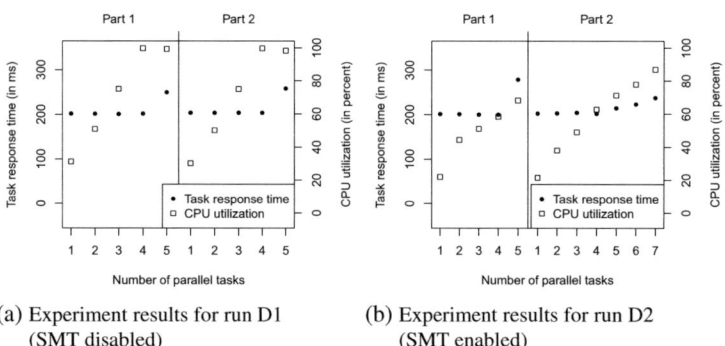

(a) Experiment results for run D1
(SMT disabled)

(b) Experiment results for run D2
(SMT enabled)

Figure 5.6.: Exemplary experiment results for experiment CPU.01 (SMT): run D1, run D2

is detected in D2. Thus, the experiment yielded the correct results when executed on machines with different operating systems.

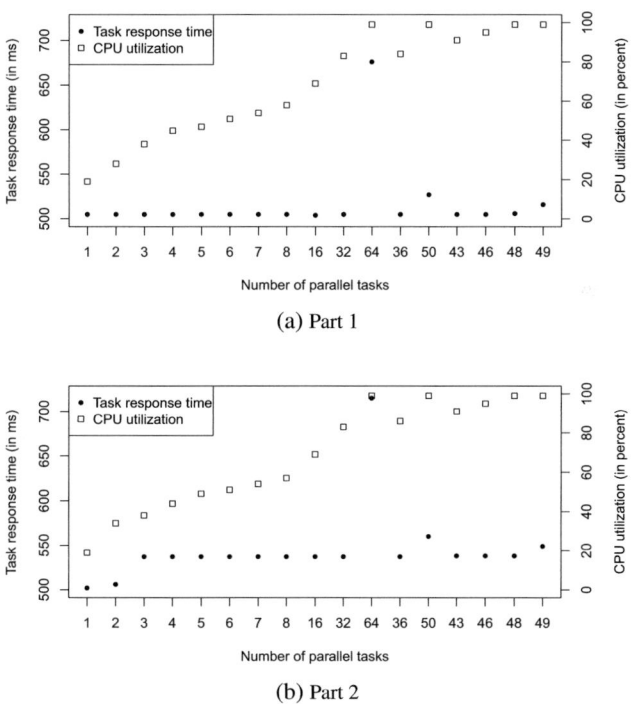

(a) Part 1

(b) Part 2

Figure 5.7.: Exemplary experiment results for experiment CPU.01 (SMT): run E

Finally, we performed the experiment on a 48-core machine to examine how the experiment performs with a larger number of CPU cores (run E). Figure 5.7 shows the experiment results for both experiment parts. The figure illustrates how the experiment continues when no result is reached after having executed 8 tasks in parallel. To minimize the number of needed runs, the experiment now uses a binary search to find the number of parallel tasks n where increased response times have been measured compared to $n - 1$. This happens for $n = 49$; in both parts, the CPU is fully utilized for this number of parallel tasks, thus the experiment detects that SMT support is missing on this machine.

In comparison to a fully linear experiment, where 49 experiment runs would be needed, run E shows that doubling the number of parallel tasks leads to a significant reduction of needed experiment runs. The experiment only needs 17 runs for each part.

5.4. Number of CPU Cores

In performance analyses, the number of CPU cores often has to be specified for a server of the system. This section introduces an experiment that detects the number of available CPU cores in a platform-independent way.

5.4.1. Motivation

For many years now, server machines are equipped with multi-core CPUs. A multi-core CPU consists of multiple identical physical processors that share the same properties, such as the processing power, or the shared address space. A symmetric multiprocessing (SMP) computer involves a multi-core CPU where a task can be executed on any available core. In contrast, asymmetric multiprocessing (AMP) denotes a multi-core CPU system where certain tasks have to be executed on dedicated cores (for example, an AMP system can distinguish between operating system tasks executed on a core on which the operating system runs on, and user tasks executed on a core reserved for executing user applications). In the following, we focus on SMP environments, as such CPUs are nowadays common for server machines and have replaced AMP environments in these fields (AMP can be seen as a predecessor technology here). However, for embedded systems or mobile devices, which gained a large momentum in recent years, AMP techniques can be an alternative to SMP and might gain more relevance in the future [Kal05].

Support for multi-core CPUs is available in different performance prediction approaches such as Palladio [RBB+11], where the number of CPU cores has to be specified in the model of the analyzed system. In performance analysis, this attribute is then regarded, for example in a simulation approach using multi-core-aware CPU scheduling strategies. In case of Palladio, simple scheduling strategies, such as first come, first served (FCFS) or processor sharing (PS) are supported [RBB+11] as well as complex multi-core CPU scheduling strategies of general-purpose operating systems [HGHR10].

As the number of available CPU cores can often be easily retrieved, specifying the number of CPU cores in the performance model is usually feasible. However, we propose an automated experiment for detecting the number of CPU cores for the following reasons:

- Querying the number of available CPU cores can only be achieved through platform-dependent system calls. The proposed experiment allows for detecting the number of available CPU cores in a platform-independent way, which also works if the information cannot be retrieved in other ways.

- As the experiment runs automated, it can be used in performance measurements on environments with a large number of machines, where the experiment can run in parallel, with no manual efforts involved, and detect the property value for every machine.

- If SMT is available, the experiment detects both the number of available physical cores and the number of virtual cores.

- The detected parameter of the experiment serves as input parameter for various experiments that aim at detecting other parameters that cannot be easily obtained otherwise. If such experiments are to be executed, this experiment is automatically executed beforehand if the parameter is not available.

The experiment logic is based on the input parameter *smt* that is detected by the CPU simultaneous multithreading (SMT) experiment CPU.01. If SMT is available, the *smt* value is set to true, otherwise it is set to false. By taking SMT availability into account, the experiment can be used for a wide range of processors and is not restricted to non-SMT processors or SMT processors only.

The experiment detects the number of available physical CPU cores, i.e. the number of CPU cores that can be used to execute CPU-bound tasks in parallel. If SMT is available, the experiment detects the number of virtual cores as well, i.e. the number of cores that appear to the operating system. For SMT, the number of virtual cores is usually a multiple of the number of physical cores. For example, current Intel CPUs that feature SMT have twice as many virtual cores as physical cores [Inta].

In the following, we describe the structure of the experiment in detail.

5.4.2. Experiment Design

The logic of the experiment is similar to the experiment CPU.01 that detects whether SMT is available for a CPU (see Section 5.3). A graphical description of the experiment is given in Figure 5.8.

As for the SMT experiment, this experiment issues a CPU load (200 ms FibonacciDemand) and iteratively increases the number of parallel tasks issuing CPU load. For the first CpuLoadTask (called *TaskMeas* in the following), the response time is measured. If *smt* is true, the CPU utilization is measured during the execution of the CpuLoadTasks. The first part of the experiment is completed based on the following conditions:

- If *smt* is false, the experiment part completes when the measured response times of *TaskMeas* are significantly higher than the measured response times of the first experiment run.

- If *smt* is true, the experiment part completes when the measured response times of *TaskMeas* are significantly higher than the measured

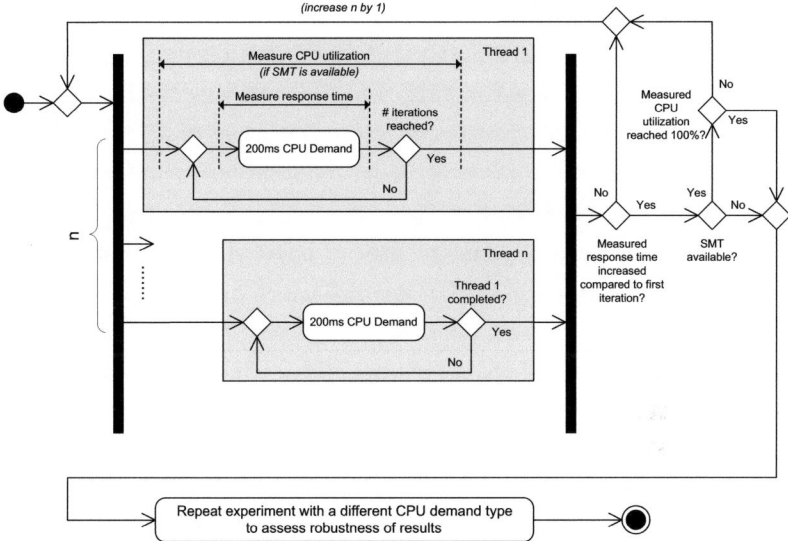

Figure 5.8.: Number of CPU cores experiment logic

response times of the first experiment run and the measured CPU utilization reached 100%.

After the first part of the experiment is completed, the collected measurements are analyzed. If *smt* is false, only response time measurements are regarded. In this case, the number of physical cores equals the number of parallel executed tasks in the second to last experiment run. As the experiment part completes once an increase of the measured response times is detected, the last iteration executed more parallel tasks than physical cores are available. Thus, the second to last iteration featured the highest number of parallel tasks that did not overutilize the available CPU cores. For this iteration, the number of parallel tasks equals the number of available physical cores. As no SMT is available, the number of available virtual cores is negligible and set by default to the number of physical cores.

If *smt* is true, the experiment part does not complete once increased response times are measured if the CPU utilization has not yet reached 100%. This is to be expected, as due to SMT, the system does not report a full CPU utilization because more virtual cores are available than physical cores (see example in Section 5.3). The experiment continues increasing the number of parallel executed tasks until the measured CPU utilization reaches 100%. When analyzing the results, the number of physical cores equals the the number of parallel tasks in the last iteration which did not yield increased response time measurements. As for the case when SMT is not available, it is assumed that increased response times appear when more parallel tasks are executed than available physical cores are available. However, as there are more virtual than physical cores available due to SMT, CPU utilization only reaches 100% if enough parallel tasks are executed to utilize all virtual cores. Thus, the number of virtual cores equals the number of parallel tasks executed in the last execution of the experiment part (which denotes the lowest number of parallel tasks needed to utilize all virtual cores).

5.4.3. Experiment Template

In this section, we give a brief overview on the experiment by using the experiment template from Section 4.6.

Experiment ID: CPU.02

Experiment name: Detect number of available CPU cores

Experiment domain: CPU

Detected experiment parameter: Number of available physical CPU cores (integer); if SMT is available, the number of available virtual CPU cores (integer) is also detected

Importance for performance analysis: The number of available CPU cores heavily influences the slowdown that can be observed for CPU requests due to parallel CPU requests. The number of cores for a CPU resource is a basic parameter this is typically reflected in performance analysis tools such as the PCM.

Configuration parameters: *smt*: SMT available (true/false); detected by Experiment CPU.01

Experiment execution logic: Iteratively increase the number of parallel executed CPU-bound tasks and measure its response time and (if *smt* is true) the CPU utilization. If response time increases and *smt* is false, stop. If *smt* is true, continue until the CPU utilization reaches 100%. The number of physical cores equals the number of parallel executed tasks in the last iteration before increased response times were measured. If *smt* is true, the number of virtual cores equals the number of parallel executed tasks in the last execution, where a CPU utilization of 100% was measured. For details, see Section 5.4.2 or the graphical description shown in Figure 5.8.

Assumptions:

- The machine is idle.

- If the CPU is a multi-core CPU, it features symmetric multi-processing (SMP). This is the case for current server CPUs.

- The OS scheduler spreads CPU load of parallel threads equally across all available CPU cores.

- If *smt* is true, the operating system reports CPU utilization based on the number of available virtual cores.

- Required sensors: Response time sensor, CPU utilization sensor (only if *smt* is true).

Experiment robustness: The experiment is being executed twice with different types of CPU demands, one focusing on integer operations, one focusing on floating-point operations. If the executions lead to the same experiment result, results can be considered robust.

Otherwise, results should be checked manually. Further checks to assess robustness:

- If *smt* is true, the detected number of virtual cores should be higher than the detected number of physical cores

- If *smt* is true, the detected number of virtual cores should be a multiple of the detected number of physical cores

Experiment performance:

If *smt* is false: $O(n)$ where n is the number of available physical CPU cores.

If *smt* is true: $O(n)$ where n is the number of available virtual CPU cores.

If the number of cores is larger than 8, the number of parallel tasks is doubled instead of linearly increased, which leads to a duration that lies in $O(\log(n))$.

5.4.4. Experiment Robustness and Performance

Similar to the SMT experiment, the experiment consists of two parts in order to assess the robustness of the experiment result. The second part closely resembles the first part with the exception of the type of CpuLoad-Task demand that is used. The first part uses FibonacciDemands to generate CPU load containing mainly integer operations, the second part uses MandelbrotDemands to generate CPU load focusing on floating-point operations. The detected experiment results are derived twice for both parts and compared. If the detected results are equal for both parts, the experiment results can be considered robust. Typically, the operating system should be able to distribute the parallel executed tasks to the available cores regardless of the executed CPU demand. Also, the assumed SMT effects (increased measured response times while the CPU is not fully utilized) should occur for any demand as long as it is CPU-bound. However, if different CPU demands lead to different detected result parameters, the experiment execution can issue a warning indicating that the results should be checked manually.

If the two parts of the experiment yield different results, we select the overall experiment result from the part where an increase of response times was measured earlier, i.e. for a smaller number of parallel tasks.

The runtime of the experiment mainly depends on the number of executed iterations. In each iteration, the number of parallel executed tasks is increased, until increased response times or a CPU utilization of 100% is measured. The runtime of one iteration is governed by 100 iterations of 200 ms CPU demands resulting in approximately 20 seconds iteration runtime if no response time slowdown occurs. Due to increased response times of the CPU demands, the duration of one iteration can be longer, but is not expected to exceed double the duration of an iteration without increased response times. Hence, the overall duration of the experiment is $O(n)$ where n is the number of needed iterations for one experiment part, which is the number of available physical CPU cores (if *smt* is false) or the number of available virtual CPU cores (if *smt* is true).

In order to reduce the number of needed experiment runs for machines equipped with a large number of physical cores, the experiment can be adapted in the same way as experiment CPU.01 (see Section 5.3.4. Once the number of parallel tasks reaches 8, the number of parallel tasks is doubled until increased response times are measured. Binary search is used to detect the number n of parallel tasks where n leads to increased response times compared to the first iteration, and $n - 1$ does not. If *smt* is true, the binary search is also used to detect the pair $m - 1$ parallel tasks and m parallel tasks where m, in contrast to $m - 1$, leads to 100% CPU utilization.

5.4.5. Example

In the following, we illustrate how the experiment detects the number of CPU cores on different platforms.

We executed the experiment on four different machines:

- Machine A: A dual-core machine with no SMT support (Intel Core 2 Duo, 2.66 GHz, 3 GB RAM) running Windows 7 (run A)

- Machine B: A dual-core machine with no SMT support (AMD Athlon64 X2 Dual Core 4600, 2.4 GHz, 4 GB RAM) running the Linux 2.6.32 kernel (run B)

- Machine C: A quad-core machine (Intel Core i7-860, 2.80 GHz, 8 GB RAM) running Windows 7, with SMT disabled (run C1) and SMT enabled (run C2)

- Machine D: A quad-core machine (Intel Core i7-860, 2.80 GHz, 8 GB RAM) running the Linux 2.6.31 kernel, with SMT disabled (run D1) and SMT enabled (run D2)

Similarly to the SMT experiments, the first two experiments have been executed on machines equipped with CPUs from different vendors (Intel, AMD), both without SMT support. For both machines, the experiment yields the correct results with both experiments parts (see results in Figure 5.9). In each part, the third run leads to increased response times, hence two cores are detected.

On the quad-core machine C, we executed the experiment twice with SMT support disabled in run C1 and enabled in run C2 (see results in Figure 5.10). In run C1, the experiment completes after five runs, as increased response times have been observed, and four cores are detected. In run C2, the experiment continues, as no full CPU utilization has been observed yet. With 8 parallel tasks, CPU utilization reaches 100%, leading to experiment completion. Here, 4 physical cores and 8 virtual cores are detected. In

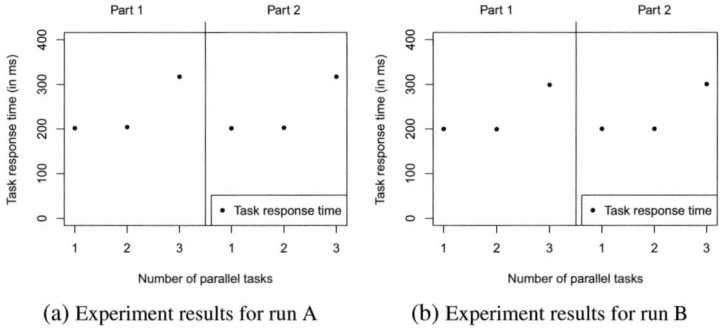

(a) Experiment results for run A   (b) Experiment results for run B

Figure 5.9.: Exemplary experiment results for experiment CPU.02 (Number of cores): run A, run B

run C2, a difference between the first and the second part of the experiment can be observed w.r.t. the increase of response times. This illustrates how different types of CPU demands can be used to obtain robust experiment results.

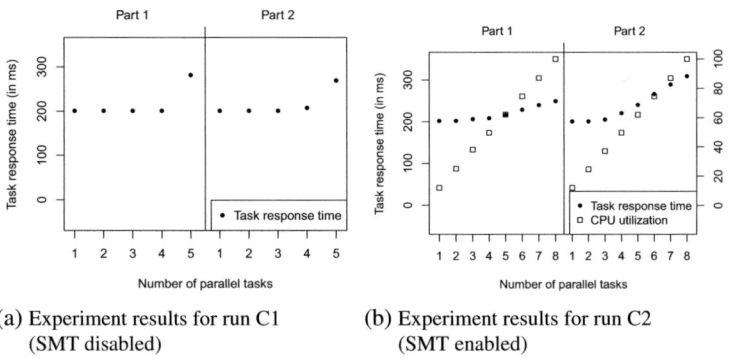

(a) Experiment results for run C1   (b) Experiment results for run C2
(SMT disabled)   (SMT enabled)

Figure 5.10.: Exemplary experiment results for experiment CPU.02 (Number of cores): run C1, run C2

Finally, we executed the experiment on machine D, which featured the same hardware resources as machine C, but a different operating system

133

(Linux 2.6.31 kernel instead of Windows 7). The results of run D1 (SMT disabled) and run D2 (SMT enabled) are shown in Figure 5.11. They are similar to the results of run C1 and run C2 and show that the experiment works with different operating systems.

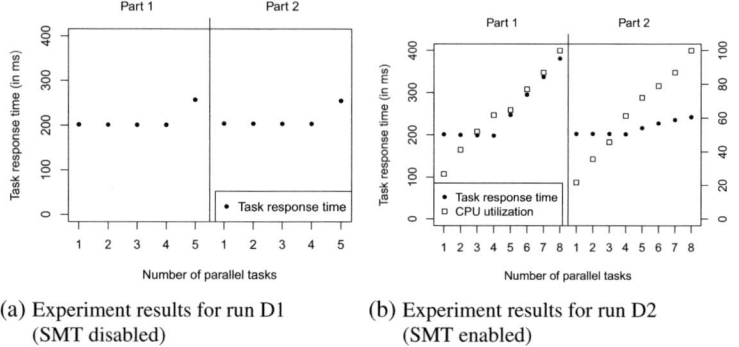

(a) Experiment results for run D1
    (SMT disabled)

(b) Experiment results for run D2
    (SMT enabled)

Figure 5.11.: Exemplary experiment results for experiment CPU.02 (Number of cores): run D1, run D2

5.5. Operating System Scheduler Timeslice Length

Based on the experiment for detecting the number of cores presented in the previous section, we can now continue with detecting performance-relevant properties of the operating system scheduler. This section deals with an experiment to detect the timeslice length of the scheduler.

5.5.1. Motivation

General-purpose operating system (GPOS) schedulers often have to deal with situations where more tasks are ready for execution on a CPU core than cores are available. Typically, GPOS schedulers use timeslices to assign a task to a CPU for a certain amount of time, and iterate through the waiting tasks in a round-robin manner to share the available processing times among all competing tasks.

In performance evaluation, typically scheduling strategies are used that are simple and abstract from timeslices, such as the processor sharing scheduling strategy used in the PCM simulation [BKR09]. Processor sharing assumes infinitesimal small timeslices. The longer the simulated resource request, the lesser impact of the OS scheduler timeslice length can be observed. In such cases, processor sharing can provide an adequate abstraction of the OS scheduler in performance simulation. However, smaller requests tend to be affected more by the timeslice length of the operating system. To accurately simulate the response time of such requests, the simulation scheduler has to reflect the timeslice length of the operating system.

However, neither can the timeslice length be easily obtained through an OS call, nor is it always available from OS specifications, as it may also depend on the actual configuration of the operating system (for example, Windows supports configuration settings in the Windows Registry that affect the scheduler timeslice length). Hence, an automated approach to detect the timeslice length is desired. In the following, we present a GINPEX experiment to detect the timeslice length on various operating systems.

5.5.2. Experiment Design

The idea of the experiment is as follows (see Figure 5.12 for a graphical description of the experiment logic): In parallel running processes, CPU load is issued on the machine. The number of parallel processes is twice as high as the number of available cores, so that every parallel task issuing CPU load is assumed to share a core with another task. One of the tasks (called *TaskMeas*) repeatedly issues small amounts of CPU load, i.e. 20 ms CPU load (to get a sufficient amount of results, the task is executed 1000 times). Between the demands, response time measurements are taken.

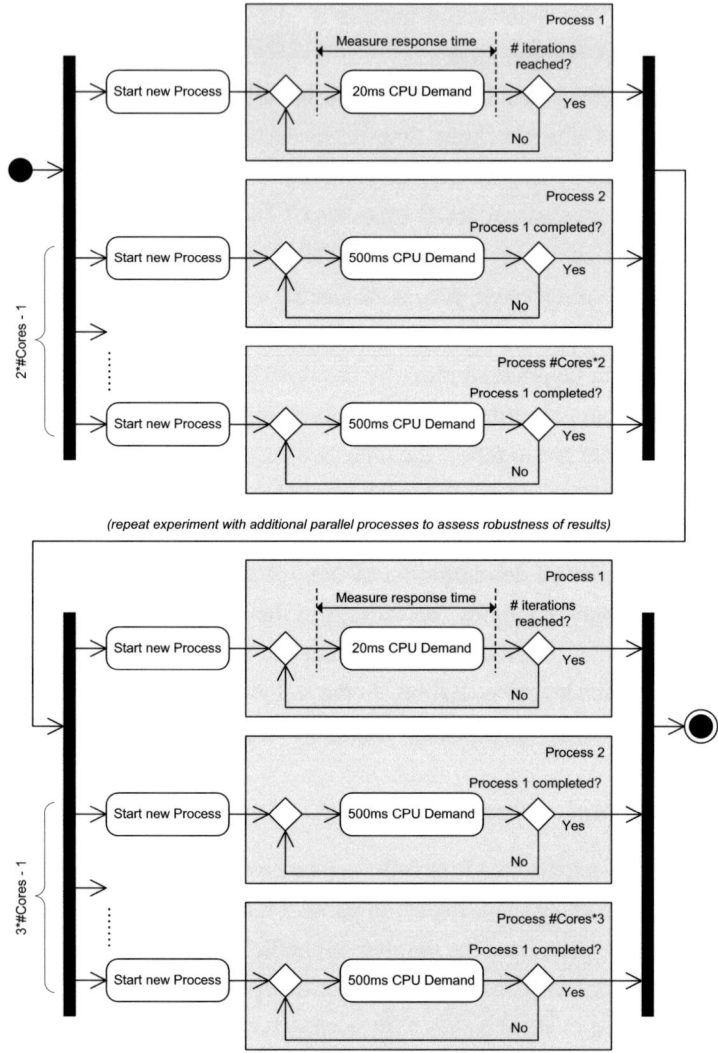

Figure 5.12.: Timeslice length experiment logic

The remaining tasks also continuously issue CPU demands in order to put load on the CPUs. On these tasks, no measurements are taken, thus, only measurement results for the first task are regarded. The experiment assumes that the measured task results fall into two clusters. One portion of results is expected to be approximately around 20 ms, i.e. the scheduler put the executed demand into one timeslice. The remaining results are expected to be a lot higher than 20 ms. In this case, the scheduler interrupted the executed demand and put the parallel running task on the CPU. As all tasks are running with the same priority, we assume that the task interrupted for exactly one timeslice. The measured result in this case includes the execution of the 20 ms demand, in addition to the interruption time of one timeslice. The difference between the average measured time of the first cluster and the average measured time of the second cluster can be interpreted as the timeslice length. We use a clustering algorithm [HKY99] for this experiment, which is a derivation of the k-means clustering method.

In a second part of the experiment, the logic is repeated with a different number of parallel tasks in order to assess the robustness of the experiment result.

5.5.3. Experiment Template

In the following, the experiment template is used to describe the experiment.

Experiment ID: OSSCHEDULER.01

Experiment name: Detect OS scheduler timeslice length

Experiment domain: OS Scheduler

Detected experiment parameter: Operating system scheduler timeslice length (integer)

Importance for performance analysis: General-purpose operating system (GPOS) schedulers split work of parallel running tasks by issuing timeslices to the tasks. Depending on the timeslice length, processing the amount of work of a task is being interrupted if it does not fit in a timeslice. On the other hand, a small amount of work may be completed within one timeslice and thus may not suffer further delays.

Configuration parameters: *number of cores*: Number of available physical CPU cores; detected by Experiment CPU.02

Experiment execution logic: Issue a small amount (20 ms) of CPU load (called *TaskMeas*) on a core and measure its response time, while additional CPU load is issued to the core by one another process. In some cases, the measured response time is then significantly larger than 20 ms, indicating that the operating system issues the CPU load of the other process in between for a timeslice. The difference to the original 20 ms is then the timeslice length used be the OS scheduler. For details, see Section 5.5.2 or the graphical description shown in Figure 5.12.

Assumptions:

- The machine is idle.

- All tasks are running with the same priority. As there is no task interactivity (e.g. I/O access), it can be assumed that all tasks are running with the same priority, and that *TaskMeas* has been interrupted for exactly one timeslice.

- The actual timeslice length is larger than 20 ms. A timeslice larger than 20 ms has to be assumed in order to yield measurements that can be used for analysis. However, given the fact that all common operating systems use average timeslice lengths between 30 ms and 200 ms (cf. [RS05, Aas05, Mol07]), this is a valid assumption.

- All CPU-bound tasks have to be equally distributed to the available cores. As GPOS schedulers aim at fully utilize the available resources, we believe this is also a valid assumption.

- The experiment is not able to detect a timeslice length that is being adjusted dynamically depending on the priority of processes. In this case, the priority management of OS processes would have to be reflected in further experiments which are subject to future work.

- Assumption for performance analysis: The performance analysis approach has to support OS timeslices during analysis.

- Required sensors: Response time sensor for *TaskMeas*.

Experiment robustness: Repeat the experiment with two parallel processes issuing CPU load instead of one parallel process. The process where response times are measured should then be interrupted for two timeslices, hence an increase of the response time should be observed that is twice as high compared to the first run.

Experiment performance:
The experiment runtime only depends on the number of iterations for *TaskMeas*.

5.5.4. Experiment Robustness

In a system with no or little measurement noise, the results of the experiments would look similar if the number of parallel processes is three times as high as the number of available cores. The only difference in the results would be a higher difference in the average measured times of the two clusters which would be twice as high as in the original experiment (as *TaskMeas* has suffered interruptions lasting two timeslices).

Thus, we repeat the experiment with the setting described above and compare the detected timeslice length of both executions. If the timeslice length of the second execution is approximately twice as high as the timeslice length of the first execution, the experiment results are considered stable.

5.5.5. Experiment Performance

As the number of parallel tasks is directly related to the number of available CPU cores, the experiment runtime does not increase with the number of available CPU cores. The experiment runtime depends on the number of iterations of *TaskMeas*, which has been set to 1000 in order to yield stable measurement results. The performance overhead of the experiment analysis (the clustering) can be neglected compared to the experiment execution.

In the first part of the experiment, *TaskMeas* shares a CPU core with one other task, which would lead to an ideal execution time of $1000 \cdot 2 \cdot 20\,\text{ms} = 40$ seconds. In the second execution of the experiment (executed for assessing the robustness of results), *TaskMeas* shares a CPU core with two other tasks, so it should take three times as long as specified, which would be $1000 \cdot 3 \cdot 20\,\text{ms} = 60$ seconds. Thus, the overall execution time of the experiment should be 100 seconds.

Exemplary execution of the experiment on a dual-core machine (Intel Core 2 Duo, 2.20 GHz, 3 GB RAM, Windows XP) took 113 seconds.

5.5.6. Example

To illustrate how the experiment detects the length of the OS scheduler timeslice, we executed the experiment on different operating systems. We executed the experiments on the following machines:

- Machine A: A dual-core machine (Intel Core 2 Duo, 2.20 GHz, 3 GB RAM) running Windows XP (run A)

- Machine B: A quad-core machine (Intel Core i7-860, 2.80 GHz, 8 GB RAM) running Windows Server 2003 (run B)

- Machine C: A quad-core machine (Intel Core i7-860, 2.80 GHz, 8 GB RAM) running Windows 7 (run C)

- Machine D: A quad-core machine (Intel Core i7-860, 2.80 GHz, 8 GB RAM) running Linux 2.6.22 (run D)

- Machine E: A quad-core machine (Intel Core i7-860, 2.80 GHz, 8 GB RAM) running Linux 2.6.31 (run E)

Figure 5.13 shows the result for run A. The diagram plots the response time of the two tasks *TaskMeas* in the two experiment runs as a cumulative distribution function. For both tasks, the two clusters that have been described in Section 5.5.2 are clearly visible in the two sharp increases in each CDF. For the first experiment run, the difference in the average results is 31 ms. The second experiment run yields a difference of 62 ms, which is exactly twice as large as the difference observed in the first run. Thus, the experiment results can be considered stable and a timeslice length of 31 ms is derived.

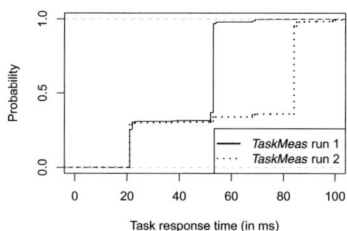

Figure 5.13.: Exemplary experiment results for experiment OSSCHEDULER.01 (Timeslice length): run A

The actual timeslice of Windows is specified as a multiple of a scheduling quantum. This quantum depends on the CPU architecture; on x86 and x64 systems, it is 15.625 ms. In Windows XP, the default timeslice is specified as two quanta, yielding an actual timeslice length of 31.5 ms [RS05].

Compared to Windows XP, much larger timeslices are used in Windows Server 2003, which is targeted at server systems. Windows Server 2003 aims at reducing context switching overhead caused by short timeslices and thus uses a default timeslice of 12 quanta (timeslice length 187.5 ms). This timeslice length is quite accurately detected by the GINPEX experiment performed in run B (see Figure 5.14): The first run yields a difference in the two cluster average results of 187 ms. The difference in the second run is 374 ms and hence is exactly twice as large.

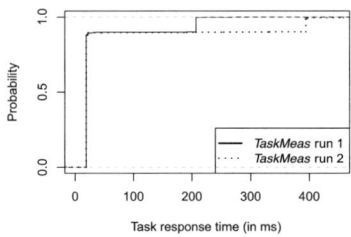

Figure 5.14.: Exemplary experiment results for experiment
OSSCHEDULER.01 (Timeslice length): run B

Finally, Figure 5.15 shows the results for run C, run D, and run E. Run C was performed on a machine with Windows 7. Here, a timeslice of 46 ms is detected, which approximates three scheduling quanta ($3 \cdot 15.625$ ms$= 46.875$ ms). Run D and run E executed on machines with Linux installations. Run D ran on a Linux 2.6.22 kernel machine, which features the Linux O(1) scheduler. This scheduler has a timeslice length of 100 ms [Aas05], which is detected by the experiment as well. Run E ran on a newer kernel (Linux 2.6.31) where the newer Linux CFS scheduler is used. According to the literature, the Linux CFS scheduler does not use the notion of timeslices [Mol07]. However, GINPEX still detects that the *TaskMeas* task is interrupted for 50 ms in the first run, and assumes a timeslice length of 50 ms.

To sum up, the example showed that the experiment works with different operating systems where different timeslice lengths are used.

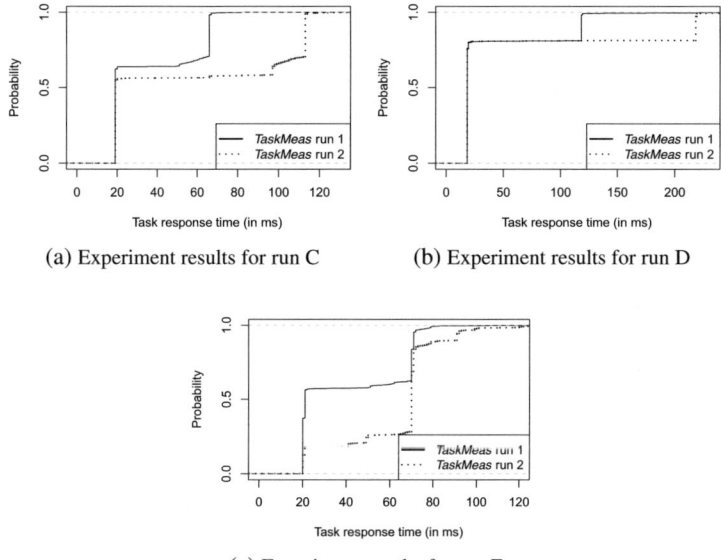

(a) Experiment results for run C   (b) Experiment results for run D

(c) Experiment results for run E

Figure 5.15.: Exemplary experiment results for experiment
OSSCHEDULER.01 (Timeslice length): run C, run D, run E

5.6. Operating System Scheduler Load-balancing Properties

In this section, we present experiments to detect properties of the OS scheduler regarding load-balancing.

5.6.1. Motivation

The load-balancing strategy of the OS scheduler defines how tasks are scheduled to the available CPU cores. Therefore, the scheduler has to decide on which CPU processor (or core) to place new tasks (initial load-balancing), and when to move tasks from one core to another in order to avoid imbalanced CPU cores and yield balanced cores (dynamic load-balancing).

For both load-balancing actions, different policies exist. Depending on the used load-balancing strategy, certain situations can occur in heavy-loaded systems where a task might suffer a stronger response time slow-down compared to other tasks due to imbalanced CPU cores. Thus, the load-balancing policies have to be reflected in software performance prediction in order to obtain accurate predictions of the real system behavior.

The experiments presented in this section aim at deriving those properties. The supported OS scheduling policies for load-balancing are based on the policies presented in [Hap08].

5.6.2. Initial Load-balancing Strategy

Initial load balancing specifies how newly created tasks are assigned to CPU processors (or cores). In [Hap08], the following policies are considered for GPOS scheduler models:

CyclicSplitting. The `CyclicSplitting` strategy assigns new tasks to the available cores based on a round-robin algorithm.

SameAsParent. The `SameAsParent` strategy assigns a new task to the same core its creator task is currently running on.

Random. The `Random` strategy assigns new tasks randomly on the available cores.

5.6.2.1. Experiment Design

The idea of the experiment to detect the initial load-balancing strategy is explained in the following and shown in the activity diagram in Figure 5.16.

The experiment has one configuration parameter which denotes the number of available CPU cores on the system. The value of this property can be detected by experiment CPU.02 (see Section 5.4). We now create N parallel processes where N is the number of CPU cores. In every process, 100 ms CPU demand is repeatedly issued and its response time is measured. Each

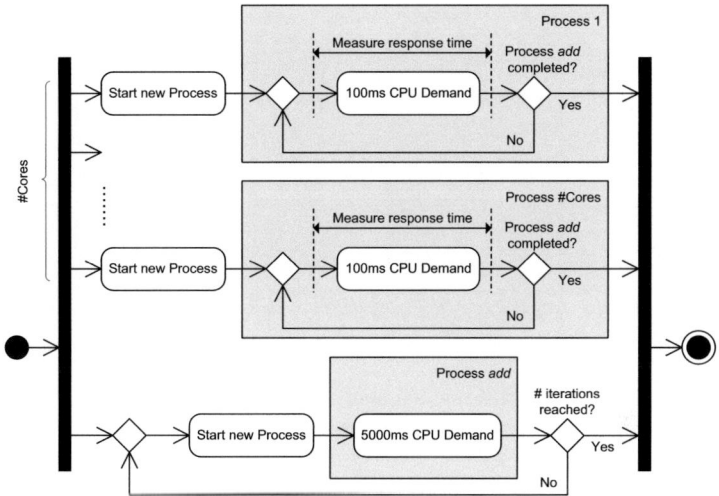

Figure 5.16.: Initial load-balancing experiment logic

of these processes is running on a dedicated core, as we have N cores and N processes. In parallel, another process is created (called process *add*), which issues a large amount of CPU demand (5000 ms). Once this demand is completed, the process completes as well and starts new. Depending on the initial load-balancing strategy of the operating system, the newly created *add* processes will be assigned to different CPU cores. The load-balancing strategy can be detected based on the response times measured in the N processes, which are running on separate cores. The response times of these processes indicate which process shared its core with the newly created *add* process.

To further illustrate this experiment, Figure 5.17 shows a schematic example of the results expected for the experiment. The time series contains the results for N tasks executed in the experiment: Task 1, ..., task j, ..., task N ($1 \leq j \leq N$). When a new *add* process is created, we expect bursts for one of the N tasks (the task whose process shares the CPU core with the newly created process). We can detect the initial load-balancing strat-

145

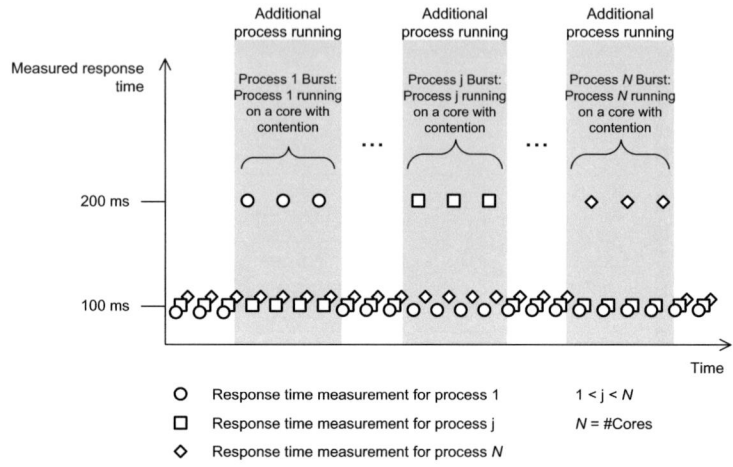

Figure 5.17.: Expected results for initial load-balancing experiment

egy by looking at the bursts and identifying the tasks whose response times have been affected: Let $burst_n$ be a burst of the measured response times of task n, i.e. a continuous set of response times of task n that are about twice as high as expected. We expect such a set to contain 50 measurements ($50 \cdot 100$ ms corresponds to the CPU demand issued in the newly created process). If a burst contains more measurements, we split the burst into several bursts. Now, we calculate the probability $p(i, j)$ of the transition $core_i \rightarrow core_j$, which denotes the probability that a $burst_j$, a burst of the task running on core j, occurs directly after a $burst_i$, a burst of the task running on core i. The probability $p(i, j)$ can be estimated by the number of $burst_j$ that occur directly after a $burst_i$, divided by the total number of $burst_j$.

To derive the initial load-balancing strategy, we use a state transition diagram representing the burst transitions. The diagram contains N nodes, where each node $i \in \{1...N\}$ denotes a CPU core. The calculated probabilities $p(i, j)$ serve as transition probabilities. In an ideal setting, without

146

any measurement noise, the experiment would detect the state transition diagrams shown in Figure 5.18 for a dual-core machine.

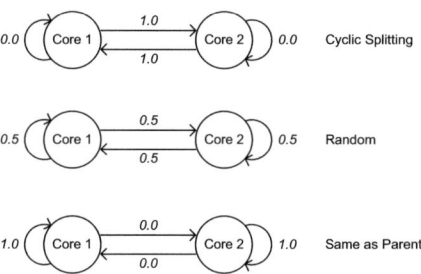

Figure 5.18.: Ideal experiment results for different initial load-balancing strategies on a dual-core machine

For some GPOS schedulers, results might be too noisy in order to detect bursts. We will present such a behavior in Section 5.6.2.4. In this case, the results indicate that the assignment of processes to cores is not fixed; the scheduler initiates further load-balancing after a new process has been created. Hence, the experiment cannot detect an initial load-balancing strategy. However, we assume that in this case, the initial load-balancing strategy can be neglected in performance prediction, as its effect is not visible in measurements. A dynamic load-balancing strategy should be detected instead that explains this effect. The corresponding experiment is presented in Section 5.6.3.

5.6.2.2. Experiment Template

A brief description of the experiment is given in the following template.

Experiment ID: OSSCHEDULER.02
Experiment name: Detect OS scheduler initial load-balancing strategy
Experiment domain: OS Scheduler

Detected experiment parameter: Operating system scheduler initial load-balancing strategy (`CyclicSplitting`, `SameAsParent`, `Random`)

Importance for performance analysis: The initial load-balancing strategy is used by the operating system to decide on which CPU core newly created tasks are placed. Depending on the used strategy, this can lead to balanced or unbalanced cores and should thus be reflected in performance analysis.

Configuration parameters: *number of cores*: Number of available physical CPU cores; detected by Experiment CPU.02

Experiment execution logic: Issue and measure CPU load in N processes where N is the number of CPU cores. Repeatedly issue a larger CPU load in a separate process *add*. Observing bursts in the measured response times of the N processes indicates which process has shared a core with the newly created process. Based on the sequence of process bursts, an initial load-balancing strategy is derived. For details, see Section 5.6.2.1 or the graphical description shown in Figure 5.16.

Assumptions:

- The machine is idle.

- The system features SMP processors where the load is equally distributed to the available cores.

- The experiment aims at detecting typical load-balancing strategies for GPOS schedulers. Real-time system schedulers might use different strategies for which the experiment would have to be adapted.

- Assumption for performance analysis: The performance analysis has to feature a notion of processes and provide support for the load-balancing strategies detected by the experiment.

- Required sensors: Response time sensors for the N tasks.

Experiment robustness: Experiment robustness can be assessed by analyzing the quality of the detected response time bursts. If the number of the detected bursts does not match the number of expected bursts, or if the measured response times are spread across a very wide range, the experiments should be repeated or it should be checked whether all experiment assumptions hold on the target platform.

Experiment performance: The experiment performance only depends on the iterations of the *add* process.

5.6.2.3. Experiment Robustness and Performance

The robustness of the experiment results can be assessed by analyzing the detected bursts and burst transitions. If results are too noisy, no bursts can be detected, as a burst only is detected if the additional process shares a CPU core only with one of the running N tasks. With more noise present on the system, either the operating system will perform additional load-balancing actions, leading to blurred response time bursts, or multiple bursts of can be observed at the same time. Both can be detected by the experiment analysis logic. In this case, the experiment can report unstable results to the user.

The runtime of this experiment mainly depends on the specified iterations of the *add* process. The more iterations of the *add* process, the more bursts can be observed, leading to more stable transition probabilities. In the current experiment setup, we perform 100 iterations of the *add* process. If we assume that the *add* process runs twice as long its specified CPU demand (as it shares the CPU core with one of the running N tasks), we can assume an experiment execution time of $1000 \cdot 2 \cdot 5000\,\mathrm{ms} = 16\,\mathrm{minutes}$ 40 seconds.

Exemplary execution of the experiment on a quad-core machine (Intel Core i7-860, 2.80 GHz, 8 GB RAM, Windows 7) took 17 min 13 seconds.

5.6.2.4. Example

We illustrate the experiment with three runs that are executed on different operating systems:

- Machine A: A quad-core machine (Intel Core i7-860, 2.80 GHz, 8 GB RAM) running Windows 7 (run A)

- Machine B: A quad-core machine (Intel Core i7-860, 2.80 GHz, 8 GB RAM) running Linux 2.6.22 (run B)

- Machine C: A quad-core machine (Intel Core i7-860, 2.80 GHz, 8 GB RAM) running Linux 2.6.31 (run C)

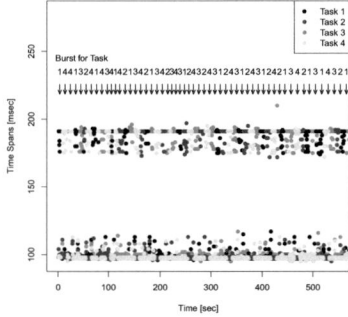

Figure 5.19.: Exemplary experiment results for experiment OSSCHEDULER.02 (Initial load-balancing strategy): run A

Figure 5.19 shows an excerpt of the timeseries containing the measurement results of example run A. For the sake of readability, we show only the first 50% of the results. However, the other half of the results looks similar.

As the experiment was performed on a quad-core machine, 4 tasks running in parallel processes where measuring issued CPU demand. For better readability, we also include marks in the diagram denoting the task bursts. The bursts in these tasks are clearly visible in the increased response time measurements that lie between 180 and 200 ms. Moreover, the burst occur in a cyclic way; thus, cyclic splitting is assumed as initial load-balancing strategy,

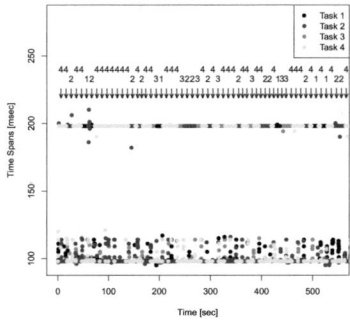

Figure 5.20.: Exemplary experiment results for experiment OSSCHEDULER.02 (Initial load-balancing strategy): run B

The scheduler of the Linux 2.6.22 kernel uses a different strategy for initial load-balancing: here, the SameAsParent strategy is used. This is also visible in the results for the experiment run B shown in the timeseries in Figure 5.20 (again, only the first part of the experiment results are shown). Here, a disproportionately large number of bursts occurs for task 4. In the experiment setup, task 4 is running in the process which forked the *add* processes. Thus, the SameAsParent is derived here.

Compared to run A and run B, run C executed on the Linux 2.6.31 kernel does not yield any continuous response time bursts (see Figure 5.21). This is due to the fact that the Linux CFS scheduler initiates further load-balancing leading to scattered response time bursts across all tasks. Hence, no initial load-balancing strategy can be derived for this scheduler. For per-

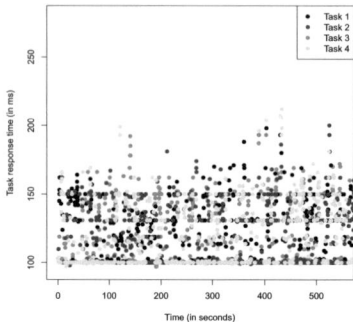

Figure 5.21.: Exemplary experiment results for experiment
OSSCHEDULER.02 (Initial load-balancing strategy): run C

formance prediction, we neglect the initial load-balancing strategy in this case, and use a dynamic load-balancing strategy explaining the observed effect. The corresponding experiment is presented in Section 5.6.3.

5.6.3. Dynamic Load-balancing Strategy

Dynamic load balancing policies are used by GPOS schedulers to provide a load-balancing of running tasks. These policies define when running tasks are moved from a busy core to a core with less contention. In [Hap08], the dynamic load-balancing policies Lazy and Active are regarded. Lazy load-balancing only initiates load balancing when a core becomes idle, and moves a task of a busy core to the idle core. On the other hand, Active load-balancing performs load-balancing upon certain events, such as task creation or completion, and in periodic intervals. While these policies cover a wide range of available GPOS schedulers, we noticed that recent schedulers (see [Mol07]) use a different scheduling strategy for dynamic load-balancing: The Linux CFS scheduler, available in the Linux kernel since kernel version 2.6.23, initiates load-balancing much earlier once the system becomes unbalanced. Thus, we enhanced the dynamic load-balancing policies presented in [Hap08] by the Immediate load-balancing strategy.

Summing up, the experiment deriving the dynamic load-balancing strategy has to be able to detect the following strategies:

Lazy load-balancing.   Load-balancing is only initiated once a CPU core becomes idle.

Active load-balancing.   Load-balancing is initiated upon certain events, such as task creation or task completion, and in periodic intervals.

Immediate load-balancing.   Load-balancing is initiated immediately once the system becomes imbalanced.

In the following, we present an experiment that detects the three different strategies.

5.6.3.1. Experiment Design

The idea of the experiment for detecting the dynamic load-balancing strategy of GPOS schedulers is as follows: We spawn three times as many parallel processes as available CPU cores. In each process, a 400 ms CPU demand task is issued and measured. In this phase, we assume that the system is in a balanced state, i.e. three tasks share one CPU core. After a fixed number of iterations, we terminate two tasks sharing a core. We then analyze the response times of the remaining tasks in order to detect the dynamic load-balancing strategy.

Once the first tasks are terminated, we expect the operating system to behave differently depending on the implemented dynamic load-balancing strategy. After the completion of two tasks sharing a core, there is only one task left running on this core. If the system employs a Lazy load-balancing strategy, no further load-balancing is performed (as no core has become idle yet). Hence, we expect one task with measured response times that indicate no CPU contention (response times lie around the specified 400 ms). In contrast, all other remaining tasks still share a CPU core with two other tasks. For these tasks, we expect that the measured response times is approximately three times as high as the specified task CPU demand.

On the other hand, if the system employs an `Active` load-balancing strategy, the imbalanced state after the two terminated tasks should lead to initiated load-balancing. In this case, we assume that one task is taken from the CPU cores where three tasks are running, and put to the CPU core where only one task is left. Hence, multiple tasks should observe a reduction of measured response times from around 1200 ms to around 800 ms, but no task should run on a CPU core without further CPU contention.

Finally, if an `Immediate` load-balancing strategy is used, we assume that load-balancing affects the response times of all tasks as soon as the first task is terminated.

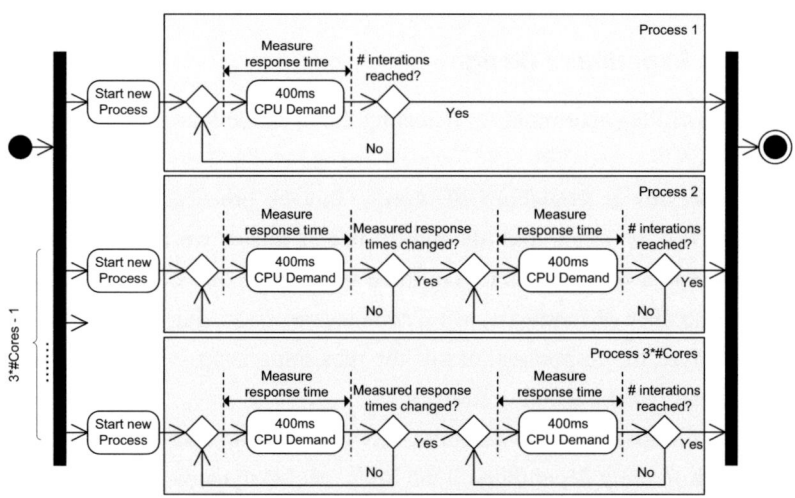

Figure 5.22.: Dynamic load-balancing experiment logic

Figure 5.22 shows the corresponding activity diagram of the experiment logic. The experiment spawns $3 \cdot N$ parallel processes where N is the number of CPU cores. The number of CPU cores is a configuration parameter and can be detected by experiment CPU.02 (see Section 5.4).

The first task issues 400 ms CPU demand in a loop which terminated after a fixed number of iterations. The other $3 \cdot N - 1$ tasks issue the same CPU demand, but do not terminate after a fixed number of iterations. Instead, the termination is triggered by changes in the measured response times. After taking a response time measurement, the measurement is compared with previous measurements. If the measurement is significantly higher or lower, the task terminates. Using this termination criteria, only those tasks are terminated that run on the same core as an earlier stopped task.

In order to prevent all tasks on the same core to stop at the same time, an additional number of task iterations is performed once a change in the measured response times is observed. This number of additional iterations varies for each of the $3 \cdot N - 1$ tasks, so that two tasks do not terminate at the same time.

Figure 5.23 shows exemplary results for the three different load-balancing strategies supported by the experiment. In the subfigures, the response times of five out of the $3 \cdot N$ tasks are shown. We assume that the first three tasks (task 1, 2, 3) are sharing one CPU core, and the other two tasks (task 4 and task 5) are sharing another CPU core. After a certain amount of time, task 1 is terminated.

In the case of Lazy load-balancing shown in Figure 5.23 (a), task 2 and task 3 observe decreased task response times. A little later, task 2 is terminated. Now, task 3 observes response times around 400 ms, which indicates that the task is running on a CPU core without further CPU contention. After termination of task 3, the operating system initiates load balancing, leading to decreased response times of task 4 and task 5. In the case of Active load-balancing (see Figure 5.23 (b)), load-balancing is initiated earlier: Here, load-balancing is performed once the cores are unbalanced after termination of task 2. Finally, Figure 5.23 (c) shows exemplary response times on a system where the Immediate load-balancing strategy is used. Here, all remaining tasks observe decreased response times once task 1 is terminated.

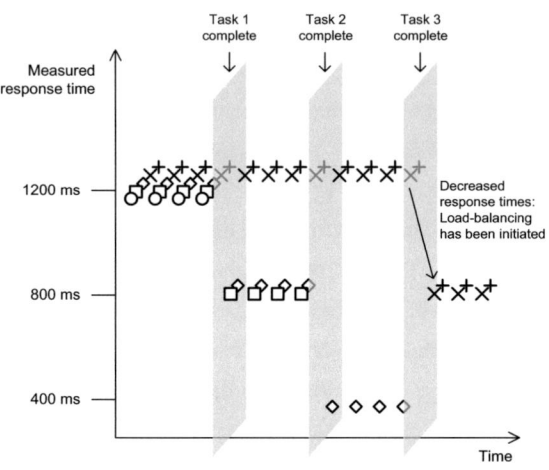

(a) Lazy load-balancing

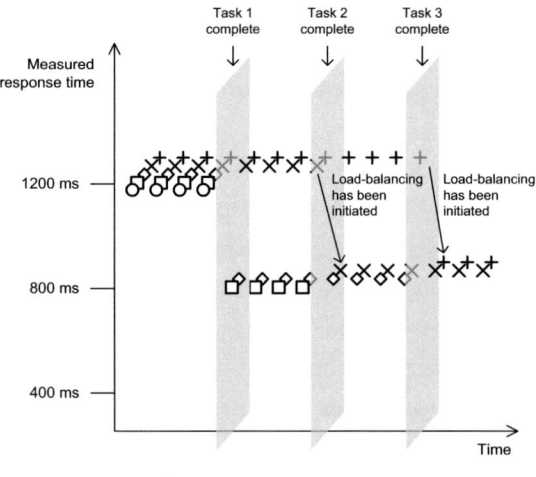

(b) Active load-balancing

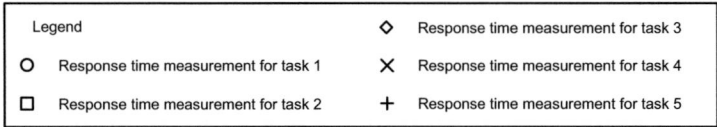

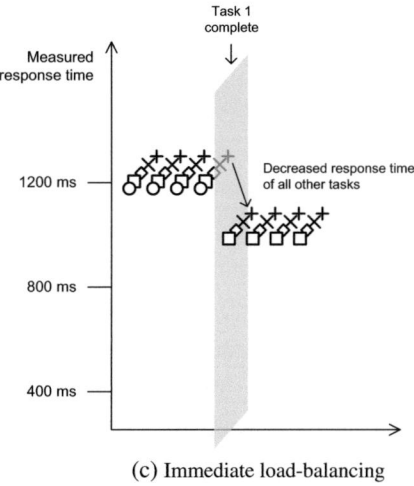

(c) Immediate load-balancing

Figure 5.23.: Expected results for dynamic load-balancing experiment

5.6.3.2. Experiment Template

In the following template, we briefly describe the experiment for detecting the dynamic load-balancing strategy.

Experiment ID: OSSCHEDULER.03

Experiment name: Detect OS scheduler dynamic load-balancing strategy

Experiment domain: OS Scheduler

Detected experiment parameter: Operating system scheduler dynamic load-balancing strategy (`Lazy`, `Active`, `Immediate`)

Importance for performance analysis: The dynamic load-balancing strategy is used by the operating system to decide when load-balancing

157

is performed to avoid imbalanced CPU cores. Depending on the used strategy, this can be done at a different frequency. If a load-balancing strategy tolerates imbalanced cores for some time, this can affect the response times of tasks that are running on the corresponding CPU cores. Hence, the load-balancing strategy should be reflected in performance analysis.

Configuration parameters: *number of cores*: Number of available physical CPU cores; detected by Experiment CPU.02

Experiment execution logic: Issue and measure CPU load in $3 \cdot N$ processes where N is the number of CPU cores. Iteratively terminate the running processes and observe the performance of the CPU load in the remaining processes. Depending on the pattern of decreased response times due to termination of processes, the used dynamic load-balancing strategy can be inferred. For details, see Section 5.6.3.1 or the graphical description shown in Figure 5.22.

Assumptions:

- The machine is idle.

- The system features SMP processors where the load is equally distributed to the available cores.

- The experiment aims at detecting typical load-balancing strategies for GPOS schedulers. Real-time system schedulers might use different strategies for which the experiment would have to be adapted.

- Assumption for performance analysis: The performance analysis has to feature a notion of processes and provide support for the load-balancing strategies detected by the experiment.

- Required sensors: Response time sensors for the $3 \cdot N$ tasks.

Experiment robustness: Experiment robustness is assessed by checking the spread of measured response times between the termination of processes. If the range of measurements is too large, the response times are too noisy in order to detect the load-balancing strategy.

Experiment performance: $O(n)$ where n is the number of available CPU cores.

5.6.3.3. Experiment Robustness and Performance

In order to assess the robustness of experiment results, the interval between the termination of processes must be large enough in order to check whether the measured response times in that interval are stable enough for obtaining useful results. We specified the first process to terminate after 50 iterations, and each other process after a minimum of 30 additional iterations once a change in the measured response times has been observed. If measurements are too noisy, we expect processes to terminate earlier or not at all in the expected time. In this case, the experiment can indicate that the observed results are not robust enough for detecting the dynamic load-balancing strategy. The performance analyst should then check whether the machine under test meets the experiment requirements, especially the assumption that the machine is idle.

The runtime of the experiments primarily depends on the number of executed processes and the duration of those processes. In the experiment, $3 \cdot N$ processes are issued, where N denotes the number of available CPU cores. The first process issues 400 ms of CPU demand and is repeated 50 times. The remaining processes issue the same demand and terminate once they detect a significant change in the measured response times, but execute a minimum of 30 additional iterations before terminating (in order to get stable results and to avoid that two processes are terminated at the same time). In the first third of the experiment, some or all processes share a CPU core with two other processes. In the second third, the processes share a CPU core with one other process. Finally, in the last third, most processes have been terminated, leaving the remaining processes on a CPU core without additional load. However, we are not interested in the measurements of the last third, as the load-balancing strategy can already be detected by looking at the measurements up to the point when the first N processes have been terminated. Hence, we specified the maximum number of iterations of all tasks as $50 + (N \cdot 3) \cdot 30 \cdot 2$ in order to get a sufficient number of additional iterations while terminating the first three processes. If we assume that during these iterations, the measured response times are three times as high as specified (because the tasks share a core with two other tasks), we can calculate the upper bound of the experiment runtime as $(50 + (N \cdot 3) \cdot 30 \cdot 2) \cdot 3 \cdot 400$ ms. On a quad-core machine, the runtime would then be not longer than $(50 + (4 \cdot 3) \cdot 30 \cdot 2) \cdot 3 \cdot 400$ ms = 15 min 24 seconds. The effective experiment runtime is expected to be considerably shorter, as the response time of the CPU tasks should decrease as more and more processes get terminated.

Exemplary execution of the experiment on a quad-core machine (Intel Core i7-860, 2.80 GHz, 8 GB RAM, Windows 7) took 9 minutes 27 seconds.

5.6.3.4. Example

For illustration, we ran the experiment on the same machines as the initial load-balancing experiment (see Section 5.6.2.4):

- Machine A: A quad-core machine (Intel Core i7-860, 2.80 GHz, 8 GB RAM) running Windows 7 (run A)

- Machine B: A quad-core machine (Intel Core i7-860, 2.80 GHz, 8 GB RAM) running Linux 2.6.22 (run B)

- Machine C: A quad-core machine (Intel Core i7-860, 2.80 GHz, 8 GB RAM) running Linux 2.6.31 (run C)

As the runs were performed on a quad-core machine, 12 parallel running processes executing CPU tasks were started in each run. As explained in Section 5.6.3.1, each CPU task issued CPU load that is expected to last 400 ms on a core without CPU contention. Figure 5.24 shows an excerpt of the timeseries with the response time measurements in run A (the Windows 7 machine). In this run, task 1 terminates after approx. 56 seconds. Now, task 5 and task 9 observe decreased response times, as they used to share a core with task 1 and now only share a core with each other. The change in response times lead to the termination of task 5 after approx. 160 seconds of experiment runtime and task 9 after approx. 255 seconds of experiment runtime. Once task 5 has been terminated, task 9 measures response times of approx. 400 ms, which indicates that task 9 now runs on a core without contention. This also indicates that the operating system employs a Lazy load-balancing strategy, as the cores already are imbalanced, but no load-balancing is performed yet. Only when task 9 terminates, the CPU core that task was running on becomes idle. Now, the operating system moves task 8 and task 12 to the idle core, which is indicated by the decreased response times measured by these tasks.

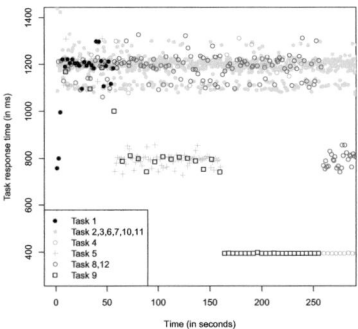

Figure 5.24.: Exemplary experiment results for experiment OSSCHEDULER.03 (Dynamic load-balancing strategy): run A

In run B (the Linux 2.6.22 machine), the results look similar at the beginning (see Figure 5.25). After approx. 58 seconds, task 1 terminates, leading to decreased response times of task 4 and task 10. Task 4 terminates after approx. 138 seconds of experiment runtime. This leads to decreased response times of task 5, 8, and 9 as well. This indicates that the OS scheduler has moved one of the three tasks to the core the remaining task 10 was running on. This behavior suggests that the OS scheduler is using an Active load-balancing strategy, i.e. load-balancing is initiated upon process completion when the cores are unbalanced.

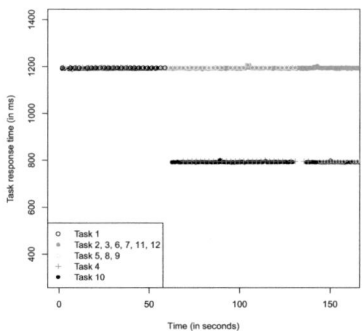

Figure 5.25.: Exemplary experiment results for experiment
OSSCHEDULER.03 (Dynamic load-balancing strategy): run B

Finally, Figure 5.26 shows the results for run C. Here, the results are quite different to the results of run A and run B. After termination of task 1, all other remaining tasks observe decreased response times. In addition, the measured response times show a much higher variance than for the other systems; for Lazy or Active load-balancing, the termination of task 1 did not affect the tasks running on the three remaining cores. This isolation does not hold for the Linux 2.6.31 system used in run C. Here, load-balancing is initiated immediately once the cores are imbalanced. Hence, the Immediate load-balancing strategy is detected here.

Detecting the `Immediate` load-balancing strategy for Linux 2.6.31 is consistent with the experiment results obtained with the initial load-balancing strategy experiment on the same machine (see Section 5.6.2.4): The `Imme-diate` load-balancing strategy explains why no bursts can be detected in the initial load-balancing strategy experiment.

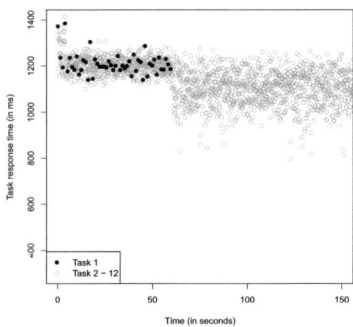

Figure 5.26.: Exemplary experiment results for experiment
OSSCHEDULER.03 (Dynamic load-balancing strategy): run C

5.7. Including Experiment Results in Performance Prediction

In the following, we explain how we adapted the performance simulation of the PCM in order to take into account the derived properties of this chapter.

Experiments CPU.01 and CPU.02 aim at deriving CPU properties. The first experiment CPU.01 derives SMT availability. This property is mainly used as a configuration parameter for the following experiment CPU.02, which detects the number of available CPU cores. The number of cores property can directly be mapped to PCM models, as the number of cores can be specified for a `ProcessingResourceSpecification`. This attribute is then used in the PCM simulation to simulate a resource with the corresponding number of resource queues. Reflecting SMT in performance prediction is not yet supported. It is still unclear how the performance impact of a CPU with SMT support should be taken into account. One could specify the number of virtual cores as number of cores for a PCM resource, if SMT availability has been detected. However, then the simulation has to be adapted in some way, as the number of virtual resources does not indicate how many CPU requests can be executed in parallel without a slowdown due to CPU contention. How large the actual performance impact of SMT is depends not only on the used CPU technology, but also on the type of CPU load that is issued to the CPU resource. Hence, in order to accurately reflect SMT in performance prediction, the way CPU load is modeled in the architecture model has to be adapted. As this probably requires changes in the performance model, as well as a study on how to reflect SMT-related CPU load at the architecture and/or design level of the software application, we leave SMT support in performance prediction to future work.

The OS scheduling properties detected by the experiments OSSCHED-ULER.01, OSSCHEDULER.02, and OSSCHEDULER.03 can be integrated into the PCM performance prediction by introducing appropriate configuration points in the PCM simulation scheduler. We included support for the properties in the simulation as follows: The timeslice length property, if specified, leads to a round-robin scheduling strategy for the corresponding CPU resource. If a process is issuing CPU demand to that resource in the simulation, the simulation puts the demand in a CPU queue. In regular intervals that correspond to the specified timeslice length, the simulation interrupts the demand that is currently executing on one of the CPU's cores, inserts the demand at the end of the CPU queue, and assigns the next CPU demand in the queue to the core. If no timeslice length is specified, the PCM simulation uses multi-queue processor sharing for scheduling CPU demands.

Initial and dynamic load-balancing strategy support has been implemented in the PCM as well. For initial load-balancing, the initial queue on which a new demand is scheduled to, is chosen based on the specified cyclic-splitting, same-as-parent, and random strategy. For lacy load-balancing strategy, load-balancing is only done in the simulation when a core becomes idle. If an active load-balancing strategy is specified, the simulation performs as soon as the length of two CPU queues differ by more than 1. If such an imbalance occurs, a random task from the longer waiting queue is transferred to the shorter waiting queue. Finally, immediate load-balancing support can be represented in the simulation by using the round-robin scheduling strategy (if the timeslice length is available) or the MPS scheduling strategy (if no timeslice length is available).

In the following section, we show how the simulation predicts the performance of a software for various operating systems while taking the OS scheduling strategies into account.

5.8. Validation

In this chapter, we presented various experiments that derive CPU and OS scheduling properties in an automated way. For each experiment, we demonstrated that the correct results could be derived on different platforms. In this section, we combine the various properties in software performance prediction and validate whether a sufficient prediction accuracy can be achieved while reflecting those properties.

The validation is based on the validation levels for model-based prediction approaches defined by Böhme and Reussner [BR08]. Here, different types of validation are distinguished. Level I validation (called metric validation) is concerned with the comparisons of predictions and measurements. The validation presented in this section resides on this level. Level II validation (called applicability validation) checks whether input data can be a obtained reliably and whether the prediction results can be interpreted by humans in a meaningful way. While the first part is validated through the examples provided for each experiments, the latter part can only be validated in a larger case study involving human participants. This is outside the scope of this thesis; however we argue that the benefits of our approach, especially the high degree of automation supported, are evident. Finally, level III validation (called benefit validation) empirically validates whether the overall approach has benefits compared to competing approaches. As this involves comparing different development projects (which partly use the approach), this involves a lot of effort which again is outside the scope of this thesis.

Every property whose value is detected by an experiment in this chapter was chosen based on existing work that motivated and validated its relevance for performance. For example, Happe [Hap08] also considered the operating system scheduling properties detected in this chapter for a performance model of operating system schedulers. However, for the set of this chapter's properties, no validation exists that compares performance predictions with measurements. In [Hap08], a performance model that consists of a larger set of properties is validated using a real-world case study. The influence of a specific property on prediction accuracy cannot be identified from this validation.

Hence, we provide a validation of performance-relevant properties detected by experiments in this chapter using a real-world case study. Validating the prediction accuracy of a performance prediction reflecting the derived properties involves the following validation questions we are answering in this section:

1. Does a performance prediction that reflects the derived properties yield a prediction with sufficient prediction accuracy?

2. How is prediction accuracy influenced by the different properties?

3. Is the prediction accuracy increased compared to a performance prediction that does not reflect those properties?

In the following, we present the validation scenario which we use to answer these questions. Afterwards we describe how we executed the case study and discuss the results.

5.8.1. Validation Scenario

For the validation, we compare the measurements of a software system's performance to the prediction results of a prediction based on a software system model. As a case study, we selected the ray tracing software POV-Ray [Per], which we deployed on a server as a service. We chose POV-Ray due to several reasons: First, it is a freely available third-party software that has been ported to various operating system platforms; second, POV-Ray has been used in validation of performance analysis before [BBB96, ENC+12]; and third, executing POV-Ray generates mainly CPU load, making it an ideal candidate for validating CPU and OS scheduling properties.

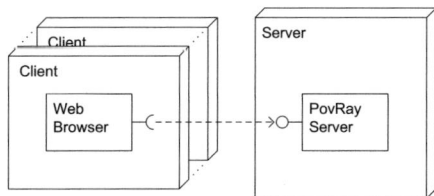

Figure 5.27.: Overall on the POV-Ray case study setup

An overview on the case study setup is given in Figure 5.27. Users can access the POV-Ray server and upload rendering scripts. The server takes rendering scripts as input to render images. These images are then transferred to the user.

When it comes to the performance of the POV-Ray server, the performance analyst might want to analyze how the server handles an increased number of parallel users requests. In this case, a model-based performance prediction approach can be applied, as it facilitates the simulation of heavy load induced by a large number of parallel users. This saves the analyst from having to generate parallel users requests on the real system. He only has to provide a model of the POV-Ray server that includes performance data which he can obtain from measuring the components when no resource contention is present. The model is then used in performance anal-

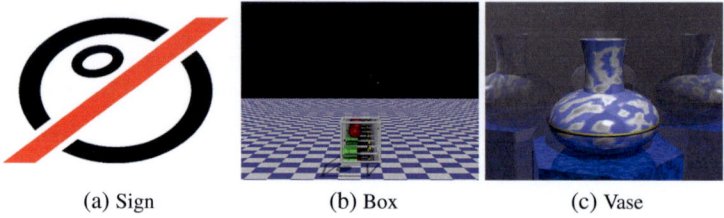

| (a) Sign | (b) Box | (c) Vase |

Figure 5.28.: Example of images for each of the three POV-Ray workload classes

ysis where the number of users is increased and the slowdown of response times due to resource contention is taken into account.

For the case study, we use three different POV-Ray workloads, each using a different rendering script:

Sign: A simple image with no complex rendering effects.

Box: A three-dimensional box with objects inside.

Vase: A vase surrounded by mirrors. This script is part of the POV-Ray benchmark.

All rendering scripts where taken from the POV-Ray sample script library. The rendered image for each workload class is shown in Figure 5.28. The three rendering scripts feature a different rendering time. Details on the workload are given in Table 5.1.

Table 5.1.: Workload of the POV-Ray case study

Request type	Mean service time	Relative frequency
Sign	408 ms	60%
Box	730 ms	30%
Vase	3590 ms	10%

5.8.2. Execution

Based on this workload information shown in Table 5.1, we created a performance model of the POV-Ray rendering server using the Palladio Component Model (see Section 2.1.4 for details on the Palladio Component Model). For this case study, we used a quad-core system (Intel Core i7-860, 2.80 GHz, 8 GB RAM) and a user workload with an arrival rate of 250 requests per minute, which resulted in a utilization of all cores. We deployed the POV-Ray rendering service on three different operating systems: Windows 7 (run A), Linux 2.6.22 kernel using the Linux O(1) scheduler (run B), and Linux 2.6.31 kernel using the Linux CFS scheduler (run C). We derived the scheduler properties using the GINPEX experiments described in Section 5.3–5.6 (see the corresponding examples for details on the experiment results). We then used the PCM with the specialized scheduler (see Section 5.7) in order to simulate the performance of the different deployment scenarios of the POV-Ray rendering server with the increased user load (Prediction A).

5.8.3. Results

In the following, we present the prediction results for the POV-Ray server case study. Figure 5.29 gives an overview on the different response time results. The subfigures show the cumulative distribution function for measurements and predictions of the different requests on the three operating systems. The prediction results are taken from the PCM simulation reflecting the derived OS scheduling properties.

The prediction error does not exceed 5% in most cases. Only for the Box rendering request under Linux 2.6.22, the error is a bit higher (6.65%), but still acceptable.

In order to answer the validation questions 2 and 3, we conducted additional predictions where only a subset of the detected properties was covered. First, we conducted a prediction with a scheduler configuration in-

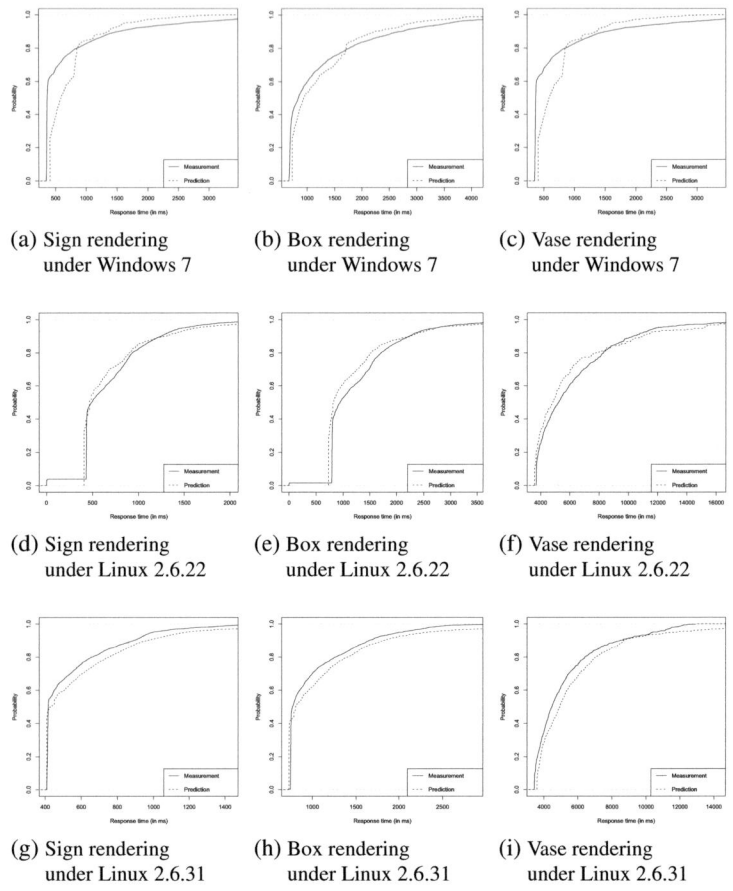

(a) Sign rendering
under Windows 7

(b) Box rendering
under Windows 7

(c) Vase rendering
under Windows 7

(d) Sign rendering
under Linux 2.6.22

(e) Box rendering
under Linux 2.6.22

(f) Vase rendering
under Linux 2.6.22

(g) Sign rendering
under Linux 2.6.31

(h) Box rendering
under Linux 2.6.31

(i) Vase rendering
under Linux 2.6.31

Figure 5.29.: Comparison of prediction and measurements for the POV-Ray services running on Windows 7, Linux 2.6.22, and Linux 2.6.31

cluding the derived load-balancing properties, but no timeslice length (prediction B). This prediction was done for the Windows 7 and the Linux 2.6.22 system. The configuration of the Linux 2.6.31 system did not use timeslices anyway, as the detected dynamic load-balancing strategy is implemented in the simulation using a MPS scheduling strategy. The prediction yielded an increased prediction error that lies between 5.23% (Sign request, Linux 2.6.22) and 27.21% (Vase request, Windows 7). The complete results are given in Table 5.2.

Table 5.2.: Detailed prediction results of the POV-Ray case study
(all results in milliseconds; in brackets: prediction error)

Request	Measured	Predicted	Predicted (no timeslices)	Predicted (using MPS)
Windows 7				
Sign	748	745 (0.40%)	795 (6.28%)	592 (20.86%)
Box	1319	1290 (2.20%)	1454 (10.24%)	1102 (16.45%)
Vase	6987	6986 (0.01%)	8888 (27.21%)	5791 (17.12%)
Linux 2.6.22				
Sign	688	686 (0.29%)	724 (5.23%)	592 (13.95%)
Box	1278	1193 (6.65%)	1191 (6.81%)	1102 (13.77%)
Vase	6282	6100 (2.90%)	5921 (5.75%)	5791 (7.82%)
Linux 2.6.31				
Sign	543	545 (0.37%)	$\rightarrow$	592 (9.02%)
Box	1014	989 (2.47%)	$\rightarrow$	1102 (8.68%)
Vase	5251	5199 (0.99%)	$\rightarrow$	5791 (10.28%)

We then predicted the POV-Ray services with a scheduling strategy that uses none of the detected properties (prediction C). Here, we used multi-queue processor sharing (MPS, a widely used scheduling strategy to predict resource behavior in software performance analysis. Compared to prediction B, the average prediction error increases slightly. The prediction errors lie between 7.82% (Vase request, Linux 2.6.22) and 20.86% (Sign request, Windows 7). However, the difference in prediction error between prediction A and prediction B was significantly larger than between prediction B and prediction C. This indicates that the reflection of the timeslice length has a stronger influence on prediction accuracy than the reflection of the load-balancing strategies. Note that for Linux 2.6.31, the scheduling strategy without using timeslices is identical to MPS, as the detected Immedi-

`ate` load-balancing strategy is covered by the MPS strategy in the PCM simulation.

5.8.4. Discussion

The POV-Ray case study showed that including fine-grained properties of the execution environment, such as the OS scheduler timeslice length and OS scheduler load-balancing strategies, can lead to improved accuracy in performance prediction. In the case study, the overall prediction error could be reduced to below 5% in most cases. A prediction not reflecting the derived properties led to a prediction error of up to 20%. In some cases, such a prediction error might be sufficient, for example if a prediction is conducted at very early stages of the software life-cycle. However, the derived properties can still be useful: For example, when predicting the performance of shorter requests than in the case study, the influence of the operating system can be stronger than for the requests that were present in the POV-Ray case study. In this case, predicting the performance with and without the derived properties can lead to a larger difference in prediction results.

For the case study, we identified the following threats to validity:

- We just executed the POV-Ray service with a subset of predefined POV-Ray rendering scripts. Different scripts might have an impact on the performance model and also on the prediction results. However, we tried to choose a balanced set of rendering scripts with different performance characteristics in order to create a realistic scenario of image rendering.

- The POV-Ray application mainly issues CPU load during execution. This leads to performance behavior where reflecting the chosen execution environment properties can yield significant improvements in the predicted performance. However, a different case study, especially a case study for a different domain, might lead to different results. Extending the validation in this way has to be left to future work. In literature, an extensive performance model with various OS scheduling properties has been validated in a case study for the domain of supply chain management (SCM) enterprise applications [Hap08]. We only cover a subset of these properties with the experiments presented in this chapter, but the SCM case study indicates that the predictions might work for different domains as well.

- We conducted the case study on three different operating systems, all having different scheduler implementations. The results of the case study may be limited to these operating systems.

5.9. Limitations and Assumptions

In the following, we discuss some limitations and assumptions of the experiments presented in this chapter.

Controlled environment. We assume that the experiments of this chapter are executed in a controlled environment, i.e. no additional load is present on the machine on which the experiments are running. This is due to the fact that additional load would disturb the measurements in a such a way that no meaningful property value can be detected. We describe how noisy results can be detected when analyzing experiment results. While detecting measurement noise during experiment analysis does not help in deriving the properties on a machine with additional load, it can alert the performance analyst who may not have monitored the system's load.

SMP systems. The experiments assume that the machine is featuring a symmetric multiprocessing (SMP) system. In SMP systems, all processors or processor cores are similar with respect to their performance properties. We assume that parallel CPU load is evenly distributed to all available CPU processors or cores. In asymmetric multiprocessor environments, CPU load might be distributed to different processors or cores depending on their capability. The performance influence of such environments needs further investigation. In addition, such environments might involve different strategies for load-balancing that are not yet reflected by our experiments.

GPOS schedulers. The experiments have been designed to derive meaningful property values for general-purpose operating system (GPOS) schedulers. Such schedulers are typically used in systems running enterprise software. However, in other domains, such as embedded systems, real-time schedulers are extensively used. Such systems, as well as performance prediction approaches for such systems (e.g. [BMdW+04, Wal03]), might involve different scheduling strategies that are not covered by the experiments. In order to apply the GINPEX approach to these systems, additional experiments may have to be defined.

Memory effects and further OS scheduling properties. When it comes to CPU and OS scheduling properties, a lot more performance-relevant properties exist that are not taken into account by the defined experiments. This includes for example memory effects in SMP environments (such as the effects of shared caches or memory buses). Here, additional research on how to model memory demand in performance models (such as the PCM) is required first of all. Then, additional experiment could be defined with GINPEX deriving additional execution environment properties concerning the memory. Other OS scheduling properties could also be taken into account by additional experiments. The current experiments do not focus on how the operating system handles processes that have different priorities, or whether the scheduler provides some mechanism to favor I/O-bound tasks over CPU-bound tasks. These properties can affect software performance to a large extent [Hap08] and are therefore also candidates for additional experiments.

5.10. Summary

In this chapter, we presented various experiments to detect CPU and OS scheduling properties of the software execution environment. Regarding CPU properties, the experiments detect simultaneous multithreading (SMT) availability and the number of CPU cores. The OS scheduling experiments detect the timeslice length of the scheduler as well as load-balancing properties.

For each experiment, we discussed why the detected property can be performance-relevant and provided a detailed description of the experiment logic. In addition, we used the experiment template presented in Chapter 4 to further illustrate the experiment, and showed in various examples how the experiment detects the corresponding property value on different platforms.

We finally performed a case study where we showed that the prediction accuracy of a performance prediction can be improved by taking the defined properties into account.

The experiments of this chapter demonstrate the GINPEX approach w.r.t. rather fine-grained execution environment properties. In the following chapter, we will apply the approach to a different experiment domain: We will cover experiments that aim at deriving properties present in virtualized environments.

6. Deriving Virtualization Properties

In the previous chapter, we presented various experiments for the automated detection of CPU and OS scheduling properties. Reflecting such properties in performance analysis can be beneficial when the analyzed software system has a strong focus on CPU load. In this case, existing work showed that such properties can have a significant impact on the software performance [Hap08, SWHB06].

In this chapter, we apply the GINPEX approach to a different experiment domain, i.e. the domain of software running in a virtualized environment. We show that the approach, including the metamodel and its underlying concepts presented in Chapter 4, can directly be reused for the experiments presented in this chapter. The following experiments derive certain properties of the virtualized environment. In different case studies, we show that reflecting these properties in performance analysis can increase the prediction accuracy.

Benevenuto et al. argued in [BFS+06] that performance analysis in virtualized environments can help to answer the following questions:

- What is the performance impact if a software is migrated from a non-virtualized to a virtualized environment?

- How many servers will be needed to run a software in a virtualized environment with acceptable performance?

- What is the best configuration of the virtualized environment for a certain software?

Existing performance prediction approaches, such as the PCM [BKR09], can be used to answer such questions. By improving the performance analysis with properties detected by the experiments in this chapter, we aim at increasing the accuracy of the predicted performance of virtualized software applications.

6.1. Experiments Overview

In this chapter, we present two experiments in detail and discuss a third experiment which all aim at detecting performance-relevant properties present in virtualized systems. The first experiment detects the overhead induced by the virtualization layer. When running in a virtual machine, accessing certain resources (such as the CPU, disk or network) might take longer compared to accessing the same amount in a non-virtualized environment. The second experiment extends the overhead model detected by the first experiment. In this experiment, we focus on additional overhead caused by the virtualization layer. This overhead can be observed when parallel requests are issued to resources at the same time. In this case, the observed overhead can depend on the parallel load and thus has to be reflected in performance prediction as well. Both experiments are validated using different case studies. Finally, we provide the concept of a third experiment that aims at deriving a simple model of additional load present on the platform. Additional load can especially be a problem in virtualized environments, as a virtual machine might share resources with a different virtual machine where load is present.

The three experiments do not depend on each other, but depend on the parameter detected by the experiment presented in Chapter 5 that detects the number of available CPU cores. An overview on the experiments and the experiment dependencies is given in Figure 6.1. As for the experiments presented in Chapter 5, the arrows between the experiments indicate a detected parameter that is used as a configuration parameter. In order to execute the experiments, either the number of cores available to the involved machines has to be specified by the user, or the corresponding experiment has to be executed first.

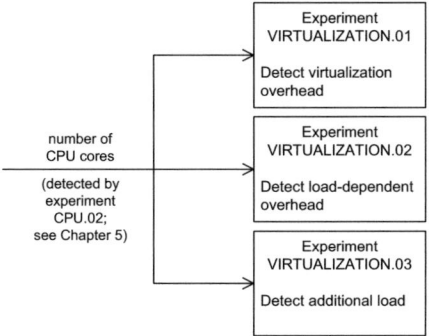

Figure 6.1.: Overview on the experiments presented in this chapter

6.2. Scientific Challenges

This chapter introduces experiments to detect performance-relevant properties that are especially relevant in virtualized systems. As for the experiments in the previous chapter, the scientific challenges outlined in Section 3.2 also apply to the experiments of this chapter. In addition, the following scientific challenges w.r.t. virtualization properties can be identified:

- How can performance-relevant factors of a virtualized environment, such as virtualization overhead, load-dependent overhead, or additional load, be derived through automated experiments?

- How can the detected properties be integrated into software performance prediction?

- What is the impact of the different properties on performance prediction accuracy?

The following Sections 6.3 to 6.5.1 deal with the different experiments in detail.

6.3. Virtualization Overhead

In this section, we present an experiment that detects the overhead that is induced by the virtualized environment. This overhead model will be extended in Section 6.4 by an experiment that detects load-dependent overhead.

6.3.1. Motivation

In a virtualized environment, the software runs inside virtualized operating systems instead of operating systems that are directly deployed on the native hardware. A virtualized operating system is running on top of a hypervisor which is responsible for managing virtual machines and delegating resource requests of virtual machines (VMs) to the actual hardware (see Section 2.3.3 for details). Compared to a software running in a non-virtualized operating system, virtualized software can only access hardware (such as CPU, disk, or network) through the hypervisor layer. This indirection of resource access can lead to significant overhead in the observed access response times. Hence, such overheads should be reflected in performance prediction of software applications running in VMs or are migrated to VMs.

Figure 6.2 gives an example for a scenario where performance overhead due to virtualization can arise. A software system is to be migrated from a non-virtualized to a virtualized system. We assume that the hardware stays the same, only a virtualization layer is introduced (for example, in order to add additional virtual machines in the future). The virtualization layer, through which resource requests of the software are being delegated, adds an overhead to the performance of such requests. The experiment presented in the following aims at quantifying this overhead.

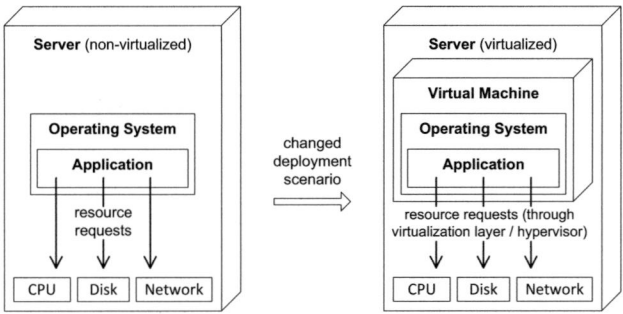

Figure 6.2.: Migration scenario introducing virtualization overhead

6.3.2. Experiment Design

The idea of the experiment is as follows: For a certain resource demand type, the same amount of resource demand is issued both on the non-virtualized machine and on the virtualized machine. As we assume identical hardware in both settings, the observed response time in the virtualized machine is not expected to be lower compared to the issued load on the non-virtualized machine. If it is higher, we calculate a response time overhead for this resource type. Afterwards, the experiment continues with a different type of resource demand.

Figure 6.3 shows the activity diagram of the experiment logic. In the first part, resource demands are issued on the non-virtualized machine. As an example, the displayed logic contains two different resource demand types. First, CPU demand is issued on the non-virtualized machine. In order to fully utilize the CPU during the experiment, all CPU cores are utilized using parallel processes (the number of parallel processes equals the number of available CPU cores that is passed to the experiment as a configuration parameter). For each issued CPU demand, response time measurements are taken. In order to gain stable measurements, CPU demand is repeatedly issued multiple times before the experiment continues with a different resource demand type. As a second demand type, disk load is issued in the

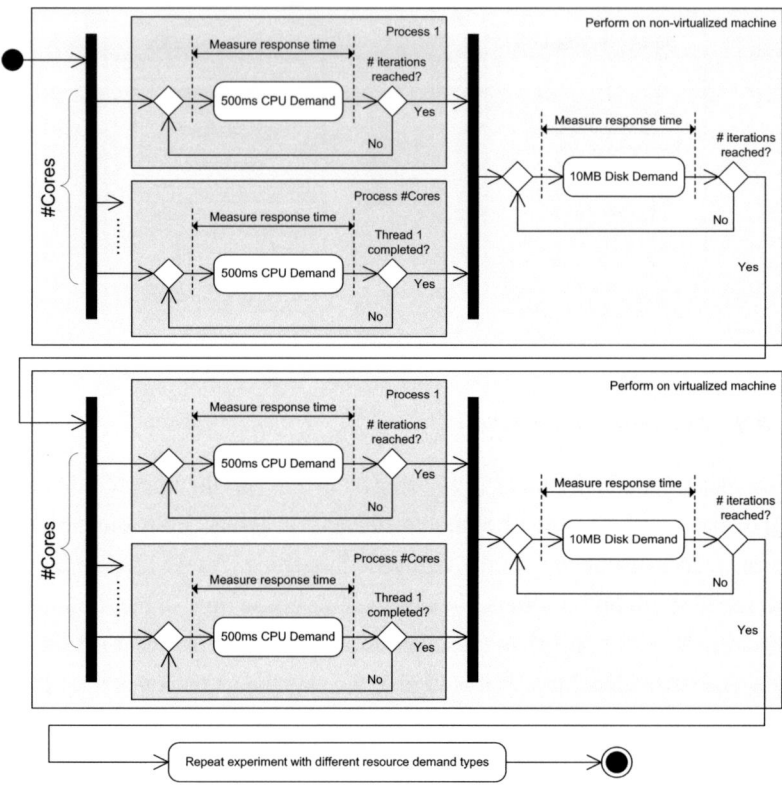

Figure 6.3.: Virtualization overhead experiment logic

experiment logic shown in Figure 6.3. This can be a disk read or a disk write demand (or a mixture of both) in order to measure the response times on the non-virtualized machine for processing the disk requests. Afterwards, the identical logic (for the CPU demands and the disk demands) is repeated on the virtualized machine. Finally, the experiment can continue with the same logic for a different type of resource demand (for example, a memory-bound demand, or a demand issued to a network device), which is omitted in the diagram. In the following, we focus on three different demands, i.e. CPU demand, disk read demand and disk write demand. However, the concept of the experiment could be reused for different demand types. For details on how the demand is generated using the GINPEX metamodel, see Section 4.4.3.

For a resource demand type *res*, let $t_{res,nonvirt}$ the average measured response time of the corresponding resource type requests on the non-virtualized machine, and $t_{res,virt}$ the average measured response time of the requests on the virtualized machine. The overhead $o(res)$ can then be calculated as

$$o(res) = \frac{t_{res,virt}}{t_{res,nonvirt}}.$$

For example, if a resource demand request yields 500 ms average response times on the non-virtualized machine, and 600 ms on the virtualized machine, the calculated overhead would be 1.2 (i.e. 20%).

6.3.3. Experiment Template

In the following template, we give a brief description of the experiment.

Experiment ID: VIRTUALIZATION.01

Experiment name: Detect virtualization overhead

Experiment domain: Virtualization

Detected experiment parameter: Virtualization overhead for each resource demand type in focus (double)

Importance for performance analysis: When a software is migrated from a non-virtualized to a virtualized environment, the virtualization layer can induce a performance overhead on issued resource demands that should be reflected in performance analysis.

Configuration parameters: *number of cores*: Number of available physical CPU cores for detecting CPU resource overhead; detected by Experiment CPU.02

Experiment execution logic: Issue and measure identical resource load on the non-virtualized machine and on the virtualized ma-

183

chine. Compare the measurement results to calculate the virtualization overhead. For details, see Section 6.3.2 or the graphical description shown in Figure 6.3.

Assumptions:

- Both machines are idle.

- Both machines are equipped with the same hardware. Otherwise, differences in the measured resource demands cannot be attributed to the virtualization layer.

- Assumption for performance analysis: The performance analysis has to provide means for including the detected overhead model in analysis. For example, the analysis could adapt issued resource demands by adding the virtualization overhead to it. Such an approach would facilitate the reuse of existing software models for predicting its performance in virtualized environments.

- Required sensors: Response time sensors for the tasks issuing resource demands on the non-virtualized and the virtualized machine.

Experiment robustness: Experiment robustness can be assessed by analyzing the dispersion of the measurement results, i.e. by calculating the interquartile range (IQR) for the measurements. If the IQR exceeds a certain threshold, the experiments should be repeated or it should be checked whether all experiment assumptions hold on the target platform.

Experiment performance: The experiment performance mainly depends on the number of resource demand types involved and the number of performed iterations for each measurement. Additional influences can stem from the performance of the accessed resource and the overhead induced by the virtualization platform.

6.3.4. Experiment Robustness

The robustness of the experiment results can primarily be assessed using a measure of statistical dispersion for the measured data. We use the interquartile range (IQR) for calculating the dispersion. This measure denotes the range of the upper and lower quartiles, it belongs to the group of robust measures (i.e. it is not strongly influenced by outliers). By setting the IQR in relation to the arithmetic mean of the measurement data, we can analyze whether the data can be considered robust.

For example, take a set of CPU measurements taken on the non-virtualized machine and on the virtualized machine. The experiment generates synthetic load that should take 500 ms on the non-virtualized machine for each taken measurement. For the results of the non-virtualized machine, we calculate a mean of 499.1 ms and an IQR of 2. This indicates very robust results, as 50% of all results lie in the range between 498 ms and 500 ms. Repeating the measurements on the virtualized machine yields a mean of 511 ms and an IQR of 9.25. The higher mean indicates that a certain overhead is introduced by the virtualization layer. The IQR is still very low. In both cases, the IQR is below 10% of the mean, which we use as a threshold for detecting noisy CPU measurements.

For different resources, the threshold can be different. When taking disk measurements on a machine without additional noise, the virtualization layer and the layout of the disk data can lead to a larger IQR compared to the mean. We performed disk read measurements on the virtual machine, where chunks of 10MB read bytes were measured. Since the specified amount of bytes can be read from disk in a short time, the dispersion of the measurements is larger compared to CPU measurements: Measurements yielded a mean of 273.7 ms and an IQR of 93. Hence, for disk requests we assume that the measurements are robust if the IQR is below 50% of the mean.

If experiment analysis detects an IQR that is higher than the threshold for the resource type, the experiment can report possible non-robust results to the user. The user can than either investigate whether the results can be considered robust anyhow, or check whether additional load was present on the platform leading to measurement noise. In the latter case, the user should remove the additional load (if possible) and repeat the experiment.

6.3.5. Experiment Performance

The performance of the experiment mainly depends on the number of resource demand types involved and the number of iterations performed for each measurement. Additionally, the performance can be influenced by the performance of the involved resources and the overhead induced by the virtualization layer.

As an example, consider four resource demand types, namely CPU, RAM, Disk read and Disk write. For CPU and RAM, we repeat each measurement 500 times. For disk demands, the measurements can be more scattered, so we increased the number of iterations for each measurement to 1000. If we assume an average response time of 500 ms for CPU and RAM requests, 200 ms for Disk read and 400 ms for Disk write requests on the non-virtualized machine, as well as a constant slowdown of 10% for each resource type, the experiment execution time would be $500 \cdot 2 \cdot 500 \,\text{ms} + 1000 \cdot (200 \,\text{ms} + 400 \,\text{ms}) + 1.1 \cdot 500 \cdot 2 \cdot 500 \,\text{ms} + 1.1 \cdot 1000 \cdot (200 \,\text{ms} + 400 \,\text{ms}) = 38$ minutes 30 seconds.

Exemplary execution of the experiment on a quad-core machine (Intel Core i7-860, 2.80 GHz, 8 GB RAM) with a non-virtualized Windows 7 and a virtualized Windows 7 using XenCenter 5.6 took 42 minutes 2 seconds.

6.3.6. Including Experiment Results in Performance Prediction

In the following, we describe how the detected virtualization overheads can be included in a performance prediction approach. For illustration, we use the Palladio Component Model (PCM) for performance prediction, which has been introduced in Chapter 2 and used in Chapter 5 as well.

In the PCM, the software architect creates a model of the software architecture that includes performance-relevant information, such as resource demands occurring in components, the usage profile for the system, or basic information on the execution environment. Virtual machines can be modeled in PCM with nested resource containers [HKKR09]. The PCM model is then transformed into a performance model that can be used for performance analysis. In our case, we use the PCM simulation SimuCom for performance analysis. When simulating the performance of software models with SimuCom, a PCM model is being transformed into Java code that plugs into the simulation framework.

In order to include the detected virtualization overheads into the PCM performance analysis, we adapted the PCM as follows. The detected overheads are stored in a configuration model that is created by GINPEX after the execution of the experiment VIRTUALIZATION.01. When conducting a performance prediction with PCM SimuCom, the software architect can select the configuration model in addition to the PCM input model. While the PCM input model is transformed into simulation code as before, in addition the configuration model is read and the simulation is configured to reflect the virtualization overheads in the simulated servers (called resource containers in PCM). Figure 6.4 illustrates this process.

Figure 6.5 shows how the PCM simulation SimuCom includes the virtualization overhead during a simulation run. During simulation, resource requests of components deployed on the containers are issued to the container's resources (e.g. CPU, disk, or a network device). Each request leads to an event indicating that the demand has to be put on the resource (step (1) in the figure). We intercept this event (2) and read the virtualization overhead from the configuration for the corresponding virtual machine the request is issued on (3). The original resource demand is multiplied with the overhead, leading to an adapted resource demand that is passed back to

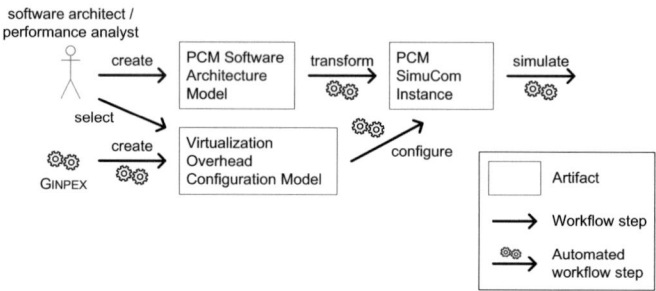

Figure 6.4.: Including virtualization overhead in PCM performance prediction

the simulation framework (4). The simulation processes the demand using queues which simulate resource scheduling logic and resource contention effects. Once a resource request is processed completely by the simulation, the simulation sends an event indicating that the control flow of the component issues the demand can be resumed (step (5) and (6)).

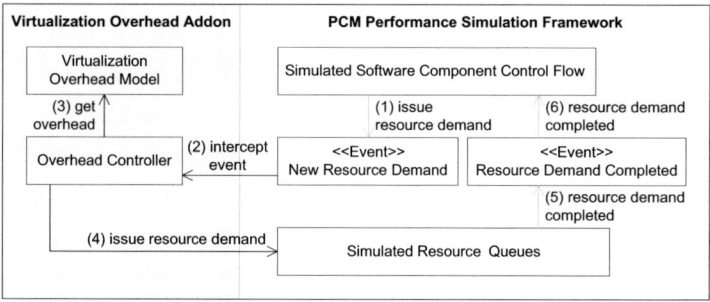

Figure 6.5.: Integration of virtualization overhead in PCM SimuCom

6.3.7. Validation

In this section, we validate whether improvements on prediction accuracy can be achieved by including the derived virtualization overhead model in performance analysis. For this validation, we first executed the experiment presented in this chapter on a machine running a non-virtualized Windows 7, and a machine with a virtualized Windows 7 running on a virtualization hypervisor (XenCenter 5.6). We then included the detected overheads in a PCM performance prediction to predict the performance of a software in the virtualized environment based on a PCM model that was calibrated for the non-virtualized environment. By taking into account the detected overheads in the PCM performance analysis, we can evaluate whether these overheads lead to increased prediction accuracy. Some experiments presented in this chapter have been initially published in [HKHR11] and [HKHR13].

6.3.7.1. Validation Scenario

As a case study, we chose an implementation of the TPC-W benchmark [Tra]. The TPC-W system specifies a web-based bookstore software application and a realistic workload mix. The implementation is based on Java servlets and a MySQL database [JMOb]. In this case study, we ran the benchmark in a non-distributed environment, i.e. we deployed the application server and the database on the same server instance. The workload is generated through emulated web browsers; the number of parallel web browsers equals the number of parallel users that are active in the system.

Figure 6.6 shows the two different deployment scenarios used in the case study. In scenario A, the server components are deployed on a non-virtualized machine (Intel Core i7-860, 2.80 GHz, 8 GB RAM) running Windows 7. In scenario B, the same hardware was used running a virtualization hypervisor (XenCenter 5.6) and a Windows 7 virtual machine in which the server components are deployed.

6.3.7.2. Execution

After setting up the execution environment, we performed the following steps:

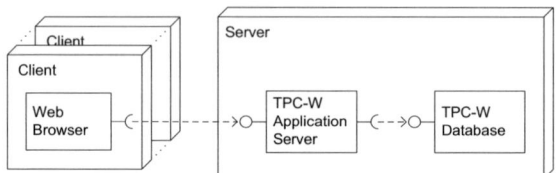

(a) TPC-W deployment on a non-virtualized machine (scenario A)

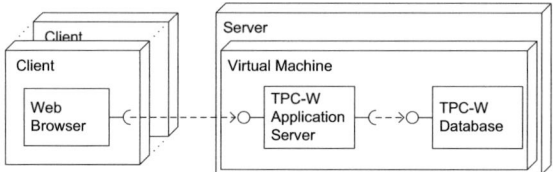

(b) TPC-W deployment on a virtualized machine (scenario B)

Figure 6.6.: TPC-W case study deployment scenario

1. Create a performance model of the TPC-W application calibrated on the non-virtualized machine

2. Conduct performance prediction for the TPC-W model (prediction 1)

3. Perform GINPEX experiment to detect virtualization overhead model

4. Conduct performance prediction for the TPC-W model using the derived virtualization overhead model (prediction 2)

5. Measure the TPC-W application to compare the application's performance with the predicted performance

6. As a cross-check, create a TPC-W model calibrated on the virtualized machine, and conduct a performance prediction with this model (prediction 3)

In the step 1, we created an initial performance prediction model of the TPC-W application using the Palladio Component Model. Component resource demands were obtained through measurements taken on the non-virtualized machine. For this model, we did not use the virtual machine for calibration, as such measurements would already contain possible virtualization overhead. Instead, we use the experiment results in performance prediction, as the experiment aims at facilitating performance predictions of software applications which do not have to be deployed on the virtual machines of the target environment.

Afterwards, we conducted a performance prediction of the TPC-W model using the PCM simulation SimuCom for different workloads (prediction 1, step 2). This prediction did not take into account any virtualization overhead, as it was based on the PCM model calibrated on the non-virtualized machine.

We then executed the GINPEX experiment on the execution environment for detecting the virtualization overhead model (step 3). We focused on three different resource demand types that are present in the TPC-W system: CPU load, disk read load, and disk write load. Figure 6.7 shows the cumulative distribution function of the measured response times for the different resource demand types on the non-virtualized and on the virtualized machine.

The average measured response times and the resulting virtualization overhead values are shown in Table 6.1. One can see that the detected overhead differs between the resource types and is significantly higher for disk read and disk write resource demands compared to CPU demands.

Table 6.1.: Measured resource demand response times and calculated overhead

Resource demand type	Avg. response time		Calculated virtualization overhead
	non-virtualized Windows 7	virtualized Windows 7	
CPU	499 ms	511 ms	1.02
Disk Read	179 ms	274 ms	1.53
Disk Write	412 ms	650 ms	1.58

The detected overheads were written into a configuration model that can be read by the PCM simulation in order to reflect the virtualization over-

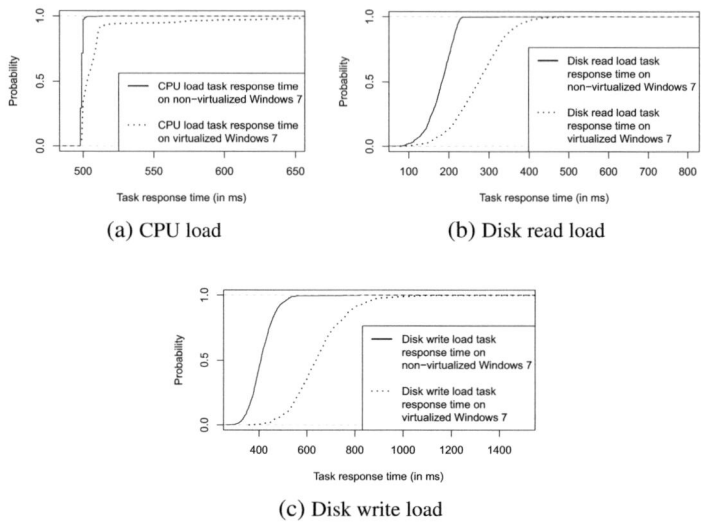

Figure 6.7.: Virtualization overhead experiment results

head during simulation (see Section 6.3.6). Using this overhead model, we repeated the PCM performance prediction (prediction 2, step 4). Afterwards, we ran a predefined workload mix (TPC-W WIPSo) on the application with different amounts of parallel users (step 5). We measured the response times of the workload requests and compared the measurements with the PCM predictions. The results are presented in the next section.

In addition, we also calibrated the TPC-W performance prediction model using TPC-W measurements on the virtualized machine (step 6). We conducted a performance prediction for this model as well to check whether the first TPC-W model, which has been calibrated using TPC-W measurements on the non-virtualized machine, yields similar results with the derived overhead model as the TPC-W model calibrated with measurements on the virtualized machine.

6.3.7.3. Results

In the following, we compare the results of the TPC-W performance prediction (with and without the virtualization overhead model) with the measurements taken on the deployed TPC-W application.

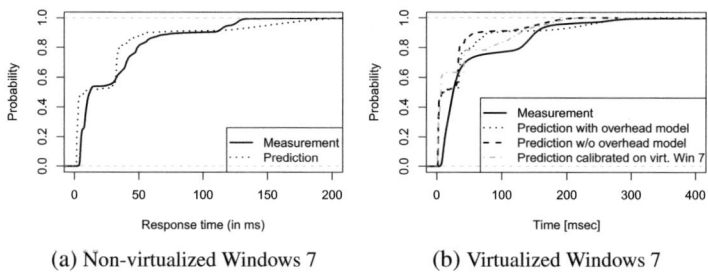

(a) Non-virtualized Windows 7   (b) Virtualized Windows 7

Figure 6.8.: Comparison of prediction and measurements for TPC-W response times of a 3-user workload running on a non-virtualized and a virtualized Windows 7

Figure 6.8 shows cumulative distribution functions of the measured and predicted response times of a 3-user TPC-W workload, i.e. the workload consisted of 3 users accessing the TPC-W application in parallel.

For the non-virtualized scenario, the predicted response times (prediction 1) are quite accurate (avg. 29.8 ms predicted vs. 32.8 ms measured), leading to a prediction error of approx. 9%. For the virtualized scenario, the measured response times are higher (avg. 57.3 ms). As the hardware environment and the software configuration was the same on both scenarios, the increase can be explained with the overhead introduced by the virtualization layer. Without the overhead model, the predicted response times apparently stay the same, leading to an increased prediction error of approx. 48%. This is an increase of 39% for the prediction error compared to the prediction for the non-virtualized scenario. When taking into account the overhead model (prediction 2), the prediction error is significantly lower (avg. predicted response time 40.3 ms, prediction error approx. 30%), but still higher than for the non-virtualized scenario prediction. Hence, the inclusion of the virtualization layer can help to reduce the prediction error for performance predictions of virtualized software, but still yields a significant higher prediction error compared to predictions of non-virtualized software. The prediction error for the TPC-W model that has been calibrated on the virtualized machine (prediction 3) is similar to the prediction error obtained by prediction 2 (avg. 36.7 ms, prediction error approx. 36%). The prediction quality of a prediction model calibrated on a non-virtualized machine using the derived overhead model is comparable to the quality of a prediction model that has been calibrated on the virtualized machine. In other words, for the TPC-W case study, the prediction results can be achieved by conducting the overhead model experimentally and calibrating the model using TPC-W measurements on the non-virtualized machine. One does not have to deploy the TPC-W on the virtualized machine for the predictions.

While the overhead model leads to a decreased prediction error, the prediction error is still higher compared to the prediction in the non-virtualized scenario. For further analysis of the prediction error, we performed both TPC-W measurements and predictions for both scenarios using different user workloads. Table 6.2 lists the average response times of measurement and predictions and the corresponding prediction error for the different workloads.

The response times show that the prediction works in the non-virtualized scenario for different amounts of parallel users: Due to resource contention, the measured response times increase with an increasing amount of parallel users. However, the prediction is able to capture this effect; the prediction error stays below 20%. For the virtualized scenario, a stronger increase in the measured response times can be observed. The single-user workload yields an average response time of 28.38 ms, which is an increase of approximately 20% compared to the non-virtualized scenario. Predicting the response times using the virtualization overhead model captures this effect.

Table 6.2.: Average response times for different numbers of parallel users (in brackets: prediction error)

	Contention (# users)	Measured	Predicted w/o overhead model	Predicted with overhead model	Predicted with model calibrated on virtualized machine
Non-virtualized	1	23.46 ms	23.71 ms (1.07%)		
	2	30.82 ms	26.22 ms (14.93%)		
	3	32.77 ms	29.79 ms (9.09%)		
	4	34.01 ms	34.46 ms (1.32%)		
	5	42.80 ms	40.87 ms (4.51%)		
	6	44.00 ms	47.58 ms (8.14%)		
	8	54.58 ms	62.00 ms (13.59%)		
	10	76.71 ms	77.50 ms (1.03%)		
Virtualized	1	28.37 ms	23.71 ms (16.43%)	28.23 ms (0.49%)	28.00 ms (1.30%)
	2	38.36 ms	26.22 ms (31.65%)	33.34 ms (13.09%)	31.71 ms (17.34%)
	3	57.26 ms	29.79 ms (47.97%)	40.32 ms (29.58%)	36.71 ms (35.89%)
	4	77.38 ms	34.46 ms (55.47%)	49.85 ms (35.58%)	43.46 ms (43.84%)
	5	118.06 ms	40.87 ms (65.38%)	60.48 ms (48.77%)	51.86 ms (56.07%)
	6	119.03 ms	47.58 ms (60.03%)	71.93 ms (39.57%)	60.94 ms (48.80%)
	8	189.48 ms	62.00 ms (67.28%)	95.66 ms (49.51%)	80.25 ms (57.65%)
	10	199.65 ms	77.50 ms (61.18%)	119.59 ms (40.10%)	100.29 ms (49.77%)

However, with increasing load the prediction underestimates the response times although the overhead model is used.

For a higher amount of parallel users, i.e. 8 or 10 parallel users, the system is under heavy load with measured response times over 6 times as high compared to the single-user scenario. In the non-virtualized scenario, this workload only yields response times 3 times as high compared to the single-user scenario. Hence, an additional increase of response times for load executed on a virtualized system can be observed. This increase is caused by the virtualization layer and depends on the amount of parallel load present in the system, because this effect is not visible for the non-virtualized scenario. The constant overhead factor that is derived by this chapter's experiment and used by the virtualization overhead model to adapt the prediction is not sufficient to capture this performance effect. It is interesting to note that the predictions with the model calibrated on the virtualized machine (last column in Table 6.2) also yield an increased prediction error with a higher amount of parallel users. In order to decrease the prediction error, the prediction has to be adapted in a way that the load-dependent overhead introduced by the virtualized environment is taken into account. In the following chapter, we provide an experiment to cope with this effect. This experiment derives a more fine-grained load-dependent model of the overhead induced by the virtualization platform.

6.4. Load-dependent Overhead

In the previous section, we introduced an experiment to detect the performance overhead that is introduced by the virtualization layer when a software is migrated from a non-virtualized to a virtualized environment. However, the case study presented in Section 6.3.7 showed that even a model calibrated on a virtualized environment based on a single-user workload underpredicts the response times (which was not the case for similar predictions for a non-virtualized environment). This can be explained by load-dependent overhead that is introduced by the virtualization layer, but is not reflected in the predictions yet. In the following, we present an experiment to derive an overhead model that reflects such load-dependent overhead of the virtualization layer.

6.4.1. Motivation

In the last section, an experiment was presented that aims at measuring resource demand overheads that occur when existing software applications are migrated from a non-virtualized machine to a virtual machine. This experiment calculated a fixed overhead for different resource demands, e.g. CPU or Disk demands. However, resource overheads depend on both the infrastructure and the current load situation of the system, i.e. the number of requests processed in parallel.

For illustration, let us return to the case study results of Section 6.3. In the case study, an implementation of the TPC-W benchmark [Tra] was deployed in a virtualized and in a non-virtualized Windows 7 environment. A workload mix with different amounts of parallel users was executed and the response times of the workload requests were measured. A run with one user (i.e. no resource contention) yielded a low overall utilization of the system, while a run with with 10 parallel users resulted in a heavily utilized system and much higher response times.

Figure 6.9 shows the average response times of the different benchmark runs. One can see that the results differ for both runs. For the first run with a small number of parallel users, the response times vary a little (mean response time 23.5 ms in the non-virtualized scenario compared to 28.4 ms in the virtualized scenario). Thus, a slowdown of approx. 20% due to the virtualization layer can be observed. However, when increasing the number of users, the difference in response times is much larger (mean response time 76.7 ms in the non-virtualized scenario compared to 199.7 ms in the virtualized scenario), resulting in a slowdown of approx. 160%. Both

197

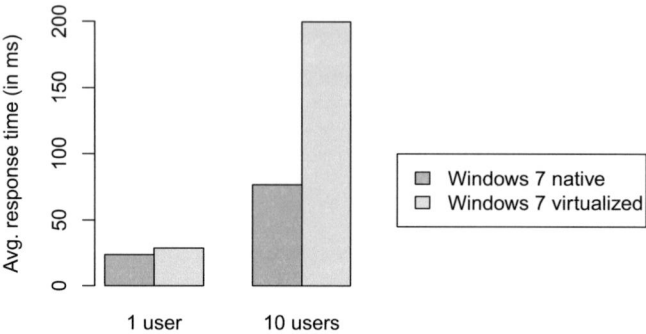

Figure 6.9.: TPC-W response times on a non-virtualised and a virtualised Windows 7

benchmark installations shared the same system setup, i.e. the used hardware resources, operating system, and middleware installed on the operating system. Hence, the results show that the virtualization layer introduces an overhead that depends on the load that is present in the system.

6.4.2. Experiment Design

In the following, we present an experiment to derive a load-dependent overhead model for resource demands issued on a virtual machine. Compared to the experiment VIRTUALIZATION.01 from Section 6.3, the following experiment has the following features:

- The detected resource demand overhead for a virtual machine is not constant, but depends on the overall load situation present in the system. Multiple resource requests that are issued in parallel are taken into account when calculating the overhead model.

- The experiment can run on multiple virtual machines and reflects load on all involved virtual machines in the overhead model.

Performance prediction of virtualized environments can benefit from a load-dependent overhead model because in such environments, overheads can occur at different levels. First, overheads can occur inside a single VM when multiple processes have to be scheduled by the operating system (similar to a non-virtualized environment). In this case, additional scheduling logic executed by the operating system to dispatch parallel requests may lead to overheads. In addition, in virtualized environments resource demands are not directly issued on a hardware resource, but forwarded to the hypervisor which deals with scheduling resource demands that can incur in multiple virtual machines. The hypervisor usually adds additional overhead which depends both on the resource type and the amount of resource requests that have to be scheduled by the hypervisor.

With increased parallel load, the combination of both resource demand overhead causers can lead to the behavior shown in Figure 6.9: In a virtualized environment, measured response times can be significantly improved compared to response times measured in a non-virtualized system.

Our experiment aims at detecting the overhead on performance that comes from different levels of the infrastructure, i.e. the operating system and the hypervisor. The experiment shares some concepts from the experiment VIRTUALIZATION.01 from Section 6.3, such as the concept of issuing demand for a certain resource, measuring its response time and comparing the measured time to a reference time for calculating an overhead value. However, the structure of the experiment is quite different from the experiment VIRTUALIZATION.01, as explained in the following.

The experiment runs on a number of virtual machines which are to be included in performance analysis, i.e. for which the overhead on resource demands should be detected. A typical experiment scenario is shown in Figure 6.10. Here, two virtual machines are deployed on a single physical server.

The experiment consists of multiple experiment runs. In one experiment run, we issue load on each machine to resources using parallel processes.

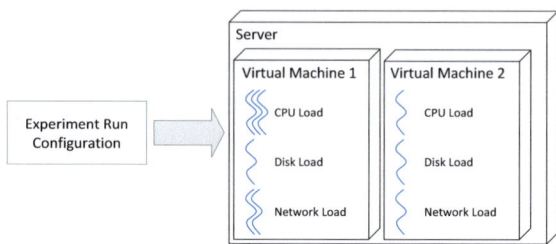

Figure 6.10.: Exemplary experiment run setup on virtual machines

In each process, load to a certain resource is issued and response times of resource requests are measured. For creating load, microbenchmarks are used. We use tasks from the GINPEX metamodel (see Section 4.4.3) for specifying the load to be issued. In particular, we use the CpuLoadTask, DiskReadTask, DiskWriteTask and NetworkLoadTask to create load to the CPU, disk, and network resource. Figure 6.10 shows how one experiment run configuration could look like. In the shown scenario, CPU resource load, disk resource load and network resource load is issued by different processes in the virtual machines. By issuing parallel requests, we aim at systematically creating resource contention for which we expect infrastructure overhead (originating from the virtualized operating system and the hypervisor).

For each resource request, the response time is measured. Based on the measured response times, we calculate the overhead for each request type with respect to the parallel load. For this purpose, we compare the measured response times to the response time of the resource request without parallel load (reference time). Let $\hat{t}_{res,m}$ be the reference time for resource res on virtual machine m. Furthermore, let $\vec{r}$ be a vector containing the number of parallel requests for each resource request in every virtual machine; $\vec{r}$ denotes the input configuration for an experiment run. Furthermore, let $t_{res,m,\vec{r}}$ be the average measured response time of requests to resource res on machine m in the experiment run denoted by $\vec{r}$, and let r_{res} be the number of parallel requests to resource res in that run. Then, the overhead $o(res,m,\vec{r})$

is calculated as follows:

$$o(res, m, \vec{r}) = 1 + \frac{\left| \frac{t_{res,m,\vec{r}}}{r_{res}} - \hat{t}_{res,m} \right|}{\hat{t}_{res,m}} \tag{6.1}$$

We vary the number of parallel processes for each resource request on each machine in multiple experiment runs. We can specify each experiment run by the number of parallel resource requests on each machine in focus. For each type of resource request and for each machine in focus, the overhead is then calculated with Equation 6.1.

Take for example, a disk request taking 200 ms if running in a VM (VM 1) with all other VMs being idle. Then, in a second experiment run, requests to other resources occur in parallel while the same amount of disk requests is issued and measured in VM 1. If the measured response time of the disk request now yields 250 ms, an overhead of 1.25 is being calculated. Now consider a third experiment run where two disk requests are issued in parallel, yielding a measured response time of 550 ms per disk request. Then, the disk request overhead would be $1 + ((550/2) - 200)/200$ = 1.375. Here, we first divide the disk response time by 2, as the slowdown due to parallel disk requests is caused by resource contention and reflected by performance analysis tools anyhow.

For the remainder of this section, we focus on three different types of resource requests, which are CPU, disk, and network requests. We chose these resource types because they are usually regarded in performance predictions of business applications [BKR09]. However, the generic approach of the experiment could also be applied to different resource requests or a more fine grained requests structure (for example, by differentiating between disk read and disk write requests).

To include load-dependent overheads of resource demands in performance analysis, we execute multiple experiment runs, each with different input parameters, i.e. a different configuration of parallel resource requests. For each resource type, we calculate an overhead that depends on the number of competing resource requests. By including the different calculations in a multi-dimensional regression model, we can estimate load-dependent resource demand overheads during performance analysis for situations (i.e. input parameter combinations) for which no experiment runs have been executed. Although we focus on deriving infrastructure overhead for virtual machines deployed on a single physical server, note that the experiment can also be executed on multiple physical machines or on a single non-virtualized machine. In the latter case, the experiment would focus on detecting load-dependent overhead that is caused by the operating system layer and the resource controllers of the machine.

In the following, we use terminology from experimental design to describe the experiment parameter variation in more detail (for more information, see [Jai91]). The *factors* of an experiment are the variables that affect the response variables and that can be varied. In our case, factors are the resource types for which load is issued by GINPEX tasks and the virtual machines in which the load is issued. The *levels* of a factor constitute the values for which a factor can be varied. To vary the amount of load, we spawn (for each resource type) multiple OS processes in parallel, each process issuing resource load.

Let R be the set of resource types and N be the set of virtual machines on which the experiment is running. Then, the set of factors F is the cartesian product of these sets: $F = R \times N$. Further, let K be the set of levels. Then, in a full-factorial experiment design, every possible combination at all levels of all factors would yield $|K|^{|R| \cdot |N|}$ experiment runs. If we consider $R = \{CPU, DISK, NETWORK\}$ and $K = \{0, 1, 2, 5\}$, a full parameter exploration cannot be performed, even for a small number of virtual machines. For example, if $|N| = 3$, then the number of needed experiment runs is $4^{3.3} - 1 = 262,143$ combinations (we can neglect the combination $((0,0,0),(0,0,0),(0,0,0))$). If we assume an average duration of 5 minutes per experiment run to gain stable measurement results of the executed microbenchmarks, 262,143 experiment runs yield an overall experiment runtime of approx. 2.5 years. In addition, the number of experiment runs grows exponentially with the number of involved machines, rendering a full-factorial experiment design infeasible.

To overcome this issue, we adapted the experiment design using a heuristic to minimize the number of needed experiment runs. The adapted design falls into two parts: First, we execute experiment runs that only create load inside a single virtual machine, while no load is issued on the remaining machines. We call the resource overhead calculated in these runs intra-machine overhead, as it only reflects influences by load issued in the same machine. Second, we execute runs issuing load across multiple virtual machines to detect inter-machine overhead. The following subsections deal present these heuristics in detail.

6.4.2.1. Determine Intra-machine Overhead

To check how response times of issued load inside a virtual machine are influenced by parallel load, we conducted measurements on microbenchmarks issuing different resource load. These benchmarks ran in one virtual machine, while the other virtual machines were left idle. All virtual machines were deployed on a XenCenter 5.6 virtualization hypervisor.

As an example, we varied CPU and Disk requests inside a single virtual machine running Windows 7 and measured the average response time (wall clock time) of the request. We spawned multiple OS processes to issue parallel requests.

Table 6.3 shows the average response times of the measured CPU requests. If no Disk load is present in the system, CPU response times take approximately twice as long when two parallel processes are issuing CPU load compared to only one process issuing CPU load. Thus, additional overhead is very low. If parallel Disk load is present, the measured CPU response times slightly increase.

Table 6.3.: Average CPU request response times for varied requests

CPU Load	No Disk	1 Disk Process	2 Disk Processes
1 CPU Process	150 ms	164 ms	175 ms
2 CPU Processes	300 ms	318 ms	336 ms

However, when we measure the response times of the Disk requests for the same scenario, we see that the Disk response times heavily depend on the parallel CPU load (see Table 6.4, note that the rows now indicate the number of disk processes). In addition, the Disk response times do not increase linearly with increasing CPU load, as it has been the case in the previous case.

Table 6.4.: Average disk request response times for varied requests

Disk Load	No CPU	1 CPU Process	2 CPU Processes
1 Disk Process	1119 ms	1791 ms	4447 ms
2 Disk Processes	2258 ms	2578 ms	5222 ms

From these experiments, we conclude that (a) different resource load overhead can occur for different resources and (b) resource overhead does not necessarily increase linearly with parallel load.

Furthermore, we repeated the experiment on a second VM running a different OS (Fedora 12 Linux instead of Windows 7). While the measured CPU results are similar to the results presented in Table 6.3, the Disk results differ, as shown in Table 6.5.

Table 6.5.: Average disk request response times for varied requests in VM2

Disk Load	No CPU	1 CPU Process	2 CPU Processes
1 Disk Process	870 ms	887 ms	889 ms
2 Disk Processes	1537 ms	1606 ms	1546 ms

For the Linux system, only little influence on Disk request response times can be observed due to parallel CPU load. Here, variations in measured response times can mainly be attributed to measurement noise. Thus, the measured resource overhead strongly depends on the guest operating system, which means that experiment results obtained for a VM with one operating system are not necessarily applicable to VMs with other operating systems.

Due to the conclusions drawn from the presented experiments presented above, we decided to use a full-factorial design for each machine in isolation, i.e. no load was issued on the remaining machines. This leads to $|N| \cdot (|K|^{|R|} - 1)$ experiment runs, were $|N|$ denotes the number of virtual machines, $|R|$ the number of involved resource types, and $|K|$ the number of used load levels (we can neglect the combination $(0, ..., 0)$ where all resources are idle). For the set of factors and levels used above, this leads to $|N| \cdot 63$ experiment runs. This number of experiments can be executed in a couple of hours, and still provides a full-factorial parameter exploration in every involved virtual machine, so that for every resource type, all influences on overheads caused by the other resource types, can be observed – as long as the resource access occurs in the same machine (intra-machine overhead). In general, if we have a limited number of resource types, the number of needed combinations for varying parameters in a single machine mainly depends on $|R|$. If $|R| = 3$, then the number of runs is $O(|K|^3)$, which is still polynomial.

6.4.2.2. Determine Inter-machine Overhead

To determine overhead that cannot be detected by the first series of experiment runs, we conduct additional experiment runs, where load is issued in parallel across multiple VMs. These experiment runs aim at provoking additional overhead that is caused by the hypervisor (inter-machine overhead). We applied a reduced 2^k factorial design to limit the number of experiment runs while still identifying all relevant influences.

For the experiments, we reduced the set of levels to $K = \{0, m\}$, where m is the number of available logical resources for a specific resource type (e.g. the number of cores for a CPU). Limiting the number of levels means that we disregard the effect of the number of parallel requests within a virtual machine on performance. Instead, we assume that the number of parallel requests to a resource inside one machine has no impact on inter-machine overheads. For example, a hypervisor schedules resource requests that occur for different virtual machines, but does not know how many parallel requests inside one virtual machine actually have been issued to the resource. We further assume that across different VMs, not all resource types have to be varied against each other. Thus, we only vary each resource type in isolation and neglect interactions between resource types. Varying only the load on one resource in different virtual machines leads to $2^{|N|} - 1$ experiment runs for each resource type, where N denotes the set of machines across which parameter values are to be varied. As a consequence, the number of experiment runs scales linearly with the number of resource types, i.e. the number of runs is $|R| \cdot (2^{|N|} - 1)$. This reduction leads to a 2^k factorial experiment design and thus a significant reduction of required experiment runs.

Another cause of inter-machine overhead can be the hypervisor requiring CPU processing time when managing VM accesses to resources. Therefore, it is quite likely that CPU load and other resource load issued in different VMs affect each other [CG05]. To capture the effect of the hypervisor, we repeat the inter-machine experiment runs for all resources (except the CPU) with full CPU load issued in one VM. As we don't know whether CPU overhead on the hypervisor is constant or depending on the number of virtual machines issuing resource requests, we vary these virtual machines, leading to another $(|R| - 1) \cdot (2^{|N|} - 1)$ experiment runs. Thus, we can observe CPU overhead that occurs on the hypervisor due to resource requests being issued in different VMs.

To sum up, the overall number of needed experiment runs can be specified as

$$|N| \cdot (|K|^{|R|} - 1) + (2|R| - 1) \cdot (2^{|N|} - 1).$$

In the case of 3 VMs, 3 resource types and 4 levels, we end up in an overall number of 224 experiment runs (compared to 262,143 runs in a full-factorial experiment design).

6.4.2.3. Experiment Implementation

We implemented the experiment with Ginpex to enable automated experiment execution and derivation of the load-dependent overheads. We specified the experiment for three different basic resource types, i.e. CPU, disk and network resource type. During execution, GINPEX generates the logic for each experiment run based on a GINPEX experiment definition. In a first step, the experiment executes experiment runs using a full factorial design (see Section 6.4.2.1) on each specified machine using a fixed set of levels ($K = \{0,1,2,5\}$). Afterwards, experiment runs are performed issuing load in parallel on multiple VMs using the experiment design presented in Section 6.4.2.2.

Issuing resource load is done by spawning one or multiple processes using the GINPEX ParallelTask. Each process independently executes a GINPEX load task repeatedly and measures the response times. For CPU load, the CpuLoadTask which performs Fibonacci calculations to generate CPU load, is used. For disk load, chunks of 5 MB random data are read and written to the disk using DiskReadTasks and DiskWriteTasks (to avoid cache effects, these tasks use a large set of files when generating disk load). For network load, random data is sent in chunks of 5 MB to a different machine not part of the system under test. For disk and network load processes, the value of k denotes the number of parallel running processes. For the CPU resource, we multiply k by the number of available cores (which is available as an experiment configuration parameter) to get the number of parallel processes. Hence, for $k = 2$ on a virtual machine that is equipped with 2 virtual CPU cores, the experiment runs 4 parallel processes issuing CPU load so that the amount of CPU load of two parallel processes is put on each available core.

6.4.3. Experiment Template

As with all experiments presented in this thesis, we use the experiment template from Section 4.6 to give a brief overview on the experiment.

In the following template, we give a brief description of the experiment.

Experiment ID: VIRTUALIZATION.02

Experiment name: Detect load-dependent virtualization overhead

Experiment domain: Virtualization

Detected experiment parameter: Load-dependent virtualization overhead for each resource demand type in focus (double)

Importance for performance analysis: The overhead induced by the virtualization layer depends on both the resource type and the load currently present on the platform. This load has to be reflected in an overhead model for performance analysis to reduce the prediction error.

Configuration parameters: *number of cores*: Number of available physical CPU cores for detecting CPU resource overhead; detected by Experiment CPU.02

Experiment execution logic: In multiple experiment runs, issue different amounts of resource load in the different virtual machines using parallel processes. Measure the response time of the resource load and compare the overhead to a reference time (the response time of the resource request when executed without parallel load).

To avoid a full parameter exploitation (number of VMs × number of resource types × number of load levels), use a set of heuristics which minimize the number of experiments without degrading prediction accuracy. For details, see Section 6.4.2.

Assumptions:

- The involved virtual machines are idle.

- The virtual machines share the involved resources, i.e. the virtual CPU cores, disk and network devices are mapped to the same physical devices.

- Assumption for performance analysis: The performance analysis has to provide means for including the detected overhead model in analysis. Similar to the overhead model detected by experiment VIRTUALIZATION.01, the analysis could adapt issued resource demands by adding the virtualization overhead to it. Such an approach would facilitate the reuse of existing software models for predicting its performance in virtualized environments.

- Required sensors: Response time sensors for the tasks issuing resource demands on the different virtual machines.

Experiment robustness: Experiment robustness can be assessed by analyzing the dispersion of the measurement results, i.e. by calculating the interquartile range (IQR) for the measurements. If the IQR exceeds a certain threshold, the experiments should be repeated or it should be checked whether all experiment assumptions hold on the target platform.

Experiment performance: The experiment performance depends on the number of experiment runs and the duration of each experiment run. The number of experiment runs depends on the number of involved virtual machines, resource demand types, and load levels.

To avoid a full parameter exploitation of these factors, we reduced the number of experiment runs as described in Section 6.4.2.

6.4.4. Experiment Robustness and Performance

Similar to the experiment VIRTUALIZATION.01 presented in Section 6.3, the robustness of the experiment results can be checked by analyzing the statistical dispersion of the measured response times. If the dispersion, for example the interquartile range (IQR) does not exceed a certain threshold, the experiment can report robust results to the user. If non-robust results are detected, additional load might be present on one of the involved virtual machines or on a different virtual machines assessing the same resources. In this case, the user should remove the additional load (if possible) and repeat the experiment. It remains to be validated whether the experiment can still yield a reasonable overhead model when measurements are taken while additional load is present on the platform. This has not been done in this thesis and is subject to future work.

The performance of the experiment depends on the number of experiment runs and the iteration of one experiment run. As described in Section 6.4.2, the overall number of experiments runs is

$$|N| \cdot (|K|^{|R|} - 1) + (2|R| - 1) \cdot (2^{|N|} - 1),$$

where N is the set of involved virtual machines, R is the set of resource types, and K is the set of load levels. The runtime of a single experiment run was set to 5 minutes. On a machine with 2 VMs, three resources (CPU, disk, network), and four load levels (0, 1, 2, 5), the experiment yielded 141 experiment runs and an overall runtime of 12 hours 51 minutes (including the time for preparing the experiment runs).

6.4.5. Including Experiment Results in Performance Prediction

In the following, we describe how performance prediction for virtualized environments can be enhanced based on the results of the experiment runs presented in Section 6.4.2. First, a load-dependent overhead model is derived based on the experiment results. This model is included in SimuCom and used during simulation for calculating the overhead of requests.

The overhead model consists of a set of regression models. For each VM, the intra-machine experiment results are used to calculate a multidimensional regression model. To derive such an overhead model, we implemented a regression model based on Classification and Regression Trees (CART) [HTF09]. A CART regression model allows for predicting the value of a dependent variable (in our case, the overhead for a resource demand) based on an input of independent variables (i.e. the number of parallel processes in the simulation accessing the different resources) and has been applied successfully in case studies on performance prediction ([WAA+04], [TZN10]). CART splits the feature space into a set of regions and predicts the output parameter as the mean of the output parameter in each region. For a set of M regions, the corresponding regression model is

$$f(x) = \sum_{m=1}^{M} c_m I(x \in \mathcal{R}_m) \qquad (6.2)$$

where c_m is the mean of the output parameter in region $\mathcal{R}_m$ and I the identity matrix ([HTF09]). For details on the CART algorithm, see [HTF09]. We used the rpart package [TAR] (for details on the implementation, see [TA13]) of the R statistical computing engine [R F] as a CART-based implementation of the regression algorithm.

For the inter-VM experiments, a CART regression model is built in the same way. The overall overhead of a resource request R in a VM can then be calculated by first predicting the overhead of the intra-machine overhead model for the VM and then predicting the inter-machine overhead of resource request R. We then multiply the request with the calculated overheads to obtain an adapted request reflecting a slowdown due to parallel load.

Take for example a scenario with two VMs, the resources *CPU*, *Disk*, *Network* shared by both VMs, and the load situation $(1,0,2),(0,1,2)$. This means that the physical CPU is fully utilized by a VM 1 process, 2 processes in VM 1 issue network requests, 1 process issues disk requests in VM 2, and 2 processes issue network requests in VM 2. Now, we assume that a new process issues network requests in VM 2.

To determine the overhead that slows down this request due to the current load situation, we compute the overhead as follows: We first compute the overhead for the request with the intra-machine overhead model. This overhead is calculated with the VM 2 intra-machine overhead model with the input parameters *CPU load* $= 0$, *Disk load* $= 1$ and *Network load* $= 3$.

Then, the inter-machine overhead is calculated. As network requests also occur in VM 1, we calculate the inter-machine network overhead for VM 2 with the input parameters *Network VM1* $= 1$ and *Network VM2* $= 1$. In addition, we have to add overhead that occurs on the hypervisor due to handling CPU and disk resource requests. This is done by first calculating overhead for VM 2 with the input parameters *CPU VM1* $= 1$ and *CPU VM2* $= 0$, and then calculating overhead for VM 2 with the input parameters *Disk VM1* $= 0$ and *Disk VM2* $= 1$. The issued network resource demand in VM 2 is then multiplied by all calculated overheads to obtain an adapted resource demand including the response time slowdown due to parallel load in the system. Similarly, overheads are calculated for the other resource requests in VM 1 and VM 2.

Figure 6.11 shows how the load-dependent overhead model is integrated into the PCM simulation SimuCom. The software architect creates a model of the software architecture and simulates its performance as described in Section 2.1.4 and Section 6.3.6.

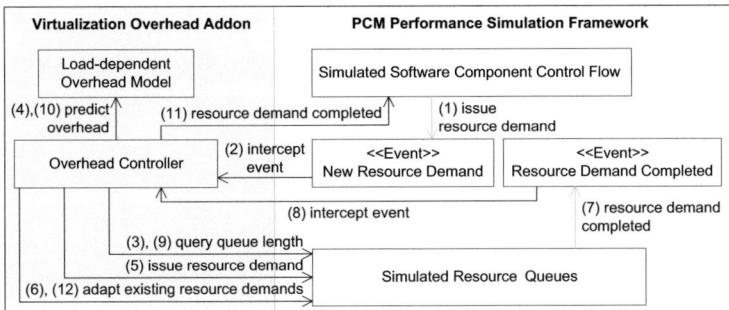

Figure 6.11.: Integration of load-dependent virtualization overhead in PCM Simu-Com

Compared to the SimuCom extension for experiment VIRTUALIZA-TION.01, we extended SimuCom as follows in order to reflect the load-dependent overhead model. For modeling virtual machines, the PCM provides the concept of nested resource containers [HKKR09]. During simulation, resource requests of components deployed on the containers are issued to the container's resources (e.g. CPU, disk, or a network device). Each request leads to an event indicating that the demand has to be put on the resource (step (1) in the figure). We intercept this event (2) and query the resources for the current load situation (3). Based on this information, we calculate the overhead as described above (4). With this information, the platform performance model can be used to predict the overhead for the issued demand based on the overall load situation. The adapted demand is then passed on to the simulation framework (5), where the demand is processed by queues which are used by the simulation to simulate resource scheduling logic and resource contention effects. At this time, we also use the platform performance model to adapt the demands of other requests currently being processed by the simulation's queues, as other demands are affected by the changed load situation as well (6).

The same procedure is done once a resource request is processed completely by the simulation. In this case, the simulation sends a different event indicating that the control flow of the component issuing the demand can be resumed (7). We again intercept this event (8), and adapt the demands of all requests that are currently processed by the corresponding queues (steps (9)–(12)).

6.4.6. Validation

In order to validate the experiment for detecting load-dependent virtualization overhead, we conducted two case studies. We applied the experiment to these case studies on a virtualized system to answer the following validation questions:

1. Does the load-dependent overhead model increase prediction accuracy?

2. Are the employed microbenchmarks suitable for deriving load-dependent overhead models?

3. Is the CART regression model suitable for calculating the overhead?

4. Is the distinction into intra-machine overhead and inter-machine overhead appropriate?

5. Can the derived overhead model be reused for predicting the performance of different software applications?

In the first case study, we first conducted the implemented experiment on a virtualized environment with two virtual machines. We then deployed the TPCW application, which has also been used in the case study for the experiment VIRTUALIZATION.01, on the virtual machines. Using the overhead model based on the experiment results, we predicted the performance of the TPC-W system and compared the results to a prediction that does not take into account any overhead information. In the second case study, we deployed a different software (an implementation of the RUBiS benchmark) on the virtual machine and conducted performance measurements and predictions for this system. Again, we compared predictions with and without the derived overhead model against performance measurements, and evaluate whether the overhead model, which has originally been derived for the first case study, can be reused for a different software while still yielding increased performance prediction results.

6.4.6.1. TPC-W Case Study

For the first case study, we reused the TPC-W implementation from the validation of experiment VIRTUALIZATION.01 (see Section 6.3.7). When predicting the performance of the TPC-W system using the simple virtualization overhead model of experiment VIRTUALIZATION.01, the prediction response times were significantly lower than the measured response times, especially for situations with increased load. In addition, as the TPC-W benchmark can be distributed to several servers, it can be used for validating the load-dependent overhead model taking into account multiple virtual machines.

Validation Scenario

As described in Section 6.3.7, the selected TPC-W implementation [Tra] is based on Java servlets and a MySQL database [JMOb].

For the case study, we selected an implementation of the TPC-W benchmark [Tra] that was presented in Section 6.4.1. We deployed the TPC-W application on a quad-core machine (Intel Core i7-860, 2.80 GHz, 8 GB RAM) that runs a virtualization hypervisor (XenCenter 5.6) with two virtual machines. On one virtual machine, we deployed the web server and the servlet components of the TPC-W benchmark application, whereas on the other virtual machine, we deployed the database server of the application. Two provide a more heterogeneous environment, we used different guest operating systems for the two virtual machines. The first virtual ma-

215

chine runs Fedora 12 Linux (kernel 2.6.31), the second virtual machine runs Windows 7. We pinned the hypervisor to one CPU core and both virtual machines to the remaining three cores. Thus, the virtual machine shared all available machine resources.

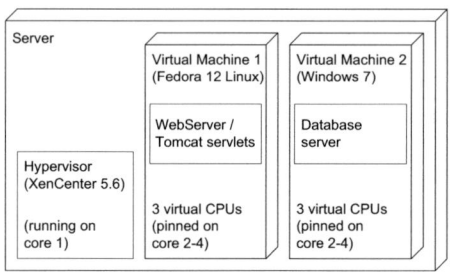

(a) Case study deployment scenario A

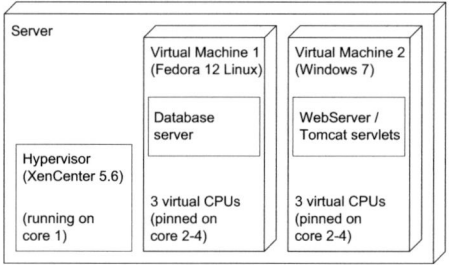

(b) Case study deployment scenario B

Figure 6.12.: TPC-W case study deployment scenarios

Figure 6.12 gives an overview of the deployment scenarios used in the case study. In the first deployment scenario (Scenario A), the web server and the servlet components ran on the Linux VM and the database server on the Windows VM. In the second deployment scenario (Scenario B), we deployed the web server and the servlet components on the Windows VM and the database server on the Linux VM.

Execution

For each deployment scenario, we created an initial PCM performance prediction model for the TPC-W application by measuring the response times of all servlet and database calls without contention, i.e. a single-user workload (the workload itself consists of 50% browsing requests and 50% ordering requests; see [Tra] for details on the WIPSo mix). Based on the derived resource demands, we created a PCM component model of the system and performed a performance simulation with the single-user workload. The predicted simulation results of the average end-to-end response time of the called services are close to the corresponding measured results, as shown in the cumulative distribution functions in Figure 6.13 (22.6 ms measured vs. 17.7 ms predicted in scenario A, 22.9 ms measured vs. 18.0 ms predicted in scenario B).

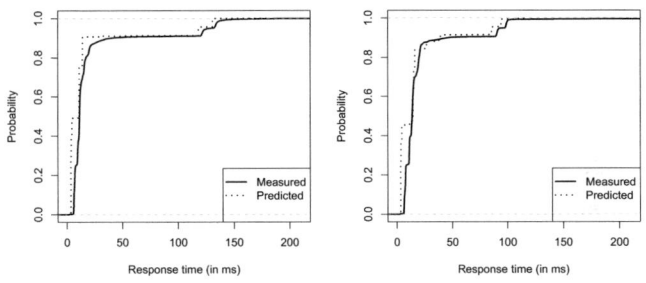

(a) Response times for deployment scenario A (b) Response times for deployment scenario B

Figure 6.13.: Case study response times for single-user workload

Using these initial performance models, we now increase the user workload to evaluate scenarios with resource contention introduced on the system.

To derive the overhead model, we executed the overhead experiments with GINPEX on both VMs. As explained before, the experiments are independent from the TPC-W system and can also be used for predicting the performance of a different system. Table 6.6 shows some examples of experiment run results for the intra-machine overhead experiment conducted on the Windows VM. The first three columns indicate the levels of the experiment runs, i.e. the amount of parallel CPU, disk and network requests. The last three columns show the calculated overhead for the requests in this experiment run. As explained above, the overhead is calculated based on the response time of the resource request executed without parallel load. For the sake of readability, we show only a subset of the experiment run results.

One can see that the CPU overhead hardly increases with parallel Disk requests, but increases with parallel network load. The calculated Network overhead also increases slightly depending on the parallel load. Compared to Network and CPU overhead, the calculated overhead of measured Disk requests grows strongly with additional parallel load (CPU as well as network load). Interestingly, when CPU load is present, the Disk overhead is

Table 6.6.: Example of measured resource demand overheads for different resource requests on the Windows 7 VM

No. of parallel requests			Calculated overhead		
CPU	Disk	Network	CPU	Disk	Netw.
1	0	0	1.0	n/a	n/a
2	0	0	1.02	n/a	n/a
0	1	0	n/a	1.0	n/a
1	1	0	1.07	2.693	n/a
0	2	0	n/a	1.144	n/a
2	2	0	1.023	2.241	n/a
0	0	1	n/a	n/a	1.0
1	1	1	2.203	3.769	1.202
0	0	2	n/a	n/a	1.023
2	0	2	2.13	n/a	1.102
0	2	2	n/a	1.145	1.733
2	2	2	1.133	3.449	1.029

Table 6.7.: Average response times for different numbers of parallel users (in brackets: prediction error)

	Contention (# users)	Measured	Predicted w/o overhead model	Predicted with overhead model
Scenario A	1	22.6 ms	17.66 ms (21.9%)	
	20	314.7 ms	116.9 ms (62.9%)	407.8 ms (29.6%)
	30	564 ms	176.4 ms (68.7%)	629.4 ms (11.6%)
	40	793.6 ms	237.3 ms (70.1%)	825.3 ms (4.0%)
	50	1065 ms	294 ms (72.4%)	1007 ms (5.4%)
	60	1257 ms	350.2 ms (72.1%)	1266 ms (0.7%)
Scenario B	1	22.9 ms	17.97 ms (21.5%)	
	20	313.2 ms	119 ms (62.0%)	301.1 ms (3.9%)
	30	466.7 ms	180.1 ms (61.4%)	449 ms (3.8%)
	40	693.8 ms	239.5 ms (65.5%)	590.8 ms (14.8%)
	50	808.6 ms	300.6 ms (62.8%)	740.9 ms (8.4%)
	60	1036 ms	356.5 ms (71.6%)	892 ms (13.9%)

lower for two parallel Disk request processes compared to a single Disk request process. One reason for this can be the Disk scheduler that creates batches for requests and thus can reduce the overhead of a single request.

As described in Section 6.4.5, the set of input and output parameters is used to build CART regression models. With the CART-based overhead model, we configured the adapted PCM simulation to look up load-dependent overheads during the simulation of resource requests (see Section 6.4.5). Then, we performed measurements and predictions of TPC-W request response times with a higher user workload to create resource contention on the system.

Results

Table 6.7 gives an overview on measurement and prediction results for both deployment scenarios. For each scenario, we varied the user workload and performed two different PCM simulations, one without the overhead model and one using the load-dependent overhead model. The performance simulation with the load-dependent overhead model yields average response times that are closer to the measured response times compared to the original simulation without an overhead model: The prediction error is decreased from 60%–70% to 15% and less except for the 20 user workload in scenario A, where the error is decreased from around 63% to 30%.

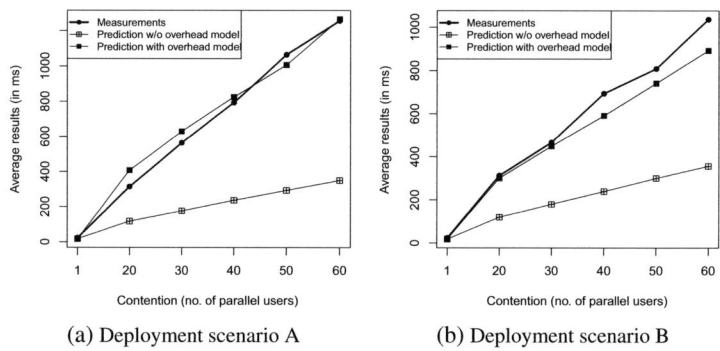

(a) Deployment scenario A (b) Deployment scenario B

Figure 6.14.: Average case study prediction results for different user workloads

The average response times for the different user workloads are shown in Figure 6.14. The figure plots the measured response times and the response times for the different prediction methods (with and without load-dependent overhead model) for the different user workloads.

From the results, one can see that the approach reduces the prediction error for all workload scenarios. Note that a workload of 50 parallel users leads to a situation in the system where a much higher resource contention occurs compared to the resource contention created during the microbenchmark-based experiment runs. Still, the derived overhead-model is able to significantly decrease the prediction error. Thus, the prediction accuracy can greatly be improved for performance predictions of software running on complex infrastructures that involve heterogeneous operating systems and virtualization layers.

To answer the fourth validation question, we now look at the impact of the intra-machine overhead model and inter-machine overhead model on prediction accuracy. For this, we performed predictions in which we used only the intra-machine overhead model or only the inter-machine overhead model. Figure 6.15 shows the average prediction results for predictions with the CART-based overhead model. Using only one of the two overhead models led to a prediction error of 40% to 55% in most cases. From the results one can see that both intra-machine overheads and inter-machine overheads contribute to the enhanced prediction accuracy, as neglecting one of the overheads leads to significantly worse prediction accuracy compared to the complete overhead model.

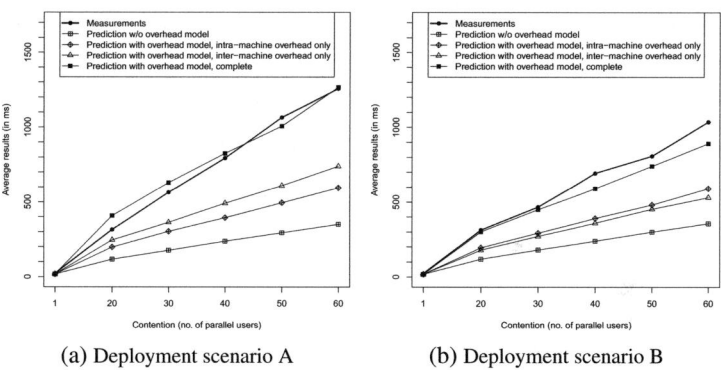

(a) Deployment scenario A   (b) Deployment scenario B

Figure 6.15.: Overhead breakdown analysis:
average prediction results with complete and partial overhead model

6.4.6.2. RUBiS Case Study

In the TPC-W case study, we illustrated how the load-dependent overhead model can lead to increased performance prediction accuracy of a software running in a virtualized environment. The case study aimed at answering the validation questions 1 to 4 that have been presented at the beginning of Section 6.4.6. It remains to be validated whether the experiment results can be reused to predict the performance of a different software (validation question 5). For this, we deployed a different software on the same execution environment and reused the derived overhead model from the TPC-W case study to predict its performance. As a software application, we chose an implementation of the RUBiS benchmark.

Validation Scenario

The RUBiS application is a web-based auctioning system modeled after eBay.com [JMOa]. The implementation is based on Java servlets and uses a MySQL database.

For deployment, we used a deployment scenario from the TPC-W case study: The web server components were deployed on the first virtual machine running Fedora 12 Linux and the database was deployed on the second virtual machine running Windows 7. The configuration of the execution environment, i.e. the hypervisor, the operating systems and the used middleware, was identical to the configuration used in the TPC-W case study.

Execution

We first created a PCM performance model of the RUBiS application by measuring servlet and database requests in a scenario without resource contention (i.e. using a single-user load scenario).

Figure 6.16 shows the results of an initial performance prediction with the model for a single-user workload. The prediction yielded average request response times of 100.8 ms compared to a measured response time average of 120 ms. This is a prediction error of approx. 16% for the initial model which we considered low enough to continue the case study with this model. Similar to the TPC-W case study, we increased the workload

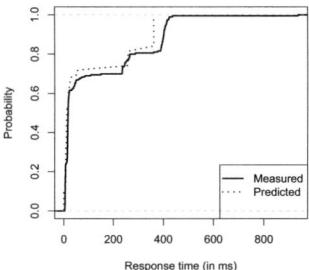

Figure 6.16.: Case study response times for single-user workload

(i.e. the number of parallel users) on the RUBiS system and compared the predicted response times with the measured response times.

Results

In this case study, we increased the number of parallel users accessing the RUBiS system up to 500. Note that the number of users is much higher than in the TPC-W benchmark although the same execution environment is used. For the case study, we used the standard workload configuration, which is shipped with the RUBiS benchmark. This workload configuration contains much larger user think times than workload model used for the TPC-W case study. Hence, the RUBiS system can serve considerably more users than the TPC-W system when running on the same execution environment.

Table 6.8.: Average response times for different numbers of parallel users (in brackets: prediction error)

Contention (# users)	Measured	Predicted w/o overhead model	Predicted with overhead model
1	120 ms	100.76 ms (16%)	
50	194.23 ms	184.47 ms (5.0%)	239.37 ms (23.2%)
100	1521.19 ms	447.63 ms (70.6%)	1218.33 ms (19.9%)
200	9590.35 ms	5277.35 ms (45.0%)	8291.42 ms (13.5%)
500	26630 ms	20506 ms (23.0%)	27692 ms (4.0%)

Table 6.8 gives an overview on the measured and predicted results for the RUBiS system with different user workloads. When using the overhead model derived by the GINPEX experiment, the prediction error is reduced in 3 out of 4 cases. For 50 parallel users, the original model still yields better predicted response times. If the number of parallel users is increased up to 500, the overhead model yields better results and reduced the prediction error from 23%–70% to 4%–20%.

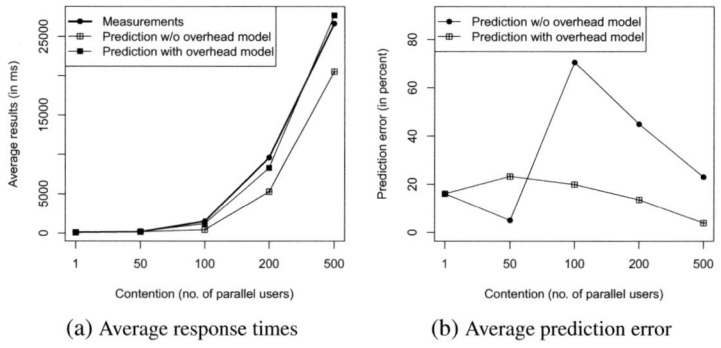

(a) Average response times   (b) Average prediction error

Figure 6.17.: Average case study prediction results and prediction error for different user workloads

A graphical illustration of the average response times and the prediction errors is given in Figure 6.17. The figures plot the results of both prediction methods (with and without the overhead model). Although using the overhead model does not yield such a strong prediction error reduction for the RUBiS predictions as for the TPC-W predictions, the prediction accuracy is still improved when using the load-dependent overhead model.

6.5. Discussion

In the previous sections, we presented two experiments which aim at detecting resource demand overheads that are introduced on a virtualization platform. In this section, we shortly discuss how the GINPEX approach can be applied to detect another factor influencing the performance in virtualized environments, which is the slowdown that can be experienced due to additional load present on the platform. In addition, we discuss several limitations and assumptions of the presented experiments for detecting virtualization properties.

6.5.1. Additional Load

Although additional load is not a direct property of the virtualization platform, it may still be useful to detect such load using an experiment in a similar way as the experiments presented so far. Often, the performance analyst has only little information concerning the load that is present on a platform, for example if he migrates a software to a server where other software services are deployed as well. In the case of virtualized environments, additional load might be present due to other virtual machines issuing load on the same hypervisor. While the latter case can be especially relevant in the context of cloud computing environments, it poses additional challenges where no extensive solution is available yet. However, we will discuss some of the challenges and possible solutions in this chapter.

6.5.1.1. Experiment Design

The idea of the experiment is as follows. For a specified duration (this is an experiment configuration parameter), different system performance counters are measured on the involved virtual machines. Typical performance counters could be CPU utilization, read and written disk load, or sent and received network load. For each performance counter, a set of measurements is obtained that is used to derive a probability density function which reflects the distribution of load during the monitoring time.

As with the other experiments provided in this thesis, this experiment can be implemented for automated execution by using the GINPEX experiment metamodel. The GINPEX experiment definition consists of WaitTasks which are executed for the specified experiment duration. For each Wait-Task, a set of sensors is specified for monitoring the relevant performance counters. For monitoring the CPU utilization, the CpuUtilizationSensor can be used (see Section 4.4.4). For additional performance counters, no appropriate sensor is specified in the core metamodel. Hence, we apply the mechanisms described in Section 4.7.3 to extend the metamodel with additional sensors and sensor logic. For providing sensor logic, we use the Sigar library [VMw], a cross-platform Java API for monitoring various system performance counters. We created additional sensor metamodel elements for monitoring the number of bytes read and written to the disk as well as elements for monitoring the number of bytes sent and received over the network. For each sensor, the corresponding experiment code generation templates were specified that provide the sensor logic (including access to the Sigar library). The metamodel extension, together with the Sigar library and the sensor logic calling the Sigar API, can be made available as a GINPEX addon that can be installed with GINPEX .

After executing the experiment, the experiment results (i.e. the derived probability density functions) are used to derive a performance model that features the load characteristics as observed on the target platform. In the case of performance prediction, the performance analyst typically should have a performance model of the software available for which he is interested in answering performance questions. Regarding our approach, the detected model of additional platform load should be seamlessly integrated into the performance analysis model. Hence, we adopted the experiment to provide a model of additional load that directly plugs into a performance prediction model of the Palladio Component Model (PCM): For each derived probability density function, a corresponding PCM component and PCM usage profile is created. The load distribution described by the function is converted into a PCM resource demand that is issued to the system resources during performance analysis. The created PCM objects can be directly joined with the existing PCM model provided by the software architect. He can then conduct a performance analysis, for example by using the PCM simulation SimuCom, to predict the performance of the software while reflecting the additional load existing on the target platform. To obtain these predictions, he does not have to deploy the software on the platform and execute it in parallel to the existing load.

6.5.1.2. Example

To illustrate how additional load can be detected experimentally and reflected in performance prediction, we conducted a small case study where we used the TPC-W system from the case studies presented in Section 6.3.7 and Section 6.4.6.1. This case study demonstrates how the experiment creates a model of the system load and how this model can be used to increase performance prediction accuracy. We deploy the TPC-W system on the same environment used in Section 6.4.6.1: On a quad-core server (Intel Core i7-860, 2.80 GHz, 8 GB RAM) running a virtualization hypervisor (XenCenter 5.6), two virtual machines were deployed. The first VM running Fedora 12 Linux (kernel 2.6.31) hosted the TPC-W web server and servlet components, the second VM running Windows 7 hosted the TPC-W database server. In addition, we set up a third VM running Fedora 12 Linux (kernel 2.6.31) that shared the same hardware resources as the other VMs. On this VM, we generated synthetic CPU and disk load. This load is not related to the TPC-W application, but expected to have a performance impact on the TPC-W response times. Figure 6.18 gives an overview on the deployment scenario.

To generate synthetic load, two processes were running on the third VM. The first process generated exponentially distributed CPU load every second yielding an average CPU utilization of 25%. The second process generated exponentially distributed disk load every second. The process yielded an average disk load of 5 MB read bytes/sec and 5 MB written bytes/sec.

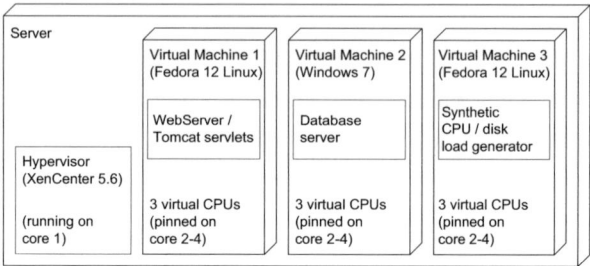

Figure 6.18.: TPC-W case study deployment scenario

We then conducted the GINPEX experiment on the virtual machine, monitoring the load situation for 15 minutes. Figure 6.19 shows the measured results of the experiment. The results are displayed a probability density functions. Based on these results, a performance model was generated that extended the PCM model of the TPC-W application in order to reflect the additional load.

We then executed the standard TPC-W WIPSo workload mix with 1 user and measured the response times whilst the synthetic load was still issued on the third VM. In addition, we conducted a PCM performance prediction of the TPC-W application both with and without the derived additional load model. The results are shown in Table 6.9. In the first prediction run, we did not include the derived load model. The predictions yielded an average response time of 17.9 ms. Compared to a measured average response time of 28.3 ms, the prediction error was higher than 36%. In the second run, the derived load model was reflected in the prediction. In this case, the prediction yielded an average response time of 25.5 ms, leading to a prediction error of approx. 10%. Hence, including the derived model in performance prediction led to a prediction error that was over three times lower compared to the original prediction.

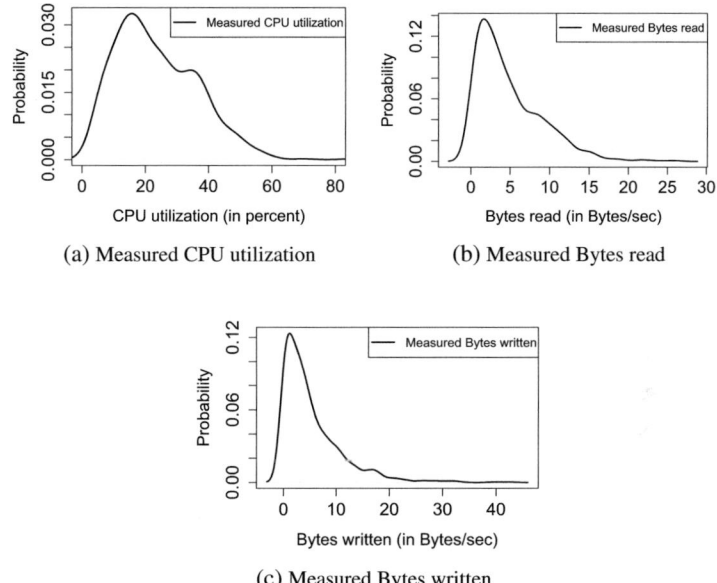

(a) Measured CPU utilization

(b) Measured Bytes read

(c) Measured Bytes written

Figure 6.19.: Results of the additional load experiment: derived probability density functions

6.5.1.3. Open Issues

In the case study presented in the previous section, the additional load performance model derived by the experiment led to a significant decrease in the response time prediction error. While the derived performance model is rather simple, it already shows how prediction accuracy can be increased by using an automatically derived model of additional load. However, its simplicity also introduces some shortcomings which we discuss in the following.

First, the approach to measure existing load for creating a model might not be appropriate in all situations. Load might change in predictable or unpredictable ways, and in most cases the software architect would then be interested to predict the performance of a software while reflecting a fu-

Table 6.9.: Average response times for the TPC-W case study (in brackets: prediction error)

Type	Avg. response time
Measured	28.3 ms
Predicted w/o additional load model	17.9 ms (36.8%)
Predicted with additional load model	25.5 ms (10%)

ture load situation. However, measuring existing load can give an initial idea on how a software behaves on a virtualized environment where existing services are competing for the same resources. In addition, in some cases services create a constant amount of load on the platform which is not about to change in the future. In this case, the performance analysts can confidently include such load in performance models.

In addition, the experiment could be extended in order to use a more sophisticated approach for detecting additional load and deriving a corresponding performance model. Such approaches have for example be proposed in [ZJY+09] and [LFG+10]. These approaches aim at taking into account workload burstiness. Such burstiness could for example be detected in a precedent experiment. After measuring the burstiness of existing system load, this information could be used to automatically adapt the duration of the experiment presented above.

Another major drawback of the experiment design is that it currently requires access to the machine for taking measurements. This is the case for all experiments presented in this thesis, however it poses additional challenges when this experiment is to be executed in different virtualized environments or cloud computing environments. In such environments, additional load is often present which may compete for shared hardware resources. In this case, including such load in performance prediction can be especially valuable, but detecting the load is much harder than in a controlled environment. For instance, access to the machine on which the load is issued is not possible in such environments. As an alternative, measurements could be taken on the hypervisor level. This might be possible if the model is to be derived by the infrastructure provider. In this case, the focus would not be on software performance prediction, but on capacity planning or infrastructure management. However, taking measurements on the hypervisor level would require adapting the experiment sensor logic, as access to performance counters inside a hypervisor strongly depends from the used hypervisor technology.

In the example presented in the previous section, we executed an instance of the TPC-W application with a single-user workload and predicted the effects of additional load. For multi-user workloads, the model of additional load should be combined with an experimentally derived model of load-dependent overhead (see Section 6.4). How both models can be combined for performance prediction is subject to future work.

6.5.2. Limitations and Assumptions

In this chapter, we presented three experiments for detecting different performance-relevant properties of the virtualization platform. This section discusses some limitations and assumptions of the experiments.

Large number of involved machines. In some environments, the number of involved virtual machines can become very large. For example, in a large grid or cloud environment, the experiment for detecting a load-dependent overhead model would require to run on all available virtual machines. In this case, the overall experiment runtime would increase strongly (see Section 6.4.2). To overcome this issue, a subset of machines should be chosen for executing the experiment. For the experiments, machines with different configurations should be selected, e.g. machines with different operating systems, different network connections, a different setup of virtual machines, or different virtualized operating systems. However, when performing the experiment on one physical machine featuring multiple virtualized machines, the experiment can be used to derive an overhead model that takes into account both hypervisor overheads and guest OS overheads. In this case, the number of needed experiment runs is acceptable.

Microbenchmark selection. The experiments for detecting the simple virtualization overhead model and the load-dependent overhead model use the microbenchmarks provided by the GINPEX metamodel. These microbenchmarks cover different types of resource load, but might not be sufficient to detect all possible patterns of overhead introduced by the virtualization platform. It is always a challenge to select a suitable set of microbenchmarks. However, the GINPEX approach allows for easily exchanging microbenchmarks, if different microbenchmarks are available that appear more suited. In the presented case studies, the chosen microbenchmarks for generating CPU, disk, and network load already yielded an overhead model that improved prediction results significantly.

Controlled environment. The experiments for detecting the simple virtualization overhead model and the load-dependent overhead model require to be executed in a controlled environment, i.e. access to all involved virtual machines is possible. In the case studies, we conducted these experiments with no additional load on the platform that might disturb the measurements. The third experiment presented in this chapter illustrates how the problem of additional load can be tackled by deriving a model of the additional load for performance prediction. However, this thesis does not investigate how additional load affects the results of the overhead model experiments. This is regarded as future work.

Additional virtualization properties. The experiment presented in this chapter only cover a subset of performance-relevant virtualization properties. Other performance-relevant properties are not yet reflected by automated experiments. For example, hypervisor scheduling properties or fine-grained resource allocation using caps, shares or priorities might influence the software performance, and should be included separately in the performance analysis in this case.

6.6. Summary

In this chapter, we presented three experiments to detect various virtualization properties. The first experiment detects overhead that is introduced when a software is migrated to a virtualized environment. The detected overhead model is quite simple: for each type of resource demand, a fixed overhead factor is calculated. A case study with an implementation of the TPC-W benchmark showed that the model can only reduce the performance prediction error for predictions with a low number of concurrent users. To improve the performance prediction for a larger number of parallel users, we extended the overhead model in the second experiment. This experiment detects a load-dependent overhead model which improved prediction accuracy significantly in the TPC-W case study. To show that the overhead model can be applied to the performance prediction of different software applications, we reused the detected overhead model in another case study. Here, we predicted the performance of a different software (an implementation of the RUBiS benchmark). In a third experiment, we illustrated how the GINPEX approach can be used to detect additional load that is present in virtualized environments, and how the derived performance model can be used to increase prediction accuracy.

Compared to the experiments presented in Chapter 5, this chapter's experiments focus on a different experiment domain and show that the GINPEX approach is not restricted to a certain part of the software execution

233

environment. In Chapter 8, we will discuss possible extensions of the GIN-PEX approach to different experiment domains.

7. Related Work

In this chapter, we discuss related work from different domains, i.e. performance engineering approaches that support modeling the execution environment, approaches that aim at deriving performance models through automated experiments, as well as work that deals with the performance analysis of CPU, OS scheduling, and virtualization properties.

7.1. Modeling the Execution Environment for Performance Prediction

In recent years, a number of software performance engineering approaches have been developed. Surveys on performance evaluation approaches can be found in [BDIS04] (model-based approaches) and [Koz10] (performance evaluation of component-based systems).

The Unified Modeling Language (UML) [Obj11c] is a widespread modeling language which is mostly used for modeling object-oriented software systems. It includes basic concepts for modeling the execution environment. Using UML profiles, UML models can be extended with domain specific models. For example, the UML Profile for Schedulability, Performance and Time (UML-SPT) [Obj05] and the UML Profile for MARTE (Modeling and Analysis of Real-time and Embedded Systems) [Obj11d] extend the UML core model with concepts for modeling resource usage and performance-relevant properties. Although the primary focus of these profiles lies on embedded systems, they can also be used to model performance aspects of business applications.

Petriu and Woodside [PW04] introduced an intermediate model that serves as a bridge between UML-SPT models and low-level models for performance analysis, such as queueing networks or timed Petri nets. However, support of performance properties of the execution environment is limited. For an active resource, only the attributes 'time per operation' and 'scheduling policy' can be specified. Detailed performance properties are not reflected by the transformations.

Other approaches use proprietary metamodels for specifying software systems and corresponding performance-relevant information for performance analysis. ROBOCOP [BMdW$^+$04] and CUTS [SBHS06] feature component models that can be used for performance prediction of real-time systems. However, as discussed in Section 3.1.3, the models do not provide a separation of the execution environment model from the software architecture model: In both models, component resource demands have to be specified in milliseconds. Hence, adopting the software model for a different execution environment requires changing the resource demands in the software model as well.

Grassi et al. [GMS07] provide a metamodel called KLAPER, which can serve as an intermediate model for different component models and performance analysis models. Due to its simplicity, it does not distinguish between component services and resource services of the execution environment. Hence, it provides only limited functionality for extending performance analysis with execution environment properties.

Furthermore, the Palladio Component Model (PCM), which has been employed in this thesis, falls into this category of metamodels for performance analysis. The PCM has been described in Chapter 2. Since it provides various ways for extending the model with execution environment properties [HKKR09, KDH$^+$12], it is suited for extending software performance predictions with execution environment properties.

7.2. Deriving Performance Models through Automated Measurements

Related work w.r.t. deriving performance models through measurements can be distinguished into the following areas: (i) approaches tightly connected to software performance engineering with the focus of a measurement-based derivation of performance models, (ii) frameworks for benchmarking automation, and (iii) tools and approaches for workload generation and performance measurements.

Software Performance Engineering Approaches

In [WFP07], Woodside argued that better software performance engineering methods are needed to converge measurement and modeling approaches. This work is targeted in this direction, but it is by far not the only one.

Liu et al. [LFG05] developed a benchmark suite for measuring certain performance-relevant parameters of the J2EE middleware platform. The measurements are fed into a performance model of the middleware. This model can then be integrated with a performance model of a software running on the J2EE platform, allowing the software architect to conduct performance analyses at early stages of the software life-cycle. While this work, like our approach, aims at decoupling the software performance model from a performance model of the execution environment, it only focuses on J2EE EJB measurements. Underlying effects stemming from the hardware or the operating system are included in the measurements, making it difficult to decouple the middleware model from the underlying platform. The approach has been extended by Zhu et al. [ZLBG07] with a tool that automatically generates a performance model based on UML diagrams and corresponding benchmarking code for benchmarking the J2EE environment. Compared to our approach, the resulting measurements are generated based on the software architecture description. We focus on the model-driven generation of execution environment experiments that are agnostic to the software system under analysis.

Woodside et al. use so-called resource functions to derive a performance model based on measured resource demands [WVCB01]. The resource functions are based on regression splines and describe a software resource demand as a function of execution environment and user workload properties. In [ZWL08], Zheng et al. use Kalman filters to estimate hidden performance-relevant parameters through performance measurements. Both approaches are based on measurements taken on the software architecture level, and the resulting model cannot be reused for a different software model.

In [KKR10], runtime measurements of Java bytecode instructions are collected in order to extend a performance model with bytecode timings that are specific to the execution environment. By mapping software resource demands to the bytecode timings, the software architecture model can be kept independent from the platform-specific timings. The identification of timing values and the subsequent configuration of the software model occurs in an automated way. While this approach shares several ideas with our approach (e.g. automatically deriving execution environment properties or separating the execution environment model from the software architecture model), it aims at a specific part of the execution environment and cannot be applied to different execution environment properties.

Thakkar et al. [THHF08] present a framework for creating performance models based on measurements. The framework encompasses the conceptual steps that are needed from taking the measurements to building the performance model. While the framework has a similar workflow as our approach (experiment preparation, execution, analysis, model building), it does not include a formal model for specifying the structure of an experiment. In addition, it is a conceptional framework only for which no implementation is available. Hence, it is unclear how the approach can be adapted for different kinds of experiments.

The Software Performance Cockpit (SoPeCo) [WHHH10] is a tool for the systematic execution of performance experiments. It provides a meta-model for specifying experiment designs. While the SoPeCo is more generic than the GINPEX approach (it can be used to derive models for any software component that can be measured using typical experiment designs), it cannot be used to model fine-grained experiment execution logic, like the experiment logic used in the OS scheduling experiments in Chapter 5. On the other hand, GINPEX experiments might benefit from the predefined logic for executing different experiment designs.

Other approaches aim at extending software architecture models using the concept of performance-related completions proposed by Woodside et al. [WPS02]. Happe et al. [HBR+10] present an approach for including middleware performance completions into model-based performance prediction. A performance model of middleware components is weaved into a software architecture model using model-driven techniques. In [Kap11], this approach is extended to general performance completions that support modeling variability of completions. Higher-order transformations are used to generate transformations for weaving the completions into the software architecture model. These approaches provide a mechanism to include execution environment properties on the model level. This means that execution environment properties are specified using elements provided by the corresponding meta-model. The performance analysis (which is based on the software architecture model) is typically left unchanged. On the other hand, some properties of the execution environment require adapting the performance analysis as well. In this case, a completion approach that is located at the model level is not sufficient. For example, the OS scheduling properties that are detected by the experiments presented in Chapter 5 require configuring the analysis part (in our case, performance simulation tooling) as well. However, other parts of the execution environment properties might be configurable using model completions. In this case, GINPEX experiments results can be used to configure a such a completion.

Benchmarking Frameworks

Compared to the approaches for automatically deriving performance models presented in the last section, the following frameworks focus on the aspect of automated benchmarking.

Courson et al. [CMMT00] define an automated benchmarking toolset that is defined around a common data format for storing benchmarking configurations and results. The toolset aims at automating the definition and execution of benchmarks. In our approach, we propose a more fine-grained model for specifying the execution logic of performance experiments. On the other hand, our approach shares with the benchmarking toolset the ability to specify automated results analysis logic for executed benchmarks or performance experiments. However, the toolset is not maintained anymore and it is not publicly available.

A generic tool for the automation of benchmark execution is presented by Kalibera et al. [KLM⁺06]. It consists of a benchmarking framework for planning benchmark executions and storing the benchmark results, and an execution framework that facilitates the automated execution of benchmarks in a distributed environment. While the tool can be used to automate the deployment and execution of benchmarks, it does not cover storing predefined benchmark runs together with automated results evaluation.

The same holds for the GridBench tool presented by Tsouloupas and Dikaiakos [TD06]. This tool aims at automating benchmarks that are to be executed in large Grid environments. Various micro-benchmarks for measuring CPU, cache, memory and I/O effects are supported, but the results have to be analyzed through human reasoning. In contrast, in this thesis we focus on the automated execution of experiments, which also includes automated evaluation of results. In addition, our approach focuses on deriving properties that can directly be included in performance engineering tools.

Weevil is a framework that supports the automated execution of experiments in highly distributed systems [WRCW05]. It shares with our approach the idea of automating and encapsulating predefined experiments and the model-based approach of specifying the experiment setup (which consists of a system under test model and a testbed model in Weevil). The authors also report various metrics to evaluate the benefits of the framework's automation features, which has not been done yet for the GINPEX approach. However, the approach has not been applied to directly enhance performance analysis methods, such as models for performance prediction. In addition, the model has a different granularity than the GINPEX metamodel: the details of the experiment logic (called workload in the Weevil framework) have to be provided by writing code. We selected various microbenchmarks for experiment execution that can be easily assembled to experiments without having to write code; we argue that using microbenchmarks in a model and extending the model with additional microbenchmarks facilitates the creation of experiments and is sufficient to provide a powerful base for specifying experiment logic.

SKaMPI is a tool for executing MPI benchmarks [RSPM98]. It provides various predefined functions for MPI measurements. Benchmarks have to be specified programatically by writing C code. Hence, it provides a powerful basis for specifying experiments, but it also requires low-level knowledge on building and executing benchmark runs. In addition, the authors note that they have no experience with running SKaMPI on machines with many processors [AW08].

Workload Generation and Performance Measurements

In the following, we discuss related tools and approaches that focus on workload generation and performance measurements.

Apache JMeter [Thea] is a tool for load-testing web applications. It can be used for specifying load-test scripts which are then executed by JMeter to issue load on a web server or a network. It can be extended with custom adapters for issuing load as well as custom analysis and results visualization logic. Our metamodel for specifying the execution logic of experiments shares some similarities with the JMeter logic controllers when it comes to specifying the order of requests. However, we focus on issuing microbenchmarks for performing experiments to automatically detect execution environment properties, whereas JMeter aims at load-testing applications. Hence, the tool does not provide predefined analysis logic of the measurement results. Instead, the user has to evaluate the results manually depending on the load-testing scenario for which he configured JMeter.

Faban is another framework for automated workload generation [Fab]. It supports the benchmark execution and workload generation in heterogeneous, distributed systems, including remote agent management, automated distribution of benchmark code, and collection of result metrics. It shares with GINPEX the focus on automating workload generation and collection of measurements, as well as the idea of formally specifying the distributed system setup. However, it does not support structuring experiments using parametric dependencies.

Iometer is a tool for generating and measuring I/O workload [Iom]. Hence, the focus is on measuring the performance of special parts of the execution environment that are related to I/O load, such as network and disk resources. It consists of a controlling component for configuration the workload and controlling its execution, and a workload generator component for generating disk or network load. Workload configuration and system setup can be configured using a graphical user interface. As it is restricted to generating network and disk load, it cannot be used for experiments that involve measuring CPU load. In addition, Iometer does not support the specification of predefined experiments which include automated analysis logic.

A classification of tools and frameworks for conducting Internet and TPC/IP measurements has been compiled at [Theb]. The taxonomy provides a fine-grained categorization and reports input and output parameters as well as the functionality of each tool. The classification has not been maintained in recent years. In addition, it is not connected to performance engineering approaches, but it could serve a starting point for evaluating tools that could be reused for GINPEX experiments detecting network properties.

The same holds for the Yahoo! Cloud Serving Benchmark (YCSB) [CST+10], which aims at facilitating performance comparisons of cloud-based systems using mainly I/O workloads for reading from and writing to cloud data stores. The workloads provide various properties to specify the I/O behavior, such as the I/O operation, which record and how many records to access, or which kind of data to write. GINPEX could benefit from these workloads, if it was applied to specifying automated experiments that focus on Cloud data serving systems.

Gropp and Lusk [GL99] describe various difficulties that can occur when measuring MPI performance characteristics. The authors provide possible solutions for some identified issues, but not for all of them. In addition, the covered issues only partially apply to generic execution environment experiments. Other parts of the execution environment properties might impose different challenges. For example, fine-grained timing measurements might not always work in virtual machines. For VMware virtualization products, extensive documentation is available on how to obtain accurate timing measurements [VMw11].

A generic approach to support the execution of performance experiments in order to yield robust, reliable, and reproducible results is DataMill, published by de Oliviera et al. [dOPRF13]. It aims at automatically quantifying the effects of hidden factors in experiment results and shielding the user from having to deal with the underlying mechanisms for detecting such hidden factors. This is done by automatically executing user-specified benchmarks while varying possible influencing factors, such as compiler flags, the reboot behavior between benchmark runs, or mechanisms to avoid memory effects, such as warm caches. GINPEX uses different techniques to support the specification of experiments yielding robust results, such as the automated iteration of tasks until a stable stop condition criteria is reached. However, GINPEX experiments might benefits from additional techniques to detect hidden performance factors, such as the ones covered by DataMill. In this case, it has to be investigated, how the highly platform-specific factors used in DataMill (for example, some of them are strongly related to Linux kernel configuration options), can be included in a GINPEX setup aiming at platform-independent execution of experiments (where the access of low-level operating system calls are avoided). Including DataMill techniques into GINPEX might be possible with less efforts if GINPEX experiments were restricted to run on Linux platforms only.

7.3. Performance Analysis Reflecting CPU and OS Scheduling Properties

The performance impact of processors and operating systems has been extensively evaluated. Especially for the domain of embedded systems, where little abstraction from CPU and OS behavior exists, detailed knowledge of the performance-relevant factors is necessary. A large body of research exists in this field. In [DB11], a survey is presented that compares and classifies different real-time scheduling strategies and discusses the performance implications of the strategies.

Brandenburg et al. [BCA08] compared different scheduling algorithms by measuring their performance and assessing the performance overhead the algorithms impose on the system. They come to the conclusion that these overheads can be significant when it comes to scaling the algorithms to higher numbers of processors. Although we focus on properties that are relevant in the area of performance analysis of business applications, this work shows that the used scheduling strategy can have a strong impact on the performance especially in multi-core environments. Schroeder et al.

[SWHB06] come to a similar conclusion. They analyzed different open and closed workloads and discovered that the selected scheduling policy can influence the performance of a software by several orders of magnitude.

On the other hand, many approaches for performance analysis only use abstract scheduling policies such as processor sharing or one of its variants, or priority preemptive scheduling. The Layered Queueing Network Solver (LQNS) provides various abstract scheduling policies, but leaves it up to the user which one to specify for the modeled processors [FMW+12]. The same holds for QPME (Queueing Petri net Modeling Environment), which provides a simulator for analyzing the performance of a software system using a queueing Petri net model [KSM10]. Here, processor sharing, first come, first served and infinite server are supported as queueing disciplines (which conform to scheduling policies if the modeled queues represent servers).

In recent years, performance models emerged which supported more fine-grained, realistic scheduling strategies.

In [Hap08], an extensive performance model of various OS scheduling properties is provided. The model covers properties which are also supported by the experiments presented in this thesis, such as the OS scheduling timeslice length or load-balancing strategies. This thesis builds on this work by extending an performance analysis approach with the automatic detection of such properties.

Another performance model for operating system scheduling has been presented by Kawasaki et al. [KGC+06]. The authors provide a Markov model of the Linux O(1) scheduler that is used for simulating the performance effects of different resource allocation policies. In [CCF+06], an analytical model of the Linux O(1) scheduler is presented for analyzing the scheduler's load balancing performance on Non-Uniform Memory Access (NUMA) systems. While both approaches also use a detailed scheduler model for performance analysis, the models are tailored towards the Linux O(1) scheduler and cannot be reused for different schedulers.

All these approaches have in common that they provide fine-grained performance models of the operating system scheduler, but they are either tailored towards a specific scheduler, or manual efforts are necessary in order to adapt the model parameters for different schedulers. Our approach uses measurements to detect the scheduler behavior on the target platform and thus facilitates the automated instantiation of scheduler models for performance prediction.

Ahmad et al. [AMM⁺94] use neural networks to predict the performance of different load-balancing strategies. The network is trained using simulation data and then used to predict parameter data for a performance model using a simple queueing network with first come, first served scheduling. While this approach is applicable to a variety of load balancing policies (depending on the parameters that are supported by the neural network and the queueing network), it only supports analysis of mean response times, and has only been validated using simulation data. The predicted results have not been compared to measurements of a real system.

Peternier et al. [PBYC13] aim at predicting the response time of software applications executed in parallel on multi-core platforms. They patched the Linux kernel to record scheduler events in order to derive a prediction model that captures performance effects of the operating system and the software application. The approach requires adapting the Linux kernel and thus only works on Linux machines. In addition, it derives a performance model that is tightly coupled to the software application. It cannot be reused for prediction the performance of a different application on the same machine. In contrast, the experiments presented in this thesis aim at separating the infrastructure model from the application model.

7.4. Performance Analysis of Virtualized Environments

In the following, approaches are discusses that are related to this thesis w.r.t. performance analysis of virtualized environments and load-dependent performance overhead.

Since the advent of virtualization products for widespread hardware platforms, various publications have been published that deal with performance modeling of virtualized environments. Menascé [Men05] modeled the performance impact of server consolidation with virtual machines using analytical queueing network models. The models are used to predict software response times, throughput, and resource utilization when multiple virtual machines are executed on a single hypervisor. Following this approach, the system is modeled at a very abstract level and, due to the use of the analytical models used for analysis, only yields rough performance estimates (i.e. average times only). The approach also requires access to the virtualization hypervisor for taking measurements in order to calculate the slowdown due to virtualization. Other approaches provide virtualization models for different performance analysis scenarios, such as predicting resource overheads due to provisioning and instantiation of virtual machines [SKF06] or virtual clusters [YMM07].

In [CG05], Cherkasova & Gardner measure the CPU overhead that occurs during I/O processing for the Xen virtualization platform. They propose a measurement and monitoring framework, but the approach is only applicable to the Xen hypervisor and is restricted to network I/O overhead only.

Wood et al. [WCOS08] use microbenchmarks to estimate performance overheads that occur when migrating a software to a virtualized environment. They focus on different kinds of virtualization overhead, but only concentrate on analyzing resource requirements, not on changes in response times. A similar approach is taken in [BFS$^+$06], where virtualization overhead is derived based on generated workload and integrated into a simple queueing model. Compared to our approach, this approach requires taking measurements on the hypervisor level and thus is not applicable in scenarios where hypervisor access is restricted. In addition, the overhead model is constant and neglects load-dependent overheads.

Iosup et al. [IOY+11] aim at measuring performance properties of cloud computing platforms. The authors focus on cloud computing services for scientific computing. However, the measurement results are not used for integration into analysis tools, e.g. for performance prediction. In [LZJ+11], an approach is presented to model the relationship of resources across virtual and physical layers in order to perform a runtime calibration for estimating resource utilization. Again, this approach requires access to the hypervisor for taking measurements.

Various approaches instrument the target software [TR12] or profile the target software [CAS+12] to obtain a performance model for predicting the performance impact on increased load. Tarvo and Reiss [TR12] simulate the performance of multi-threaded software applications using a very fine-grained application model that is derived using a combination of manual program analysis and instrumentation of program code and the Linux kernel. The model reflects the performance effects of multiple parallel requests to the operating system and hardware resources. The Kismet tool [JGLT11] uses code instrumentation to estimate the parallel speedup that can achieved for unparallelized programs. This is done using an extension of the critical path analysis method. Chen et al. [CAS+12] create a load-dependent queueing model based on the measured CPU utilization, the number of held spin locks, and the disk throughput during program execution. The model is then solved using an adapted mean value analysis algorithm to predict the response times of concurrently executed applications. These approaches are not restricted to virtualized environments, but they are related to the load-dependent overhead model presented in Chapter 6. However, our approach does not require instrumenting or measuring the target software in order to gain a model that explains the effects on high concurrency levels. We include such effects in performance analysis by deriving a load-dependent overhead model based on measuring microbenchmarks.

Mian et al. [MMVP13] generate a performance model of data-intensive workloads running in Cloud environments through sampling and taking measurements. A linear model is used as a performance model in the first instance. If the measurements show a non-linear behavior, non-linear modeling based on radial basis functions is used. The authors focus on measuring effects on the software level that cannot be easily mapped to effects stemming from the execution environment. Also, no tool support is available for adopting the technique. However, starting with linear models first in order to reduce the overhead for deriving the model seems to be a promising approach that could also be used for obtaining certain execution environment properties experimentally.

7.5. Summary

In this chapter, we discussed related work for different areas. While the presented approaches cover a wide range of functionality necessary for automatically deriving performance-relevant execution environment properties, they also have certain limitations:

- Many approaches require manual analysis of experiment results and/or manually including the results in performance prediction.

- Only a few approaches are applicable to a wide range of execution environment properties; many approaches focus on a certain part or property of the execution environment.

- Some approaches have not been implemented, but are only defined on a conceptional level.

8. Conclusions

In this chapter, we first summarize the contributions of this thesis. Then, we give an overview on the discussions on limitations and assumptions provided in this thesis. We continue with presenting additional application areas where the approach or parts of the approach can be or have been applied. Finally, we present several directions for future research.

8.1. Summary

This thesis introduced GINPEX, a novel approach for deriving performance-relevant execution environment properties through automated experiments. The experiments can be executed by a performance analyst who is shielded from having to deal with internal details of the execution environment or the design of experiments. In the following, we summarize the contributions of this thesis.

An approach for the automated derivation of execution environment properties. In this thesis, we introduced an approach which aims at encapsulating domain knowledge that is needed for retrieving execution environment properties into automated experiments. Following the approach, an experiment designer can design such experiments in advance which are then stored for later reuse by performance analysts. For executing experiments, the performance analyst has to deploy a small application called Load Driver on the target platform(s) which is responsible for retrieving the experiment specification and executing the experiment. Every experiment aims at deriving the value of a certain execution environment property, e.g. a CPU property (such as the number of CPU cores), a property of the operating system (such as the timeslice length of the scheduler), or a property of the virtualization environment. During an experiment, certain load patterns are issued on the target platform and simple performance metrics, such as response times or CPU utilization, are measured. The measured results reported by the Load Driver are then used to execute predefined experiment analysis. The analysis derives the execution environment property value based on the measured results using predefined algorithms. To fully automate the process of reflecting execution environment properties in performance analysis, the experiment results can be automatically integrated into a performance analysis approach. In this thesis, we utilized the Palladio Component Model (PCM) for performance prediction, which we adapted for supporting the specification of execution environment properties in a model that is independent from the software architecture model. This way, the derived execution environment properties can be reused for the performance analysis of a different software without the need to repeat the executed experiments. The approach regards the execution environment as a black box, i.e. it does not require access to low-level (technology-specific) resources. Instead, it aims at provoking an execution environment behavior through specific load patterns using microbenchmarks. From observing the influence of the execution environment on measurements, conclusions about the property in focus can be drawn. A black box approach supports the definition of experiments that are platform-independent and thus widely applicable. Furthermore, this thesis introduced different concepts in order to implement the approach:

- A workflow describes how to apply the approach for designing and executing experiments;

- A metamodel for the specification of experiments (see below);

- Concepts for structuring execution environment domains and storing predefined experiments;

- A concept for coupling experiments through parametric experiment dependencies.

A metamodel for the specification of execution environment experiments. In order to facilitate the efficient specification of experiments, this thesis introduces a metamodel for specifying experiments and experiment logic. The former part of the metamodel provides constructs for grouping experiments in experiment domains as well as specifying experiments, experiment dependencies, and the involved machines of the execution environment. The latter part focuses on specifying the experiment logic which includes the control flow of the experiment, tasks for generating load through microbenchmarks, as well as sensors indicating at which part of the experiment certain measurements have to be taken. In addition, the following contributions were made:

- An experiment template for describing and documenting experiments in a non-formal way;

- A discussion of various possibilities for extending the approach with additional experiment domains, experiments, experiment metamodel tasks and sensors, as well as experiment analysis logic;

- A discussion on the performance overhead of executing experiments.

Experiment designs for detecting CPU, OS scheduling, and virtualization properties. In this thesis, we applied the GINPEX approach to various experiments that aim at detecting properties from different parts of the execution environment. The execution environment properties in focus comprise CPU, OS scheduling and virtualization properties. These experiments show (i) that execution environment properties can be detected automatically using predefined experiments, and (ii) that the experiments can be run on different platform technologies. For example, we applied the OS scheduling experiment to different Windows and Linux schedulers and showed that the experiment detects the correct property value on all included platforms. In detail, the thesis contributes automated experiments to detect the following properties:

- The CPU experiments detect simultaneous multithreading (SMT) and the number of available physical and virtual CPU cores;

- The OS scheduling experiments detect the OS scheduler timeslice length as well as the OS load-balancing policy used for initial and dynamic load-balancing;

- The virtualization experiments detect the response time overhead on resource demands introduced by the virtualization hypervisor; in addition the design of an experiment for detecting additional load on the virtualization platform is briefly discussed.

The detected properties differ w.r.t. their prominence in software performance engineering (SPE): While the importance of CPU and operating system scheduling policies for SPE is well known, this thesis provides a novel model reflecting load-dependent virtualization overhead that can be included in software performance analysis. In all cases, the derived model of the execution environment features properties that are independent from the software model.

Validation. We validated the contributions of this thesis in multiple steps. First we evaluated the applicability of the general approach by defining experiments that aim at detecting properties of different parts of the execution environment. Although the properties in focus differed in their level of granularity (for example, the operating system timeslice length is a very fine-grained property compared to virtualization overhead), values of these properties can be detected using the model-based approach presented in this thesis. In addition, the experiments have been validated as follows: For the CPU and OS scheduling experiments, the experiments were executed on different platforms and the detected properties were compared with the CPU and OS specifications. Furthermore, we conducted a case study to evaluate how the set of derived properties impacts the performance prediction accuracy. In the case study, the prediction error could be reduced from over 20% to below 5% in most cases. For the virtualization experiments, different case studies have been performed to evaluate the impact of the derived overhead model on performance prediction. With the simple overhead model derived by the first experiment, the prediction error can only be reduced for a low number of parallel users accessing the software system. With the enhanced overhead model derived by the second experiment, the prediction error could be reduced in most cases from 60%–70% to below 15%. To validate the applicability of the derived overhead model for multiple software applications, we conducted another case study in which we predicted the performance of a different software application. In this case study, the derived overhead model yielded a reduced prediction error from 23–70% to 4%–20%.

8.2. Limitations and Assumptions

We discussed limitations and assumptions of the general approach and the presented experiments in the corresponding chapters. Limitations and assumptions of the general approach have been discussed in Section 3.5. For the CPU and OS scheduling experiments, limitations and assumptions have been covered in Section 5.9. Similarly, limitations and assumptions for the virtualization experiments can be found in Section 6.5.2. Finally, more fine-grained assumptions for each presented experiment can be found in the "Assumptions" section of the corresponding experiment template. All presented experiment templates are also compiled in Appendix B.

8.3. Further Application Areas

In this thesis, we used the GINPEX approach to support the performance analyst in conducting performance analyses. However, the approach (or parts of it) can be applied in different scenarios. In the following, we briefly discuss three of them.

Supporting middleware developers. Automated experiments could also be used to support middleware developers in testing middleware implementations. As experiments detect the properties by observing the execution environment's effects on issued load, they can be applied to new implementations of the execution environment: The developer can run an experiment and check if the derived property value is consistent with the requirements. For instance, the presented experiments for detecting operating system scheduling properties could not only be used to derive such properties for software performance prediction, but also for testing if a new implementation of an operating system scheduler meets certain requirements.

Measuring performance effects in scalable platforms. In an evaluation of scalability effects of virtualization platforms [vK11, KHvKR11], the GINPEX tooling has been used to generate workloads on an IBM z10 machine. The automated GINPEX experiment was executed to measure the effects of elastic virtual CPU resources on microbenchmark response times.

Evaluating approaches to resource demand estimation. In [Spi11], different approaches to resource demand evaluation are discussed and compared. For evaluating these approaches, artificial workloads have been defined using GINPEX, as GINPEX provides the possibility to specify workloads with fixed, predefined resource demands using the different microbenchmark tasks. The resource demands were issued through automated GINPEX experiments and the resulting resource demands estimated by the different resource demand estimation approaches were monitored and evaluated.

8.4. Future Work

In the following, we discuss several possibilities for future work. Future work can be grouped into work regarding the approach in general, and work that extends the presented experiments.

GINPEX Approach for Deriving Execution Environment Properties

Model-based specification of analysis logic. In this thesis, we proposed a metamodel for specifying the structure and logic of experiments. The analysis logic has to be implemented in Java code. Specifying the analysis logic using a metamodel could lead to a more efficient development of experiments. In this case, it has to be investigated which analysis tasks are typically recurring among multiple experiments so that encapsulating these analysis tasks into a metamodel makes sense. It also has to be investigated how a meaningful structure of the analysis logic metamodel should look like.

Mapping performance model constructs to experiments. With an increased number of predefined experiments, an automated approach would be useful to select required experiments based on the software performance model. Automating the selection of experiments could shield the performance analyst from deciding which experiments are needed. Furthermore, the expressiveness of the performance model and the performance analysis approach could also be taken into account when selecting experiments: some parts of the infrastructure might not be relevant for performance analysis (e.g. virtualization experiments can be neglected if the modeled software system is not running in a virtualization environment), or might not be supported by the performance analysis approach (e.g. if the analysis approach does not support the reflection of fine-grained execution environment properties). Automating the experiment selection could for example be obtained by specifying OCL constraints for performance model elements. Constraint checks are then automatically executed for performance model instances and based on the results of the constraint checks, the required experiments are selected.

Additional validation. Additional validation of the approach introduced in this thesis could for instance comprise an empirical investigation of the possible speedup that can be obtained through automated derivation of execution environment properties. This requires a case study involving human participants where one group conducts a performance prediction for a software system using the approach to derive execution environment properties, and another group conducts the same prediction while identifying the performance-relevant execution environment properties manually.

Another validation activity could be a level-III validation [BR08], in which the approach is compared to other performance analysis methods not following the approach w.r.t. the overall improvements of the software development process. Such a validation involves a lot effort, as it requires the execution of two identical projects in an industrial setting, one project applying the approach, and one project neglecting it. Such a validation is rarely performed in practice, but we argue that validating the different benefits of the approach separately (i.e. the importance of deriving execution environment properties for performance prediction, and the speedup of deriving such properties automatically) could also help in assessing the advantages of the approach.

Extending GINPEX Experiments

Extending CPU experiments. The CPU and OS scheduling experiments presented in this thesis only deal with a subset of the major performance-relevant CPU and OS scheduling properties. To derive additional properties, further experiments are needed. For example, CPU power management properties such as dynamic frequency scaling can have an impact on software performance, but it is hard to quantify in performance models just by consulting CPU specifications. For the CPU simultaneous multithreading (SMT) property value detected by an experiment presented in this thesis, additional research efforts are necessary in order to establish an approach of reflecting SMT in performance prediction properly.

Extending OS scheduling experiments. OS scheduling properties that are candidates for further automated experiments are properties

259

related to priority handling: OS scheduler implementations strongly differ in how they dynamically manage the scheduling priorities of running tasks. Performance models such as the ones presented by [Hap08] already support scheduling priorities, but no platform-independent experiment is yet available to detect such properties automatically.

Extending virtualization experiments. Regarding the experiments to detect virtualization properties, extensions with regard to additional hypervisor and virtual machine properties might be helpful. For example, experiments could be used to detect virtual CPU configurations of virtual machines, such as CPU priorities or caps. Properties regarding the hypervisor scheduling policy, i.e. how the hypervisor manages the concurrent access to shared resources from different virtual machines, might also lead to improved performance prediction and thus can be a good candidate for additional experiments. In addition, further research is necessary on how to automatically detect a reasonable model of additional load present in virtualized environments. The experiment concept presented in Section 6.5.1 can serve as a starting point here.

Designing experiments for different experiment domains. In addition to CPU, OS scheduling, and virtualization experiments, performance prediction can also benefit from experiments detecting totally different execution environment properties. Software performance prediction approaches often use simple performance models of disk or network resources. Typically, they only support the specification of a simple performance property, such as throughput or latency. For both kinds of resources, additional performance-relevant properties are present which are assumed to lead to better prediction results if reflected in performance prediction.

In large software systems, caching effects are also an important factor regarding software performance and should therefore be reflected in performance prediction. Again, experiments to detect hardware caching properties or middleware caching properties (for instance, the speedup of an in-memory database compared to a traditional disk-based database) might be useful. In all those cases, it has to be investigated how these properties can be detected automatically using a predefined experiment, and how the detected property values can be reflected in performance prediction.

As a last point, the approach can also be applied to the domain of embedded systems. In this thesis, we focused on the domain of business information systems and dealt with properties of the execution environment used for such systems. For embedded systems, a different infrastructure is typically used, where for example real-time properties are much more important. The approach can applied to this domain as well, but it has to be explored to which degree existing experiments can be reused for embedded system and for which properties new experiments are needed.

A. GINPEX Metamodel

In the following, we provide an overview on the GINPEX metamodel that has been implemented in the GINPEX tooling[1], and give additional details on the metamodel part regarding the different experiment tasks and sensors.

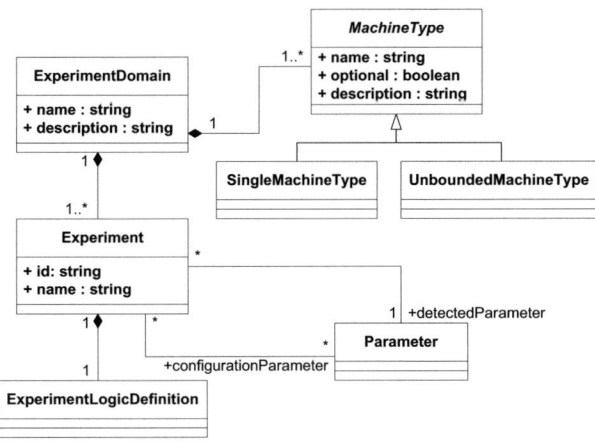

Figure A.1.: GINPEX experiments metamodel

The GINPEX experiment metamodel is shown in Figure A.1, the experiment logic definition metamodel is shown in Figure A.2. The concepts of these metamodel elements can be found in Section 4.4.1 and Section 4.4.2.

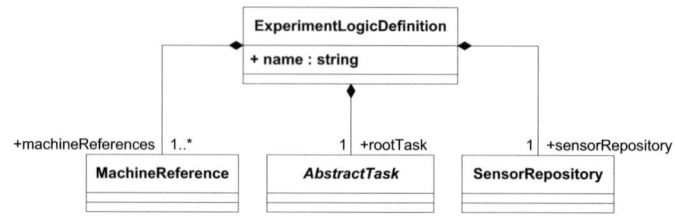

Figure A.2.: GINPEX experiment logic definition metamodel

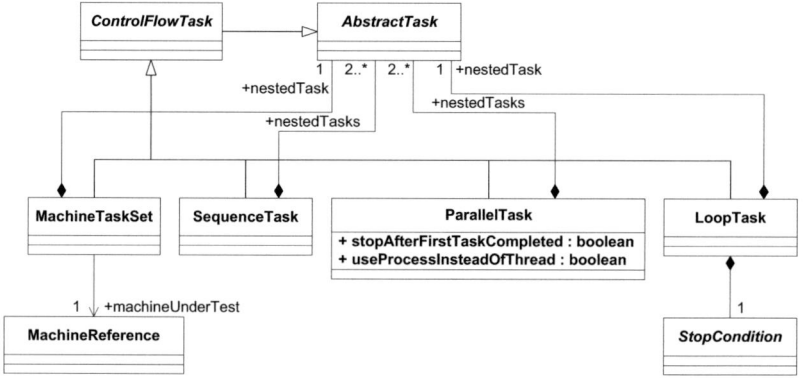

Figure A.3.: GINPEX control flow tasks metamodel

A.1. Control Flow Tasks

Figure A.3 gives an overview on the control flow tasks of the GINPEX metamodel. In the following, these metamodel elements are described in detail.

SequenceTask Executes multiple nested task in a sequence. Nested tasks are ordered; a nested task is being executed once its predecessor task has been completed.
Activity Diagram Syntax:

---

[1]see http://ginpex.ipd.kit.edu/

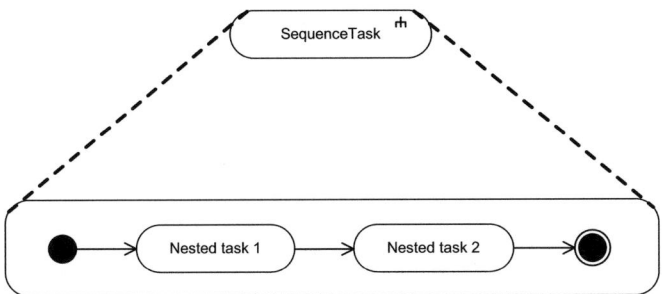

Attributes:

- *nestedTasks*: An ordered list of nested tasks.

ParallelTask   Executes multiple nested task in parallel.

Activity Diagram Syntax:

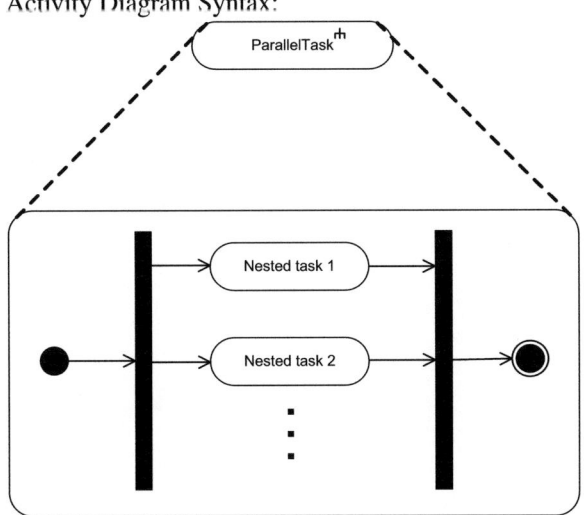

Attributes:

- *nestedTasks*: A list of nested tasks.

- boolean *stopAfterFirstTaskCompleted*: Indicates whether the
  ParallelTask should stop once the first nested task has

completed. Otherwise, the `ParallelTask` waits until all nested tasks have completed.

- boolean *useProcessInsteadOfThread*: Indicates whether the task should execute the nested tasks in different OS processes. If set to false (default), threads are used.

`LoopTask`   Executes a nested task multiple times.

Activity Diagram Syntax:

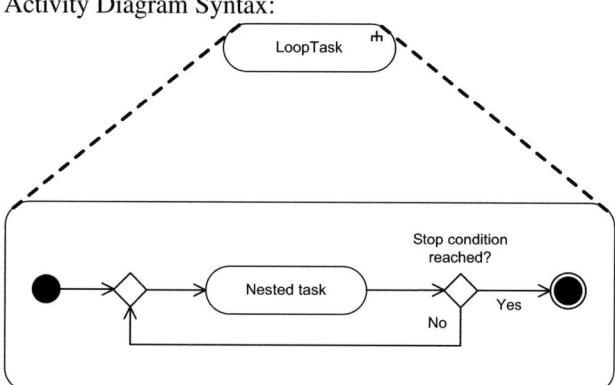

Attributes:

- *nestedTask*: The nested task which has to be executed in a loop.

- *stopCondition*: The stop condition is specified by one of the stop condition model elements (see below).

`MachineTaskSet`   Executes a set of tasks on a specified machine.

Activity Diagram Syntax:

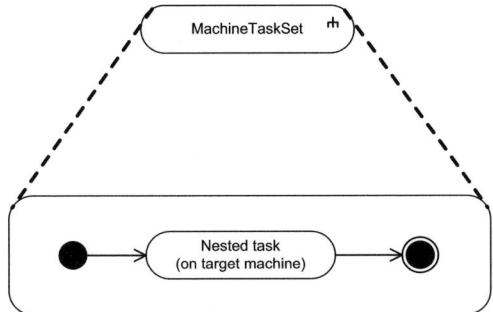

Attributes:

- *nestedTask*: The root task to be executed on the machine.

- MachineReference *targetMachine*: The machine on which the nested task is to be executed.

- MachineReference *calibrationFilesFromDifferentMachine*: If specified, nested task uses calibration files from this machine, instead of the calibration files from the target machine.

A.2. Stop Conditions

The following metamodel elements inherit from StopCondition and can be used to specify the condition for terminating a LoopTask.

FixedNumberOfIterationsReached   Executes the loop for a specified number of iterations.
Attributes:

- *numberOfIterations*: The number of iterations.

- *randomized*: An optional distribution that specifies a randomization of the number of iterations (see Distribution elements below).

`InternalTimesStable`   Executes the loop until the response times of a nested task are stable, i.e. if the average response time lies in a specified confidence interval.
Attributes:

- *taskForInternalTimes*: The nested task whose response times are used for determining the stop condition.

- *confidence*: The statistical confidence.

- *halfWidth*: The half width of the confidence interval.

- *minimumNumberOfIterations*: A minimum number of loop iterations that is to be executed independent from the stop criteria.

- *maximumNumberOfIterations*: A maximum number of loop iterations that is to be executed, even if the stop criteria is not met.

`InternalTimesChanged`   InternalTimesChangedSymbol.gif Executes the loop until there is a significant change in the measured response times of the nested task.
Attributes:

- *numberOfLastTimesRegarded*: A number indicating the number of previous iterations that should be taken into account when determining a difference in response times. A higher number means that the condition is more robust to outliers.

- *finalNumberOfIterationsToDo*: Number of loop iterations to perform after detecting an internal times change before completing the loop.

- boolean *finalNumberOfIterationsToDoRandomized*: Indicates whether the actual number of loop iterations to perform after detecting an internal times change before completing the loop is random. If set, this number is greater than 0 and lower than finalNumberOfIterationsToDo.

- boolean *resetFinalNumberOfIterationsIfInternalTimesChangedAgain*: Indicates whether the final number of iterations to be executed is to be reset if the internal times change again a second time during the final number of iterations are executed.

- *maximumNumberOfIterations*: A maximum number of loop iterations that is to be executed, even if the stop criteria is not met.

UserAbort Executes the loop until the user manually aborts execution

EndlessLoop Executes the loop without a specific stop condition. Instead, the loop has to be aborted from outside. Endless loops can for example be used in a ParallelTask that aborts the loop after another nested task has been completed.

A.3. Machine Tasks

Figure A.4 gives an overview on the machine tasks of the GINPEX metamodel. In the following, these metamodel elements are described in detail.

CpuLoadTask Executes CPU-bound load on the machine.
   Attributes:

- *duration*: The amount of load that is to be executed is specified in duration in milliseconds. This attribute corresponds to the duration the load execution would take if executed without contention on the platform.

269

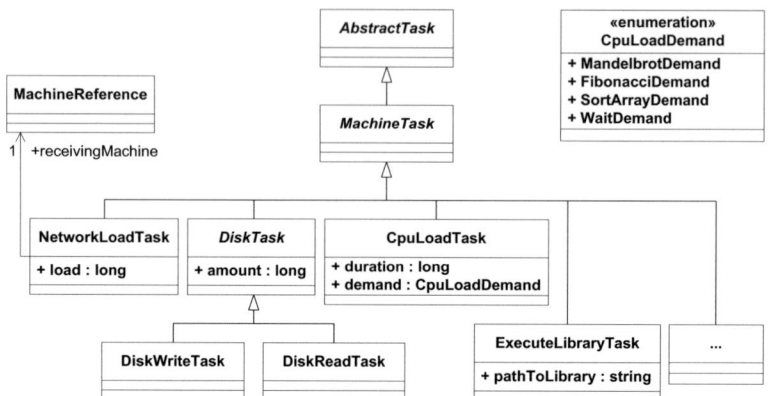

Figure A.4.: GINPEX machine tasks metamodel

- *demand*: The type of CPU load to be executed. The user can choose between `FibonacciDemand`, `MandelbrotDemand` (both CPU-related), `SortArrayDemand` (CPU/RAM-related), and `WaitDemand` (sleep).

- *randomized*: An optional distribution that specifies a randomization of the amount of load (see `Distribution` elements below).

`DiskReadTask` Issues disk read load. Data is read from a large number of 10 MB large disk files, all containing random data. Attributes:

- *amount*: Inherited from abstract `DiskTask`: The amount of bytes to read. .

`DiskWriteTask` Issues disk write load. Random data is written to a large number of 10 MB large disk files. Attributes:

- *amount*: Inherited from abstract `DiskTask`: The amount of bytes to write.

NetworkLoadTask   Issues network load by sending raw random data to another machine.

Attributes:

- MachineReference *targetMachine*: The target machine to which load is to be sent to.

- *load*: The amount of load to be sent in bytes.

ExecuteLibraryTask   Execute task logic that is provided by a Java JAR library. This allows for executing task logic without extending the metamodel or code-generation templates.

Attributes:

- *libraryPath* Absolute path to the JAR file on the controller machine. The JAR file will be transferred to the Load Driver for execution.

- *className* The fully qualified class name which provides the task logic implementation.

A.4. Distributions

The following metamodel elements inherit from the abstract Distribution element which is currently used in the LoopTask and the CpuLoadTask element for specifying randomized behavior. The value which is to be randomized is available in the metamodel element for which the distribution is specified.

UniformDistribution   Use randomized values based on a uniform distribution. The minimum value is 0 and the maximum value is the vlaue to be randomized.

NormalDistribution   Use randomized values based on a normal distribution (Gaussian distribution). For both distribution parameters μ (mean) and σ (standard deviation), the value to be randomized is used.

ExponentialDistribution   Use randomized values based on an exponential distribution. For the distribution parameter λ (rate), the value to be randomized is used.

A.5. Sensors

The sensors which can be specified for GINPEX tasks are shown in Figure A.5.

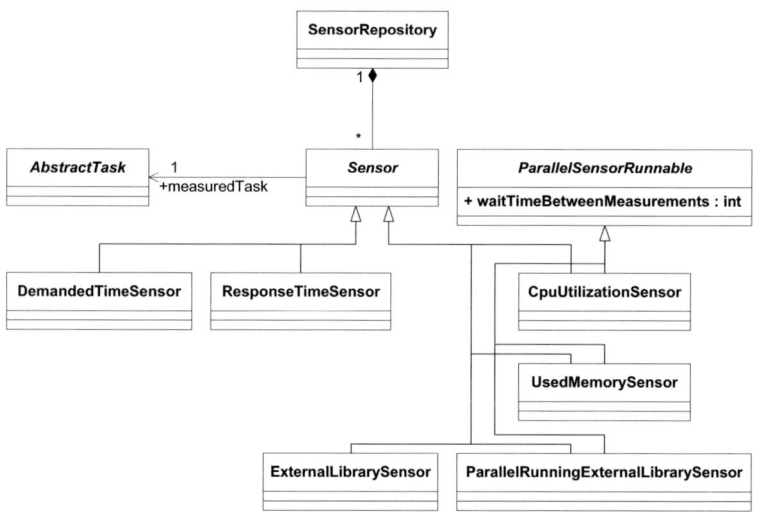

Figure A.5.: GINPEX sensors metamodel

`ResponseTimeSensor`   Measures the response time of a task execution by taking system time stamps before and after the task. Attributes:

- *measuredTask*: Inherited from abstract `Sensor`: The task to be measured.

`DemandedTimeSensor`   For a task using random times, for example a random duration of a CpuLoadTask, this sensor monitors the demanded (random) times. Attributes:

- *measuredTask*: Inherited from abstract `Sensor`: The task to be measured.

`CpuUtilizationSensor`   Measures CPU utilization during a task in a parallel thread. 100% means all cores have been utilized. On a quad-core machine, 25% means that only one core has been fully utilized during the last measurement period, or multiple cores have been partly utilized, yielding an overall 25% utilization. Attributes:

- *measuredTask*: Inherited from abstract `Sensor`: The task to be measured.

- *waitTimeBetweenMeasurements*: Inherited from abstract `ParallelSensorRunnable`: Indicates the wait time in milliseconds between taking sensor measurements.

`UsedMemorySensor`   Measures the used physical memory in percent during a task in a parallel thread. 100% means no free memory is available at the time of the measurement. Attributes:

- *measuredTask*: Inherited from abstract `Sensor`: The task to be measured.

- *waitTimeBetweenMeasurements*: Inherited from abstract `Par-allelSensorRunnable`: Indicates the wait time in milliseconds between taking sensor measurements.

`ExternalLibrarySensor`   Executes sensor logic that is provided by a Java JAR library. This allows to execute sensor logic without extending the metamodel or code-generation templates. The sensor library has to provide logic that is called before the measured task is executed, and logic that is called after the measured task is executed. Attributes:

- *measuredTask*: Inherited from abstract `Sensor`: The task to be measured.

`ParallelRunningExternalLibrarySensor`   Executes sensor logic that is provided by a Java JAR library. The sensor logic is executed in a parallel thread while the measured task is executed. Attributes:

- *measuredTask*: Inherited from abstract `Sensor`: The task to be measured.

- *waitTimeBetweenMeasurements*: Inherited from abstract `Par-allelSensorRunnable`: Indicates the wait time in milliseconds between taking sensor measurements.

B. Presented Experiments

In the following, all experiment templates that have been presented throughout this thesis are listed. For an explanation on the experiment template structure, see Section 4.6.

B.1. CPU Simultaneous Multithreading

Experiment ID: CPU.01

Experiment name: Detect simultaneous multithreading (SMT)

Experiment domain: CPU

Detected experiment parameter: SMT available (true/false); default: false

Importance for performance analysis: A performance speedup for parallel CPU-bound workloads possible due to virtual CPU cores. However, the performance gain of x virtual cores is typically lower than x physical cores. If SMT is available, the observed CPU utilization of an application is based on the available virtual cores.

Configuration parameters: None.

Experiment execution logic: Iteratively increase the number of parallel executed CPU-bound tasks and measure its response times and the CPU utilization. If response time increases, stop. If the measured CPU utilization has not reached 100% once increased response times have been measured, we assume that SMT is available.

For details, see Section 5.3.2 or the graphical description shown in Figure 5.3.

Assumptions:

- The machine is idle.

- The operating system reports CPU utilization based on the number of available virtual cores.

- Required sensors: Response time sensor, CPU utilization sensor.

Experiment robustness: The experiment is being executed twice with different types of CPU demands, one focusing on integer operations, one focusing on floating-point operations. If at least one of the demands yields measurements that indicate SMT availability, the experiment result is set to true (SMT available).

Experiment performance: $O(n)$ where n is the number of available CPU cores. If the number of cores is larger than 8, the number of parallel tasks is doubled instead of linearly increased, which leads to a duration that lies in $O(\log(n))$.

B.2. Detect Number of Available CPU Cores

Experiment ID: CPU.02

Experiment name: Detect number of available CPU cores

Experiment domain: CPU

Detected experiment parameter: Number of available physical CPU cores (integer); if SMT is available, the number of available virtual CPU cores (integer) is also detected

Importance for performance analysis: The number of available CPU cores heavily influences the slowdown that can be observed for

CPU requests due to parallel CPU requests. The number of cores for a CPU resource is a basic parameter this is typically reflected in performance analysis tools such as the PCM.

Configuration parameters: *smt*: SMT available (true/false); detected by Experiment CPU.01

Experiment execution logic: Iteratively increase the number of parallel executed CPU-bound tasks and measure its response time and (if *smt* is true) the CPU utilization. If response time increases and *smt* is false, stop. If *smt* is true, continue until the CPU utilization reaches 100%. The number of physical cores equals the number of parallel executed tasks in the last iteration before increased response times were measured. If *smt* is true, the number of virtual cores equals the number of parallel executed tasks in the last execution, where a CPU utilization of 100% was measured. For details, see Section 5.4.2 or the graphical description shown in Figure 5.8.

Assumptions:

- The machine is idle.

- If the CPU is a multi-core CPU, it features symmetric multiprocessing (SMP). This is the case for current server CPUs.

- The OS scheduler spreads CPU load of parallel threads equally across all available CPU cores.

- If *smt* is true, the operating system reports CPU utilization based on the number of available virtual cores.

- Required sensors: Response time sensor, CPU utilization sensor (only if *smt* is true).

Experiment robustness: The experiment is being executed twice with different types of CPU demands, one focusing on integer operations, one focusing on floating-point operations. If the executions

277

lead to the same experiment result, results can be considered robust. Otherwise, results should be checked manually. Further checks to assess robustness:

- If *smt* is true, the detected number of virtual cores should be higher than the detected number of physical cores

- If *smt* is true, the detected number of virtual cores should be a multiple of the detected number of physical cores

Experiment performance:

If *smt* is false: $O(n)$ where n is the number of available physical CPU cores.

If *smt* is true: $O(n)$ where n is the number of available virtual CPU cores.

If the number of cores is larger than 8, the number of parallel tasks is doubled instead of linearly increased, which leads to a duration that lies in $O(\log(n))$.

B.3. Detect OS Scheduler Timeslice Length

Experiment ID: OSSCHEDULER.01

Experiment name: Detect OS scheduler timeslice length

Experiment domain: OS Scheduler

Detected experiment parameter: Operating system scheduler timeslice length (integer)

Importance for performance analysis: General-purpose operating system (GPOS) schedulers split work of parallel running tasks by issuing timeslices to the tasks. Depending on the timeslice length, processing the amount of work of a task is being interrupted if it does not fit in a timeslice. On the other hand, a small amount of work may be completed within one timeslice and thus may not suffer further delays.

Configuration parameters: *number of cores*: Number of available physical CPU cores; detected by Experiment CPU.02

Experiment execution logic: Issue a small amount (20 ms) of CPU load (called *TaskMeas*) on a core and measure its response time, while additional CPU load is issued to the core by one another process. In some cases, the measured response time is then significantly larger than 20 ms, indicating that the operating system issues the CPU load of the other process in between for a timeslice. The difference to the original 20 ms is then the timeslice length used be the OS scheduler. For details, see Section 5.5.2 or the graphical description shown in Figure 5.12.

Assumptions:

- The machine is idle.

- All tasks are running with the same priority. As there is no task interactivity (e.g. I/O access), it can be assumed that all tasks are running with the same priority, and that *TaskMeas* has been interrupted for exactly one timeslice.

- The actual timeslice length is larger than 20 ms. A timeslice larger than 20 ms has to be assumed in order to yield measurements that can be used for analysis. However, given the fact that all common operating systems use average timeslice lengths between 30 ms and 200 ms (cf. [RS05, Aas05, Mol07]), this is a valid assumption.

- All CPU-bound tasks have to be equally distributed to the available cores. As GPOS schedulers aim at fully utilize the available resources, we believe this is also a valid assumption.

- The experiment is not able to detect a timeslice length that is being adjusted dynamically depending on the priority of processes. In this case, the priority management of OS processes would have to be reflected in further experiments which are subject to future work.

- Assumption for performance analysis: The performance analysis approach has to support OS timeslices during analysis.

- Required sensors: Response time sensor for *TaskMeas*.

Experiment robustness: Repeat the experiment with two parallel processes issuing CPU load instead of one parallel process. The process where response times are measured should then be interrupted for two timeslices, hence an increase of the response time should be observed that is twice as high compared to the first run.

Experiment performance:

The experiment runtime only depends on the number of iterations for *TaskMeas*.

B.4. Detect OS Scheduler Initial Load-balancing Strategy

Experiment ID: OSSCHEDULER.02

Experiment name: Detect OS scheduler initial load-balancing strategy

Experiment domain: OS Scheduler

Detected experiment parameter: Operating system scheduler initial load-balancing strategy (CyclicSplitting, SameAsParent, Random)

Importance for performance analysis: The initial load-balancing strategy is used by the operating system to decide on which CPU core newly created tasks are placed. Depending on the used strategy, this can lead to balanced or unbalanced cores and should thus be reflected in performance analysis.

Configuration parameters: *number of cores*: Number of available physical CPU cores; detected by Experiment CPU.02

Experiment execution logic: Issue and measure CPU load in N processes where N is the number of CPU cores. Repeatedly issue a larger CPU load in a separate process *add*. Observing bursts in the measured response times of the N processes indicates which process has shared a core with the newly created process. Based on the sequence of process bursts, an initial load-balancing strategy is derived. For details, see Section 5.6.2.1 or the graphical description shown in Figure 5.16.

Assumptions:

- The machine is idle.

- The system features SMP processors where the load is equally distributed to the available cores.

- The experiment aims at detecting typical load-balancing strategies for GPOS schedulers. Real-time system schedulers might use different strategies for which the experiment would have to be adapted.

- Assumption for performance analysis: The performance analysis has to feature a notion of processes and provide support for the load-balancing strategies detected by the experiment.

- Required sensors: Response time sensors for the N tasks.

Experiment robustness: Experiment robustness can be assessed by analyzing the quality of the detected response time bursts. If the number of the detected bursts does not match the number of expected bursts, or if the measured response times are spread across a very wide range, the experiments should be repeated or it should be checked whether all experiment assumptions hold on the target platform.

Experiment performance: The experiment performance only depends on the iterations of the *add* process.

B.5. Detect OS Scheduler Dynamic Load-balancing Strategy

Experiment ID: OSSCHEDULER.03

Experiment name: Detect OS scheduler dynamic load-balancing strategy

Experiment domain: OS Scheduler

Detected experiment parameter: Operating system scheduler dynamic load-balancing strategy (Lazy, Active, Immediate)

Importance for performance analysis: The dynamic load-balancing strategy is used by the operating system to decide when load-balancing is performed to avoid imbalanced CPU cores. Depending on the used strategy, this can be done at a different frequency. If a load-balancing strategy tolerates imbalanced cores for some time, this can affect the response times of tasks that are running on the corresponding CPU cores. Hence, the load-balancing strategy should be reflected in performance analysis.

Configuration parameters: *number of cores*: Number of available physical CPU cores; detected by Experiment CPU.02

Experiment execution logic: Issue and measure CPU load in $3 \cdot N$ processes where N is the number of CPU cores. Iteratively terminate the running processes and observe the performance of the CPU load in the remaining processes. Depending on the pattern of decreased response times due to termination of processes, the used dynamic load-balancing strategy can be inferred. For details, see Section 5.6.3.1 or the graphical description shown in Figure 5.22.

Assumptions:

- The machine is idle.

- The system features SMP processors where the load is equally distributed to the available cores.

- The experiment aims at detecting typical load-balancing strategies for GPOS schedulers. Real-time system schedulers might use different strategies for which the experiment would have to be adapted.

- Assumption for performance analysis: The performance analysis has to feature a notion of processes and provide support for the load-balancing strategies detected by the experiment.

- Required sensors: Response time sensors for the $3 \cdot N$ tasks.

Experiment robustness: Experiment robustness is assessed by checking the spread of measured response times between the termination of processes. If the range of measurements is too large, the response times are too noisy in order to detect the load-balancing strategy.

Experiment performance: $O(n)$ where n is the number of available CPU cores.

B.6. Detect Virtualization Overhead

Experiment ID: VIRTUALIZATION.01
Experiment name: Detect virtualization overhead
Experiment domain: Virtualization

Detected experiment parameter: Virtualization overhead for each resource demand type in focus (double)

Importance for performance analysis: When an application is migrated from a non-virtualized to a virtualized environment, the virtualization layer can induce a performance overhead on issued resource demands that should be reflected in performance analysis.

Configuration parameters: *number of cores*: Number of available physical CPU cores for detecting CPU resource overhead; detected by Experiment CPU.02

Experiment execution logic: Issue and measure identical resource load on the non-virtualized machine and on the virtualized machine. Compare the measurement results to calculate the virtualization overhead. For details, see Section 6.3.2 or the graphical description shown in Figure 6.3.

Assumptions:

- Both machines are idle.

- Both machines are equipped with the same hardware. Otherwise, differences in the measured resource demands cannot be attributed to the virtualization layer.

- Assumption for performance analysis: The performance analysis has to provide means for including the detected overhead model in analysis. For example, the analysis could adapt issued resource demands by adding the virtualization overhead to it. Such an approach would facilitate the reuse of existing software models for predicting its performance in virtualized environments.

- Required sensors: Response time sensors for the tasks issuing resource demands on the non-virtualized and the virtualized machine.

Experiment robustness: Experiment robustness can be assessed by analyzing the dispersion of the measurement results, i.e. by calculating the interquartile range (IQR) for the measurements. If the IQR exceeds a certain threshold, the experiments should be repeated or it should be checked whether all experiment assumptions hold on the target platform.

Experiment performance: The experiment performance mainly depends on the number of resource demand types involved and the number of performed iterations for each measurement. Additional influences can stem from the performance of the accessed resource and the overhead induced by the virtualization platform.

B.7. Detect Load-dependent Virtualization Overhead

Experiment ID: VIRTUALIZATION.02

Experiment name: Detect load-dependent virtualization overhead

Experiment domain: Virtualization

Detected experiment parameter: Load-dependent virtualization overhead for each resource demand type in focus (double)

Importance for performance analysis: The overhead induced by the virtualization layer depends on both the resource type and the load currently present on the platform. This load has to be reflected in an overhead model for performance analysis to reduce the prediction error.

Configuration parameters: *number of cores*: Number of available physical CPU cores for detecting CPU resource overhead; detected by Experiment CPU.02

Experiment execution logic: In multiple experiment runs, issue different amounts of resource load in the different virtual machines using parallel processes. Measure the response time of the resource load and compare the overhead to a reference time (the response time of the resource request when executed without parallel load). To avoid a full parameter exploitation (number of VMs × number of resource types × number of load levels), use a set of heuristics which minimize the number of experiments without degrading prediction accuracy. For details, see Section 6.4.2.

Assumptions:

- The involved virtual machines are idle.

- The virtual machines share the involved resources, i.e. the virtual CPU cores, disk and network devices are mapped to the same physical devices.

- Assumption for performance analysis: The performance analysis has to provide means for including the detected overhead model in analysis. Similar to the overhead model detected by experiment VIRTUALIZATION.01, the analysis could adapt issued resource demands by adding the virtualization overhead to it. Such an approach would facilitate the reuse of existing software models for predicting its performance in virtualized environments.

- Required sensors: Response time sensors for the tasks issuing resource demands on the different virtual machines.

Experiment robustness: Experiment robustness can be assessed by analyzing the dispersion of the measurement results, i.e. by calculating the interquartile range (IQR) for the measurements. If the IQR exceeds a certain threshold, the experiments should be repeated or it should be checked whether all experiment assumptions hold on the target platform.

Experiment performance: The experiment performance depends on the number of experiment runs and the duration of each experiment run. The number of experiment runs depends on the number of involved virtual machines, resource demand types, and load levels. To avoid a full parameter exploitation of these factors, we reduced the number of experiment runs as described in Section 6.4.2.

List of Figures

Bibliography

[Aas05]   J. Aas, "Understanding the Linux 2.6.8.1 CPU Sched-
             uler," 2005. http://citeseerx.ist.psu.edu/viewdoc/summary?
             doi=10.1.1.59.6385, last retrieved: 2013-06-05.

[AMM+94]   I. Ahmad, K. Mehrotra, C. K. Mohan, S. Ranka, and
             A. Ghafoor, "Performance Modeling of Load-balancing
             Algorithms using Neural Networks," *Concurrency: Practice
             and Experience*, vol. 6, no. 5, pp. 393–409, 1994.

[AW08]   W. Augustin and T. Worsch, "The SKaMPI 5 Manual,"
             2008. http://liinwww.ira.uka.de/~skampi/download/skampi.
             pdf, last retrieved: 2013-06-12.

[BBB96]   J. E. Baldeschwieler, R. D. Blumofe, and E. A. Brewer, "AT-
             LAS : An Infrastructure for Global Computing," in *Proceed-
             ings of the 7th ACM SIGOPS European Workshop: Systems
             Support for Worldwide Applications*, 1996, pp. 165–172.

[BCA08]   B. B. Brandenburg, J. M. Calandrino, and J. H. Anderson,
             "On the Scalability of Real-Time Scheduling Algorithms on
             Multicore Platforms: A Case Study," in *Proceedings of the
             2008 Real-Time Systems Symposium (RTSS 2008)*.   IEEE
             Computer Society, 2008, pp. 157–169.

[BDH08]   S. Becker, T. Dencker, and J. Happe, "Model-driven
             Generation of Performance Prototypes," in *Proceedings
             of the SPEC International Workshop on Performance*

Evaluation: Metrics, Models and Benchmarks (SIPEW 2008). Springer-Verlag, 2008, pp. 79–98.

[BDIS04] S. Balsamo, A. Di Marco, P. Inverardi, and M. Simeoni, "Model-based Performance Prediction in Software Development: A Survey," *IEEE Transactions on Software Engineering*, vol. 30, no. 5, pp. 295–310, 2004.

[Bec08] S. Becker, "Coupled Model Transformations for QoS Enabled Component-based Software Design," PhD Thesis, University of Oldenburg, Germany, 2008.

[BFS⁺06] F. Benevenuto, C. Fernandes, M. Santos, V. Almeida, J. Almeida, G. J. Janakiraman, and J. R. Santos, "Performance Models for Virtualized Applications," in *Frontiers of High Performance Computing and Networking - ISPA 2006 Workshops*. Springer-Verlag, 2006, pp. 427–439.

[BHK06] S. Becker, J. Happe, and H. Koziolek, "Putting Components into Context: Supporting QoS-Predictions with an explicit Context Model," in *Proceedings of the 11th International Workshop on Component-Oriented Programming (WCOP 2006)*, 2006.

[BKNT11] C. Baun, M. Kunze, J. Nimis, and S. Tai, *Cloud Computing: Web-based Dynamic IT Services*. Springer-Verlag, 2011.

[BKR09] S. Becker, H. Koziolek, and R. Reussner, "The Palladio Component Model for Model-driven Performance Prediction," *Journal of Systems and Software*, vol. 82, pp. 3–22, 2009.

[BMdW⁺04] E. Bondarev, J. Muskens, P. de With, M. Chaudron, and J. Lukkien, "Predicting Real-Time Properties of

Component Assemblies: a Scenario-Simulation Approach," in *Proceedings of the 30th EUROMICRO Conference (EUROMICRO 2004)*. IEEE, 2004, pp. 40–47.

[BR08] R. Böhme and R. Reussner, "Validation of Predictions with Measurements," in *Dependability Metrics*. Springer-Verlag, 2008, pp. 14–18.

[BW01] A. Burns and A. Wellings, *Real-Time Systems and Programming Languages*, 3rd ed. Addison-Wesley, 2001.

[CAS⁺12] L. Y. Chen, D. Ansaloni, E. Smirni, A. Yokokawa, and W. Binder, "Achieving Application-centric Performance Targets via Consolidation on Multicores: Myth or Reality?" in *Proceedings of the 21st International Symposium on High-Performance Parallel and Distributed Computing (HPDC 2012)*, 2012, pp. 37–48.

[CCF⁺06] R. Chanin, M. Corrêa, P. Fernandes, A. Sales, R. Scheer, and A. F. Zorzo, "Analytical Modeling for Operating System Schedulers on NUMA Systems," *Electronic Notes in Theoretical Computer Science*, vol. 151, no. 3, pp. 131–149, Jun. 2006.

[CDI01] V. Cortellessa, A. D'Ambrogio, and G. Iazeolla, "Automatic Derivation of Software Performance Models from CASE Documents," *Performance Evaluation*, vol. 45, pp. 81–105, 2001.

[CG05] L. Cherkasova and R. Gardner, "Measuring CPU Overhead for I/O Processing in the Xen Virtual Machine Monitor," in *Proceedings of the USENIX Annual Technical Conference (ATEC 2005)*. USENIX Association, 2005, pp. 387–390.

[CMMT00]   M. Courson, A. Mink, G. Marçais, and B. Traverse, "An Automated Benchmarking Toolset," in *Proceedings of the 8th International Conference on High Performance Computing and Networking (HPCN 2000)*. Springer-Verlag, 2000, pp. 497–506.

[CPU]   CPUID, "CPU-Z." http://www.cpuid.com/softwares/cpu-z. html, last retrieved: 2013-06-08.

[CS01]   V. Claus and A. Schwill, Eds., *Duden Informatik: Ein Fachlexikon für Studium und Praxis*, 3rd ed. Dudenverlag, 2001.

[CST⁺10]   B. F. Cooper, A. Silberstein, E. Tam, R. Ramakrishnan, and R. Sears, "Benchmarking Cloud Serving Systems with YCSB," in *Proceedings of the 1st ACM Symposium on Cloud computing (SoCC 2010)*. ACM, 2010, pp. 143–154.

[DB11]   R. I. Davis and A. Burns, "A survey of hard real-time scheduling for multiprocessor systems," *ACM Computing Surveys*, vol. 43, no. 4, pp. 1–44, Oct. 2011.

[DES]   DESMO-J Development Team, "DESMO-J." http://desmoj. sourceforge.net, last retrieved: 2013-06-14.

[DG08]   J. Dean and S. Ghemawat, "MapReduce: Simplified Data Processing on Large Clusters," *Communications of the ACM*, vol. 51, no. 1, pp. 107–113, 2008.

[dOPRF13]   A. B. de Oliveira, J.-C. Petkovich, T. Reidemeister, and S. Fischmeister, "DataMill : Rigorous Performance Evaluation Made Easy," in *Proceedings of the 4th ACM/SPEC International Conference on Performance Engineering (ICPE 2013)*. ACM, 2013, pp. 137–148.

[EHK⁺02]   F. N. Eskesen, M. Hack, T. Kimbrel, M. S. Squillante, R. J. Eickemeyer, and S. R. Kunkel, "Performance Analysis of Simultaneous Multithreading in a PowerPC-based Processor," in *Proceedings of the 1st Annual Workshop on Duplicating, Deconstructing, and Debunking (WDDD 2002)*, 2002.

[ENC⁺12]   V. C. Emeakaroha, M. A. S. Netto, R. N. Calheiros, I. Brandic, R. Buyya, and C. A. F. De Rose, "Towards Autonomic Detection of SLA Violations in Cloud Infrastructures," *Future Generation Computer Systems*, vol. 28, no. 7, pp. 1017–1029, Jul. 2012.

[Ern]   J. Ernst, "What is metamodeling, and what is it good for?" http://infogrid.org/trac/wiki/Reference/WhatIsMetaModeling, last retrieved: 2013-06-16.

[Fab]   Faban Development Team, "Faban." http://www.faban.org/, last retrieved: 2013-06-05.

[Fer78]   D. Ferrari, *Computer Systems Performance Evaluation*. Prentice Hall International, 1978.

[FMW⁺12]   G. Franks, P. Maly, C. M. Woodside, D. C. Petriu, A. Hubbard, and M. Mroz, "Layered Queueing Network Solver and Simulator User Manual," Department of Systems and Computer Engineering, Carleton University, Tech. Rep., 2012. http://www.sce.carleton.ca/rads/lqns/LQNSUserMan.pdf

[Gar]   Gartner, Inc., "Gartner IT Glossary – Virtualization." http://www.gartner.com/it-glossary/virtualization/, last retrieved: 2013-06-17.

[GL99]   W. Gropp and E. Lusk, "Reproducible Measurements of MPI Performance Characteristics," in *Proceedings of the 6th Eu-*

ropean PVM/MPI Users' Group Meeting (PVM/MPI 1999). Springer-Verlag, 1999, pp. 11–18.

[GM00]   H. Gomaa and D. A. Menascé, "Design and Performance Modeling of Component Interconnection Patterns for Distributed Software Architectures," in *Proceedings of the 2nd International Workshop on Software and Performance (WOSP 2000)*.   ACM, 2000, pp. 117–126.

[GMS07]   V. Grassi, R. Mirandola, and A. Sabetta, "Filling the Gap between Design and Performance/Reliability Models of Component-based Systems: A Model-driven Approach," *Journal of Systems and Software*, vol. 80, no. 4, pp. 528–558, Apr. 2007.

[Gol74]   R. P. Goldberg, "Survey of Virtual Machine Research," *IEEE Computer*, vol. 7, no. 6, pp. 34–45, 1974.

[Gra93]   J. Gray, Ed., *The Benchmark Handbook for Database and Transaction Processing Systems*, 2nd ed.   Morgan Kaufmann, 1993.

[Gro09]   R. C. Gronback, *Eclipse Modeling Project: A Domain-specific Language (DSL) Toolkit*.   Addison-Wesley, 2009.

[Hap08]   J. Happe, "Predicting Software Performance in Symmetric Multi-core and Multiprocessor Environments," PhD Thesis, University of Oldenburg, Germany, 2008.

[HBR^{+}10] J. Happe, S. Becker, C. Rathfelder, H. Friedrich, and R. Reussner, "Parametric Performance Completions for Model-Driven Performance Prediction," *Performance Evaluation*, vol. 67, no. 8, pp. 694–716, 2010.

[HGHR10]   J. Happe, H. Groenda, M. Hauck, and R. H. Reussner, "A Prediction Model for Software Performance in Symmetric Multiprocessing Environments," in *Proceedings of the 7th International Conference on the Quantitative Evaluation of Systems (QEST 2010).* IEEE Computer Society, 2010, pp. 59–68.

[HHR10]   M. Hauck, J. Happe, and R. H. Reussner, "Automatic Derivation of Performance Prediction Models for Load-balancing Properties Based on Goal-oriented Measurements," in *Proceedings of the 18th IEEE International Symposium on Modeling, Analysis and Simulation of Computer and Telecommunication Systems (MASCOTS 2010).* IEEE Computer Society, 2010, pp. 361–369.

[HHR11]   M. Hauck, J. Happe, and R. H. Reussner, "Towards Performance Prediction For Cloud Computing Environments Based on Goal-oriented Measurements," in *Proceedings of the 1st International Conference on Cloud Computing and Services Science (CLOSER 2011).* SciTePress, 2011, pp. 616–622.

[HKHR11]   M. Hauck, M. Kuperberg, N. Huber, and R. Reussner, "Ginpex: Deriving Performance-relevant Infrastructure Properties Through Goal-oriented Experiments," in *Proceedings of the 7th International Conference on the Quality of Software Architectures (QoSA 2011).* ACM, 2011, pp. 53–62.

[HKHR13]   M. Hauck, M. Kuperberg, N. Huber, and R. Reussner, "Deriving Performance-relevant Infrastructure Properties Through Model-based Experiments with Ginpex," *Software & Systems Modeling*, 2013.

[HKKR09]   M. Hauck, M. Kuperberg, K. Krogmann, and R. Reussner, "Modelling Layered Component Execution Environments for Performance Prediction," in *Proceedings of the 12th International Symposium on Component Based Software Engineering (CBSE 2009)*. Springer-Verlag, 2009, pp. 191–208.

[HKY99]   L. J. Heyer, S. Kruglyak, and S. Yooseph, "Exploring Expression Data: Identification and Analysis of Coexpressed Genes," *Genome Research*, vol. 1999.9, pp. 1106–1115, 1999.

[HTF09]   T. Hastie, R. Tibshirani, and J. Friedman, *The Elements of Statistical Learning: Data Mining, Inference, and Prediction*, 2nd ed., ser. Springer Series in Statistics. Springer-Verlag, 2009.

[Inta]   Intel Corporation, "Intel Hyper-Threading Technology." https://www-ssl.intel.com/content/www/us/en/architecture-and-technology/hyper-threading/hyper-threading-technology.html, last retrieved: 2013-06-05.

[Intb]   Intel Corporation, "Intel Processor Frequency ID Utility." http://www.intel.com/p/en_US/support/highlights/processors/frequencyid, last retrieved: 2013-06-08.

[Intc]   Intel Corporation, "Intel Processor Identification Utility." http://www.intel.com/p/en_US/support/highlights/processors/toolspiu, last retrieved: 2013-06-08.

[Iom]   Iometer Development Team, "Iometer." http://www.iometer.org/, last retrieved: 2013-06-05.

[IOY+11]   A. Iosup, S. Ostermann, N. Yigitbasi, R. Prodan, T. Fahringer, and D. Epema, "Performance Analysis of Cloud Computing Services for Many-Tasks Scientific Computing," *IEEE Transactions on Parallel and Distributed Systems (to appear)*, vol. 22, no. 6, pp. 931–945, 2011.

[Jai91]   R. Jain, *The Art of Computer Systems Performance Analysis.* Wiley, 1991.

[JGLT11]   D. Jeon, S. Garcia, C. Louie, and M. B. Taylor, "Kismet: Parallel Speedup Estimates for Serial Programs," in *Proceedings of the 2011 ACM International Conference on Object Oriented Programming Systems Languages and Applications (OOPSLA 2011).* ACM, 2011, pp. 519–536.

[JMOa]   JMOB Project, "RUBiS: Rice University Bidding System Implementation." http://rubis.ow2.org/, last retrieved: 2013-06-05.

[JMOb]   JMOB Project, "TPC-W Benchmark Implementation." http://jmob.ow2.org/tpcw.html, last retrieved: 2013-06-05.

[Jon]   M. T. Jones, "Inside the Linux 2.6 Completely Fair Scheduler." http://www.ibm.com/developerworks/library/l-completely-fair-scheduler/, last retrieved: 2013-08-06.

[Kal05]   D. Kalinsky, "Who's Afraid of Asymmetric Multiprocessing?" 2005. http://rtcmagazine.com/articles/view/100404/, last retrieved: 2013-06-05.

[Kap11]   L. Kapová, "Configurable Software Performance Completions through Higher-Order Model Transformations," Ph.D. dissertation, Karlsruhe Institute of Technology, 2011.

[KB03]   S. Kounev and A. Buchmann, "Performance Modeling and Evaluation of Large-Scale J2EE Applications," in *Proceedings of the CMG 2003 International Conference*, 2003, pp. 273–283.

[KDH⁺12]   M. Kramer, Z. Durdik, M. Hauck, J. Henß, M. Küster, P. Merkle, and A. Rentschler, "Extending the Palladio Component Model using Profiles and Stereotypes," in *Proceedings of the Palladio Days 2012*, 2012.

[KGC⁺06]   R. Y. Kawasaki, L. A. Guedes, D. L. Cardoso, C. R. L. Francês, G. H. S. Carvalho, S. V. Carvalho, J. C. W. A. Costa, and M. S. Silva, "A Markovian Sensibility Analysis for Parallel Processing Scheduling on GNU / Linux," in *Frontiers of High Performance Computing and Networking - ISPA 2006 Workshops*. Springer-Verlag, 2006, pp. 269–278.

[KH06]   H. Koziolek and J. Happe, "A QoS Driven Development Process Model for Component-Based Software Systems," in *Proceedings of the 9th International Symposium on Component Based Software Engineering (CBSE 2006)*. Springer-Verlag, 2006, pp. 336–343.

[KHvKR11]   M. Kuperberg, N. R. Herbst, J. G. von Kistowski, and R. Reussner, "Defining and Quantifying Elasticity of Resources in Cloud Computing and Scalable Platforms," Tech. Rep., 2011. http://digbib.ubka.uni-karlsruhe.de/volltexte/1000023476

[KKR10]   K. Krogmann, M. Kuperberg, and R. Reussner, "Using Genetic Search for Reverse Engineering of Parametric Behaviour Models for Performance Prediction," *IEEE Transactions on Software Engineering*, vol. 36, no. 6, pp. 865–877, 2010.

[KLM⁺06]   T. Kalibera, J. Lehotsky, D. Majda, B. Repcek, M. Tomcanyi, A. Tomecek, P. Tůma, and J. Urban, "Automated Benchmarking and Analysis Tool," in *Proceedings of the 1st International Conference on Performance Evaluation Methodolgies and Tools (VALUETOOLS 2006)*, vol. 180. ACM, 2006.

[Kop11]   H. Kopetz, *Real-Time Systems: Design Principles for Distributed Embedded Applications*.   Springer, 2011.

[Koz10]   H. Koziolek, "Performance Evaluation of Component-based Software Systems: A Survey," in *Performance Evaluation*, vol. 67, no. 8.   Elsevier Science Inc., 2010, pp. 634–658.

[KSM10]   S. Kounev, S. Spinner, and P. Meier, "QPME 2.0 - A Tool for Stochastic Modeling and Analysis using Queueing Petri Nets," in *From Active Data Management to Event-Based Systems and More*.   Springer-Verlag, 2010, pp. 293–311.

[Lee12]   T. Leemhuis, "What's new in Linux 3.2," 2012. http://www.h-online.com/open/features/What-s-new-in-Linux-3-2-1400680.html, last retrieved: 2013-06-24.

[LFG05]   Y. Liu, A. Fekete, and I. Gorton, "Design-Level Performance Prediction of Component-Based Applications," *IEEE Transactions on Software Engineering*, vol. 31, no. 11, pp. 928–941, 2005.

[LFG⁺10]   M. Lassnig, T. Fahringer, V. Garonne, A. Molfetas, and M. Branco, "Identification, Modelling and Prediction of Non-periodic Bursts in Workloads," in *Proceedings of the 10th IEEE/ACM International Conference on Cluster, Cloud and Grid Computing (CCGRID 2010).* IEEE Computer Society, 2010, pp. 485–494.

[LZJ⁺11]   L. Lu, H. Zhang, G. Jiang, H. Chen, K. Yoshihira, and E. Smirni, "Untangling Mixed Information to Calibrate Resource Utilization in Virtual Machines," in *Proceedings of the 8th ACM International Conference on Autonomic Computing (ICAC 2011)*, ser. ICAC '11. ACM, 2011, pp. 151–160.

[MAD04]   D. A. Menascé, V. A. Almeida, and L. W. Dowdy, *Performance by Design : Computer Capacity Planning by Example.* Prentice Hall International, 2004.

[Mal12]   M. Malohlava, "Variability of Execution Environments for Component-based Systems," PhD Thesis, Charles University in Prague, 2012.

[Mar05]   V. Maraia, *The Build Master: Microsoft's Software Configuration Management Best Practices.* Addison-Wesley, 2005.

[Men05]   D. A. Menascé, "Virtualization: Concepts, Applications, and Performance Modeling," in *Proceedings of the CMG 2005 International Conference*, 2005.

[MM07]   M. Marzolla and R. Mirandola, "Performance Prediction of Web Service," in *Proceedings of the 3rd International Conference on the Quality of Software Architectures (QoSA 2007).* Springer-Verlag, 2007, pp. 127–144.

[MMM⁺05]   H. M. Mathis, A. E. Mericas, J. D. McCalpin, R. J. Eickemeyer, and S. R. Kunkel, "Characterization of Simultaneous Multithreading (SMT) Efficiency in POWER5," *IBM Journal of Research and Development*, vol. 49, no. 4/5, pp. 555–564, 2005.

[MMVP13] R. Mian, P. Martin, and J. L. Vazquez-Poletti, "Towards Building Performance Models for Data-intensive Workloads in Public Clouds," in *Proceedings of the 4th ACM/SPEC International Conference on Performance Engineering (ICPE 2013)*. ACM, 2013, pp. 259–270.

[Mol07] I. Molnar, "Modular Scheduler Core and Completely Fair Scheduler (CFS)," 2007. http://lwn.net/Articles/230501/, last retrieved: 2013-06-05.

[Obj05] Object Management Group (OMG), "UML Profile for Schedulability, Performance and Time, Version 1.1," 2005. http://www.omg.org/spec/SPTP/1.1/, last retrieved: 2013-06-10.

[Obj11a] Object Management Group (OMG), "OMG Meta Object Facility (MOF) Core Specification, Version 2.4.1," 2011. http://www.omg.org/spec/MOF/2.4.1/PDF, last retrieved: 2013-06-10.

[Obj11b] Object Management Group (OMG), "OMG Unified Modeling Language (OMG UML), Infrastructure, Version 2.4.1," 2011. http://www.omg.org/spec/UML/2.4.1/Infrastructure/PDF/, last retrieved: 2013-06-10.

[Obj11c] Object Management Group (OMG), "OMG Unified Modeling Language (OMG UML), Superstructure, Version 2.4.1," 2011. http://www.omg.org/spec/UML/2.4.1/Superstructure/PDF/, last retrieved: 2013-06-10.

[Obj11d] Object Management Group (OMG), "UML Profile for Modeling and Analysis of Real-Time and Embedded systems (MARTE), Version 1.1," 2011. http://www.omg.org/spec/MARTE/1.1/, last retrieved: 2013-06-10.

[Obj12]   Object Management Group (OMG), "OMG Object Constraint Language (OCL), Version 2.3.1," 2012. http://www.omg.org/spec/OCL/2.3.1/PDF/

[Os]   Operating-system.org, "IBM Company History." http://www.operating-system.org/betriebssystem/_english/fa-ibm.htm, last retrieved: 2013-06-24.

[PBYC13]   A. Peternier, W. Binder, A. Yokokawa, and L. Chen, "Parallelism Profiling and Wall-time Prediction for Multi-threaded Applications," in *Proceedings of the 4th ACM/SPEC International Conference on Performance Engineering (ICPE 2013)*. ACM, 2013, pp. 211–216.

[Per]   Persistence of Vision Pty. Ltd., "Persistence of Vision (TM) Raytracer." http://www.povray.org/, last retrieved: 2013-06-05.

[PSG08]   M. Polte, J. Simsa, and G. Gibson, "Comparing Performance of Solid State Devices and Mechanical Disks," in *Proceedings of the 3rd Petascale Data Storage Workshop (PDSW 2008)*. IEEE, 2008.

[PW04]   D. B. Petriu and M. Woodside, "A Metamodel for Generating Performance Models from UML Designs," in *Proceeedings of the 7th International Conference on the Unified Modeling Language (UML 2004)*. Springer-Verlag, 2004, pp. 41–53.

[R F]   R Foundation for Statistical Computing, "R: A Language and Environment for Statistical Computing." http://www.r-project.org, last retrieved: 2013-06-05.

[RBB⁺11]   R. Reussner, S. Becker, E. Burger, J. Happe, M. Hauck, A. Koziolek, H. Koziolek, K. Krogmann, and M. Kuperberg,

"The Palladio Component Model," Karlsruhe Institute of Technology, Department of Informatics, Tech. Rep., 2011. http://digbib.ubka.uni-karlsruhe.de/volltexte/1000022503

[RS05]   M. E. Russinovich and D. A. Solomon, *Microsoft Windows Internals: Microsoft Windows Server 2003, Windows XP, and Windows 2000*, 4th ed.   Microsoft Press, 2005.

[RSPM98]   R. Reussner, P. Sanders, L. Prechelt, and M. Müller, "SKaMPI: A Detailed, Accurate MPI Benchmark," in *Recent Advances in Parallel Virtual Machine and Message Passing Interface*.   Springer-Verlag, 1998, pp. 52–59.

[SAF05]   M. Shao, A. Ailamaki, and B. Falsafi, "DBmbench: Fast and Accurate Database Workload Representation on Modern Microarchitecture," in *Proceedings of the 2005 Conference of the Centre for Advanced Studies on Collaborative Research (CASCON 2005)*.   IBM Press, 2005, pp. 254–267.

[SBHS06]   J. Slaby, S. Baker, J. Hill, and D. Schmidt, "Applying System Execution Modeling Tools to Evaluate Enterprise Distributed Real-time and Embedded System QoS," in *Proceedings of the 12th IEEE International Conference on Embedded an Real-Time Computing Systems and Applications (RTCSA 2006)*.   IEEE Computer Society, 2006, pp. 350–362.

[SJT05]   V. S. Sharma, P. Jalote, and K. S. Trivedi, "Evaluating Performance Attributes of Layered Software Architecture," in *Proceedings of the 8th International Symposium on Component Based Software Engineering (CBSE 2005)*.   Springer-Verlag, 2005, pp. 66–81.

[SKF06]   B. Sotomayor, K. Keahey, and I. Foster, "Overhead Matters: A Model for Virtual Resource Management," in *Proceedings of the 2nd International Workshop on Virtualization Technology in Distributed Computing (VTDC 2006)*.   IEEE Computer Society, 2006.

[SL04]   C. Smith and C. Llado, "Performance model interchange format (PMIF 2.0): XML definition and implementation," in *Proceedings of the 1st International Conference on the Quantitative Evaluation of Systems (QEST 2004)*.   IEEE Computer Society, 2004, pp. 38–47.

[Smi90]   C. U. Smith, *Performance Engineering of Software Systems*. Addison-Wesley, 1990.

[SN05]   J. E. Smith and R. Nair, *Virtual Machines: Versatile Platforms for Systems and Processes*.   Morgan Kaufmann, 2005.

[Spi11]   S. Spinner, "Evaluating Approaches to Resource Demand Estimation," Master Thesis, Karlsruhe Institute of Technology, 2011.

[SQ]   P. Shirley-Quirk, "The Windows Scheduler." http://www.slideshare.net/PeterSQ/the-windows-scheduler-presentation,   last   retrieved: 2013-06-08.

[Sta73]   H. Stachowiak, *Allgemeine Modelltheorie*.   Springer-Verlag, 1973.

[SV06]   T. Stahl and M. Völter, *Model-driven Software Development: Technology, Engineering, Management*.   Wiley, 2006.

[SW02]   C. U. Smith and L. G. Williams, *Performance Solutions: A Practical Guide to Creating Responsive, Scalable Software*, 1st ed.   Addison-Wesley, 2002.

[SWHB06]   B. Schroeder, A. Wierman, and M. Harchol-Balter, "Open Versus Closed: A Cautionary Tale," in *Proceedings of the 3rd Conference on Networked Systems Design & Implementation (NSDI 2006)*. USENIX Association, 2006, pp. 239–252.

[TA13]   T. M. Therneau and E. J. Atkinson, "An Introduction to Recursive Partitioning Using the RPART Routines," Mayo Foundation, Tech. Rep., 2013. http://cran.r-project.org/web/packages/rpart/vignettes/longintro.pdf

[Tan01]   A. S. Tanenbaum, *Modern Operating Systems*, 2nd ed. Prentice Hall International, 2001.

[TAR]   T. M. Therneau, E. J. Atkinson, and B. Ripley, "R Package RPART." http://cran.r-project.org/web/packages/rpart/, last retrieved: 2013-06-05.

[TD06]   G. Tsouloupas and M. D. Dikaiakos, "Characterization of Computational Grid Resources Using Low-Level Benchmarks," in *Proceedings of the 2nd IEEE International Conference on e-Science and Grid Computing (E-SCIENCE 2006)*. IEEE Computer Society, 2006.

[TEL95]   D. M. Tullsen, S. J. Eggers, and H. M. Levy, "Simultaneous Multithreading: Maximizing On-Chip Parallelism," in *Proceedings of the 22nd Annual International Symposium on Computer Architecture (ISCA 1995)*. ACM, 1995, pp. 392–403.

[Thea]   The Apache Foundation, "Apache JMeter." http://jmeter.apache.org/, last retrieved: 2013-06-05.

[Theb]   The Cooperative Association for Internet Data Analysis, "Internet Tools Taxonomy." http://www.caida.org/tools/taxonomy/, last retrieved: 2013-06-05.

[Thec]   The Eclipse Foundation, "Eclipse EMF Ecore Metamodel API." http://download.eclipse.org/modeling/emf/emf/javadoc/2.7.0/org/eclipse/emf/ecore/package-summary.html, last retrieved: 2013-06-05.

[Thed]   The Eclipse Foundation, "Eclipse Equinox OSGi." http://www.eclipse.org/equinox/, last retrieved: 2013-06-05.

[Thee]   The Eclipse Foundation, "Eclipse Model To Text (M2T) Framework." http://www.eclipse.org/modeling/m2t/, last retrieved: 2013-06-05.

[Thef]   The Eclipse Foundation, "Eclipse Modeling Project." http://www.eclipse.org/modeling/, last retrieved: 2013-06-16.

[THHF08]   D. Thakkar, A. E. Hassan, G. Hamann, and P. Flora, "A Framework for Measurement Based Performance Modeling," in *Proceedings of the 7th International Workshop on Software and Performance (WOSP 2008)*, 2008, pp. 55–66.

[TR12]   A. Tarvo and S. P. Reiss, "Using Computer Simulation to Predict the Performance of Multithreaded Programs," in *Proceedings of the 3rd ACM/SPEC International Conference on Performance Engineering (ICPE 2012)*.   ACM, 2012, pp. 217–228.

[Tra]   Transaction Processing Performance Council (TPC), "TPC-W: Benchmarking An Ecommerce Solution." http://www.tpc.org/tpcw/TPC-W_wh.pdf, last retrieved: 2013-06-05.

[TZN10]   E. Thereska, A. X. Zheng, and P. Nobel, "Practical Perfor-
             mance Models for Complex, Popular Applications," in *Pro-
             ceedings of the ACM SIGMETRICS International Confer-
             ence on Measurement and Modeling of Computer Systems
             (SIGMETRICS 2010).*   ACM, 2010.

[vK11]   J. G. von Kistowski, "Defining and Measuring Workloads for
             Elasticity Benchmarking," Bachelor Thesis, Karlsruhe Insti-
             tute of Technology, 2011.

[VMw]   VMware Inc., "Hyperic SIGAR API." http://www.hyperic.
             com/products/sigar, last retrieved: 2013-06-05.

[VMw11]   VMware Inc., "Timekeeping in VMware Virtual Ma-
             chines," Tech. Rep., 2011. http://www.vmware.com/
             resources/techresources/238

[WAA⁺04]   M. Wang, K. Au, A. Ailamaki, A. Brockwell, C. Faloutsos,
             and G. R. Ganger, "Storage Device Performance Prediction
             with CART Models," in *Proceedings of the 12th IEEE
             International Symposium on Modeling, Analysis, and
             Simulation of Computer and Telecommunications Systems
             (MASCOTS 2004).*   IEEE Computer Society, 2004, pp.
             588–595.

[Wal03]   K. C. Wallnau, "Volume III: A Technology for Pre-
             dictable Assembly from Certifiable Components," Soft-
             ware Engineering Institute, Carnegie Mellon University,
             Tech. Rep., 2003. http://www.sei.cmu.edu/library/abstracts/
             reports/03tr009.cfm

[WCOS08]   T. Wood, L. Cherkasova, K. Ozonat, and P. Shenoy,
             "Profiling and Modeling Resource Usage of Virtualized
             Applications," in *Proceedings of the 9th ACM/IFIP/USENIX*

International Conference on Middleware (Middleware 2008). Springer-Verlag, 2008, pp. 366–387.

[WFP07] C. M. Woodside, G. Franks, and D. C. Petriu, "The Future of Software Performance Engineering," in *Future of Software Engineering (FOSE 2007)*, 2007, pp. 171–187.

[WHHH10] D. Westermann, J. Happe, M. Hauck, and C. Heupel, "The Performance Cockpit Approach: A Framework for Systematic Performance Evaluations," in *Proceedings of the 36th EUROMICRO Conference on Software Engineering and Advanced Applications (SEAA 2010)*. IEEE Computer Society, 2010, pp. 31–38.

[Wik] Wikipedia, Die freie Enzyklopädie, "Hyper-Threading." http://de.wikipedia.org/w/index.php?title=Hyper-Threading&oldid=116699596, last retrieved: 2013-06-05.

[WPS02] C. M. Woodside, D. Petriu, and K. Siddiqui, "Performance-related Completions for Software Specifications," in *Proceedings of the 24th International Conference on Software Engineering (ICSE 2002)*, 2002, pp. 22–32.

[WRCW05] Y. Wang, M. J. Rutherford, A. Carzaniga, and A. L. Wolf, "Automating Experimentation on Distributed Testbeds," in *Proceedings of the 20th IEEE/ACM International Conference on Automated Software Engineering (ASE 2005)*. ACM, 2005, pp. 164–173.

[WVCB01] C. M. Woodside, V. Vetland, M. Courtois, and S. Bayarov, "Resource Function Capture for Performance Aspects of Software Components and Sub-systems," in *Performance*

Engineering: State of the Art and Current Trends. Springer-Verlag, 2001, pp. 239–256.

[WW04] X. Wu and C. M. Woodside, "Performance Modeling from Software Components," in *Proceedings of the 4th International Workshop on Software and Performance (WOSP 2004)*. ACM, 2004, pp. 290–301.

[YMM07] S. Yamasaki, N. Maruyama, and S. Matsuoka, "Model-based Resource Selection for Efficient Virtual Cluster Deployment," in *Proceedings of the 3rd International Workshop on Virtualization Technology in Distributed Computing (VTDC 2007)*. ACM, 2007.

[ZJY$^+$09] H. Zhang, G. Jiang, K. Yoshihira, H. Chen, and A. Saxena, "Resilient Workload Manager: Taming Bursty Workload of Scaling Internet Applications," in *Proceedings of the 6th International Conference Industry Session on Autonomic Computing and Communications (ICAC-INDST 2009)*. ACM, 2009.

[ZLBG07] L. Zhu, Y. Liu, N. B. Bui, and I. Gorton, "Revel8or: Model Driven Capacity Planning Tool Suite," in *Proceedings of the 29th International Conference on Software Engineering (ICSE 2007)*. IEEE Computer Society, 2007, pp. 797–800.

[ZWL08] T. Zheng, C. M. Woodside, and M. Litoiu, "Performance Model Estimation and Tracking Using Optimal Filters," *IEEE Transactions on Software Engineering*, vol. 34, no. 3, pp. 391–406, 2008.

The Karlsruhe Series on Software Design and Quality

Edited by Prof. Dr. Ralf Reussner // ISSN 1867-0067

Band 1   **Steffen Becker**
Coupled Model Transformations for QoS Enabled
Component-Based Software Design. 2008
ISBN 978-3-86644-271-9

Band 2   **Heiko Koziolek**
Parameter Dependencies for Reusable Performance
Specifications of Software Components. 2008
ISBN 978-3-86644-272-6

Band 3   **Jens Happe**
Predicting Software Performance in Symmetric
Multi-core and Multiprocessor Environments. 2009
ISBN 978-3-86644-381-5

Band 4   **Klaus Krogmann**
Reconstruction of Software Component Architectures and
Behaviour Models using Static and Dynamic Analysis. 2012
ISBN 978-3-86644-804-9

Band 5   **Michael Kuperberg**
Quantifying and Predicting the Influence of Execution
Platform on Software Component Performance. 2010
ISBN 978-3-86644-741-7

Band 6   **Thomas Goldschmidt**
View-Based Textual Modelling. 2011
ISBN 978-3-86644-642-7

Die Bände sind unter www.ksp.kit.edu als PDF frei verfügbar oder als Druckausgabe bestellbar.

The Karlsruhe Series on
Software Design and Quality

Edited by Prof. Dr. Ralf Reussner // ISSN 1867-0067

Band 7   **Anne Koziolek**
            Automated Improvement of Software Architecture Models
            for Performance and Other Quality Attributes. 2013
            ISBN 978-3-86644-973-2

Band 8   **Lucia Happe**
            Configurable Software Performance Completions through
            Higher-Order Model Transformations. 2013
            ISBN 978-3-86644-990-9

Band 9   **Franz Brosch**
            Integrated Software Architecture-Based Reliability
            Prediction for IT Systems. 2012
            ISBN 978-3-86644-859-9

Band 10   **Christoph Rathfelder**
            Modelling Event-Based Interactions in Component-Based
            Architectures for Quantitative System Evaluation. 2013
            ISBN 978-3-86644-969-5

Band 11   **Henning Groenda**
            Certifying Software Component
            Performance Specifications. 2013
            ISBN 978-3-7315-0080-3

Band 12   **Dennis Westermann**
            Deriving Goal-oriented Performance Models
            by Systematic Experimentation. 2014
            ISBN 978-3-7315-0165-7

Die Bände sind unter www.ksp.kit.edu als PDF frei verfügbar oder als Druckausgabe bestellbar.

The Karlsruhe Series on
Software Design and Quality

Edited by Prof. Dr. Ralf Reussner // ISSN 1867-0067

Band 13   **Michael Hauck**
Automated Experiments for Deriving Performance-relevant
Properties of Software Execution Environments. 2014
ISBN 978-3-7315-0138-1

Die Bände sind unter www.ksp.kit.edu als PDF frei verfügbar oder als Druckausgabe bestellbar.